CONTENTS

ACKNOWLEDGEMENTS   *4*

PREFACE   *5*

1   SOMERSET'S AGE OF STEAM   *7*

2   FARMING IN THE INDUSTRIAL AGE   *15*

3   SOMERSET STONE   *19*

4   LIME BURNING   *25*

5   MINING FOR METALS   *31*

6   COAL MINING AND OTHER FUELS   *37*

7   CLAY INDUSTRIES   *43*

8   CORN MILLING   *49*

9   BREWING AND MALTING   *59*

10   CIDER AND CREAM   *67*

11   TEXTILES   *69*

12   LEATHER INDUSTRIES   *79*

13   FOUNDERS AND ENGINEERS   *83*

14   PAPER MAKING   *91*

15   ROADS   *95*

16   CANALS AND RIVER NAVIGATIONS   *103*

17   RAILWAYS AND TRAMWAYS   *115*

18   PORTS AND SHIPPING   *127*

19   WATER SUPPLY AND DRAINAGE   *135*

20   LIGHT, HEAT AND POWER   *143*

21   HOUSING AND RECREATION   *147*

SELECTED FURTHER READING   *152*

INDEX   *157*

ACKNOWLEDGEMENTS

This book is not intended as a definitive work on the subject, yet it would not have been possible without the immense amount of work that has gone before, especially that undertaken by the Somerset Industrial Archaeological Society and others. All the SIAS publications are available in the Somerset Studies Library in Taunton and a visit is recommended. Researching Somerset's industrial sites has taken me to some truly beautiful parts of the county and the rich diversity of its rural landscape, industrial or otherwise, has been a true revelation. I would particularly like to thank those owners who have shown an interest and allowed access when requested.

A chance conversation with Derrick Warren started my progress on this book and his help and encouragement throughout have been much appreciated. Brian Murless has also come up with answers at a moment's notice. In addition, I would like to thank the following, who have all been of particular help: Charlie and Yvonne Back, Martin Bodman, David Bromwich, Roger Carter, Mike Dixon, Geoff Fitton, Nick Griffiths, Phil Jacques, Douglas Marshall, Michael Messenger, Iain and Mary Miles, Chris Tilley, Martin Watts and John Willows. Organisations which have been especially forthcoming include the Chard and District Museum, Radstock Museum, Somerset Studies Library (Taunton), Wellington Museum, Wessex Water, Westonzoyland Engine Trust and Yeovil Library. I apologise for any omission from this list; it was unintentional.

Unless otherwise stated, most of the photographs were taken in 2003 and provide a useful record of the state of industrial archaeology in that year. Acknowledgements are made with the captions to the British Geological Survey, Chard Museum, Betty Deavin, Bruce Howard, Michael Messenger, Iain and Mary Miles, Chris Tilley, Wellington Museum, Martin Watts, Derrick Warren and the Wessex Water Archive. All others are my own. The maps were drawn by Nick Griffiths.

I have been a fairly inactive member of the Somerset Industrial Archaeological Society for some ten years, so now I hope to put something back. The work of SIAS over the last three decades deserves full recognition and if I may be allowed to dedicate this book to anyone, then it is to all the members of that Society since its formation in 1972.

Peter Stanier
July 2003

PREFACE

The principal manufactures are those of woollen, worsted and silk goods at Frome and Wellington; of gloves at Yeovil, Stoke, Martock and Taunton; of lace at Chard; linen shirts and sailcloth at Crewkerne; shirt collars at Ilminster and Taunton and Shepton Mallet; horsehair seating at Castle Cary, Bruton and Crewkerne; brushes at Wells; of bricks, draining pipes, and the celebrated Bath brick, at Bridgwater, where are also extensive coach building factories; also manufactories of spades, shovels and edge tools. The chief mineral productions are coal, brown ironstone, zinc, limestone and freestone... Ham Hill stone is found in this county and Doulting stone... The iron ore is obtained mostly from the Brendon Hills, known as Spathose ore, and exported to Ebbw Vale... There are lead mines near Wellington [sic], and lead is washed from the old mines on the Mendip hills. There are slate quarries at Wiveliscombe and at Treborough, near Williton. The coal beds contain the most southern deposit of that mineral in England.

KELLY & CO.'S DIRECTORY OF SOMERSET, 1889

Somerset's 'Age of Steam' was the period of c.1750–1950, two centuries during which the Industrial Revolution took hold and transformed parts of the country for ever, reaching a climax in late-Victorian times before declining in the twentieth century. Steam power was present but did not always dominate. Somerset is noted for its scenic beauty, from the open wilds and steep valleys of Exmoor in the west to the high limestone plateau of the Mendip Hills in the east. Between them are the Quantocks, Blackdowns and gentler hills and vales while the flat landscape of the Levels is a unique feature of the West Country. It is hard to believe there was ever any industry here except perhaps in the larger towns.

Many industries were connected with the land: the products of its rocks, minerals or agriculture. Mendip mines yielded lead, silver and zinc, while the high hills in the west have given up iron and some copper ores. Coal mining thrived in the north-east and there were once hopes for an oil shale industry on the Quantock coast. Today's giant Mendip roadstone quarries contrast with the hundreds of small quarries formerly worked on a more human scale for freestone, building stone and slate throughout the county. The levels and moors have their own special industries like peat extraction, withy growing or the drainage pumping engines. Farming has produced the raw materials for processing industries such as malt, beer, cider, butter and cheese, textiles, tanning and leather products. Somerset's rivers were harnessed for power, with corn mills in abundance as well as textile and other industrial mills. Textiles included woollens, silk, lace, horsehair, sailcloth and twine. The county has two preserved windmills.

A wide network of turnpike roads was established after the mid-eighteenth century, some of which were surveyed by the celebrated road engineer John Loudon McAdam. There were river navigations and the county's canals featured innovative lifts and inclined planes. Only the restored Bridgwater & Taunton Canal is open today. Railway developments have left their mark, from I.K. Brunel's Bristol & Exeter Railway to the many abandoned lines including the much-loved Somerset & Dorset Railway and a massive inclined plane on the Brendon Hills. Bridgwater had Somerset's only true dock, but there were other harbours too. Somerset can be proud of its aviation history, from the pioneer of the first powered flight at Chard to Yeovil's Westland helicopters. Yeovil was also home to leading glove makers, Petter oil engines and the St Ivel creamery. Clarks of Street are world famous manufacturers of shoes.

Although it was by no means the only source of power, steam played a significant part in many industries following its first application at the collieries in the 1740s. From around 1800 onwards, steam engines were used increasingly at mines, farms, mills, textile factories, brick-works, pumping stations and on the railways. Steam continued beyond 1950. Steam locomotives ran on the Somerset & Dorset Railway right up to closure in 1966, and paddle-steamers plied the Bristol Channel with occasional visits to Minehead until 1967. But steam is not dead. Steam trains now rule on the preserved East Somerset and West Somerset Railways, the latter the longest of its kind in England, and an unusual steam pumping engine has been restored at Westonzoyland.

Somerset's rich legacy of industrial archaeology was steadily eroded in the closing decades of the twentieth century. The saving of sites and the recording of those lost to us are due in no small part to the involvement of the Somerset Industrial Archaeological Society whose extensive publications have borne witness to their commitment to the county's industrial heritage since 1972. SIAS was formed in response to challenges such as the demolitions of the Devon & Somerset Railway's Waterrow Viaduct and the three magnificent Hoffmann kilns at Wellington brickworks. Since then SIAS has worked closely with local authorities by commenting on planning applications and, where appropriate, encouraging their adaptive re-use rather than demolition. Through the Society's hard work, significant industrial monuments have been 'listed' as worthy of statutory protection.

A derelict industrial complex does not have to be flattened. With vision, a site can find a new lease of life while retaining something of its origins to enhance the local heritage. While writing this book in 2003, I have been surprised by the number of active conversions under way. If well thought out, such developments can only be good if they save an element of the industrial landscape where the alternative is oblivion. In the latter case, sound recording practices are the alternative. Members of SIAS have been actively involved with other research and restoration groups in the county, including the Brendon Hills Mining Group, Exmoor Mines Research Group, Grand Western Canal Trust and the Westonzoyland Engine Trust.

After outlining the principal industries of the Age of Steam this book describes their surviving physical remains: the industrial archaeology. It is intended as a broad overview, aimed especially at all who are concerned for Somerset's heritage, and it is thereby hoped to introduce a new generation of potential industrial archaeologists to the subject. Many sites are hidden gems, known only to industrial archaeologists (and perhaps not all of them in some cases!).

The historic Somerset during the Age of Steam was larger than today and its boundary extended to the River Avon at Bristol and Bath. This area was partitioned off in 1974 to form the new county of Avon, which has subsequently become Bath and North East Somerset and North Somerset. Unless otherwise stated the 'Somerset' of this book is the present county dating from 1974. Six-figure grid references identify the location of sites mentioned in this book, but their inclusion should not imply automatic right of access, and the reader is reminded that many are on private property. However, a polite request or enquiry will often be rewarded with permission to visit.

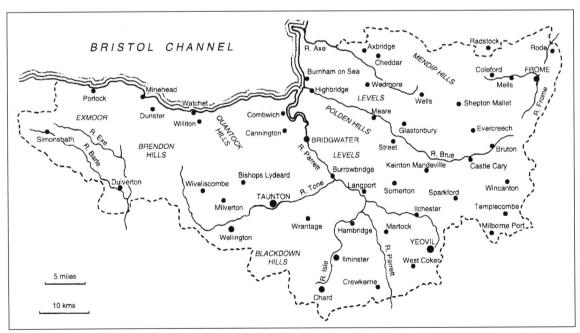

A map of Somerset, showing the post-1974 county boundary. This is the area covered by this book, although Somerset extended further to the northeast in the Age of Steam. N. GRIFFITHS

1
SOMERSET'S AGE OF STEAM

There were industries in Somerset long before the Age of Steam. The Romans mined and smelted lead and silver on the Mendip Hills and worked iron on Exmoor, the Brendons and Blackdown Hills. They also quarried freestone at Ham Hill and salt was extracted in the lower Brue valley.

Metal mining became important again in medieval times. The Mendip lead industry, which was subject to its own laws and customs, increased in Elizabethan times but declined by the end of the seventeenth century. Medieval ironworking sites are known on the western hills. Stone quarries were opened for churches and other prestigious buildings and freestone quarries were worked vigorously at Ham Hill and Doulting, the latter supplying Glastonbury Abbey and Wells Cathedral. Other quarries were worked widely for more common building stones.

The harnessing of water and wind power for corn milling in the medieval period is well documented. The historic county of Somerset had the third greatest number of corn mills in all England in 1086. A windmill was first recorded in 1212. Water-powered fulling mills, for processing woven cloth, are known from at least 1219 in Taunton. Despite this minor industrial revolution in the textile trade, hand spinning and weaving remained domestic activities.

Daniel Defoe indicated the extent of industry and trade in the 1720s, on the eve of the Industrial Revolution. He described profitable woollen trades at Frome, Shepton Mallet and Taunton. Stockings were manufactured at Wells, Shepton Mallet and Glastonbury, and gloves were the main business at Yeovil. Minehead was 'the best port, and safest harbour,' proven in the great storm of 1703 when ships there suffered little damage. The chief trade was with Ireland, and Minehead had been the main place into which Irish wool was imported. Watchet and Porlock were too shallow for the larger ships of the day. At the 'very considerable town and port' of Bridgwater was 'a very good bridge of stone' but the high tidal range and bore in the River Parrett were inconveniences not remedied for more than a century with the opening of a floating dock. The new Tone

Navigation was noted as a considerable asset to the traders of Taunton.

By 1750 the first stirrings of the Industrial Revolution were taking hold in Somerset. Steam power was being introduced for pumping in the coal mines (in historic Somerset) and new turnpike trusts of the 1750s and '60s established a wide network of improved roads. Work was begun in the 1790s on a coalfield branch of the Dorset & Somerset Canal, although it was never completed. Although writing on agricultural matters at the end of the century, John Billingsley also commented on related industries. He acknowledged that new inventions such as carding and spinning machinery would soon become universal in the textile industries despite the initial protests from workers fearful for their livelihoods. This was a time when large numbers of people were employed in the trade at Frome and Shepton Mallet.

Certain early maps, although limited by scale, are invaluable sources of information for the industrial archaeologist. For example, the first Ordnance Survey 1-inch scale maps published in 1809–17 give a tentative idea of the distribution of industries, by showing coal works, copper mines, mills (many of them named), windmills, mill factory (at Chard), Fussells' edge tool mill (at Nunney), a brewery and factory at Crewkerne, brick kilns and yards, limekilns, turnpike gates, the unfinished course of the Dorset & Somerset Canal, a lock on the Tone Navigation, a dock at Bridgwater and a lighthouse at Burnham. The Ham Hill quarries are marked but not named. The 6-inch and 25-inch scale maps published from the 1880s give unprecedented detail of developments when many industries were at their height.

This book examines the history and archaeology of the primary, extractive, manufacturing, transport and service industries during the Age of Steam, c.1750–1950. Farms, estates and woodland industries relied on the power of horses, water and steam in the nineteenth century. Machinery and implements were manufactured as labour-saving improvements, while some larger farms were planned and laid out as experiments in high farming, using steam power. Many farms, however, still relied on water-wheels to provide their motive power for barn-based machinery. Sawmills were found on larger estates, worked by water power or the occasional portable steam engine. The internationally renowned Kelway's nursery near Langport is a reminder that horticulture is also part of the farming industry. The withy industry, with its curious boilers, is unique to the Levels and moors.

Stone quarrying is the oldest of all the extractive industries. Somerset's varied geology has yielded countless quarries and pits for local building needs but finer freestones were worked at Ham Hill and Doulting, with the blue lias around Keinton Mandeville supplying kerbs and paving. Devonian slates were quarried around the edges of Exmoor. Roadstone has been quarried almost everywhere but the Carboniferous limestone of the Mendips expanded from the late-nineteenth century because of its quality, availability and access to road and rail transport. Steam-powered cranes, crushing plant and sawing machines worked in the larger or more progressive quarries. Lime has been burnt since the Roman period for building mortar and, especially in the eighteenth and nineteenth centuries, for agriculture. Abandoned limekilns are found on all outcrops of limestone suitable for burning. Cement manufacturing took place at Dunball near Bridgwater, with access to the main railway line. Gypsum was quarried from the cliffs near Watchet for cement making.

Extensive areas of 'gruffy ground' on the Mendips show where lead miners and smelters were active since the Roman period. Some mining was attempted in the nineteenth century but most activity was concentrated on the re-smelting of ancient slags, such as at Charterhouse and Priddy. Iron mines on Exmoor may also date back to the Romans and there was activity here down to the nineteenth century. The Brendon Hills saw the greatest metal mines in Somerset when the Ebbw Vale Iron Co. sent thousands of tons down to Watchet for shipment to smelters in South Wales. The mines worked for thirty years and their ruins have been the subject of recent investigations. Copper was mined on the Quantocks where the Buckingham Mine has the earliest complete beam engine house in the South West. Other Mendip minerals were zinc (calamine), mined at Shipham, and ochre at Axbridge.

The landscape of the Somerset coalfield is hard to match anywhere else in England. Colliery sites to the south of Radstock around Coleford and the Nettlebridge valley include seventeenth- and eighteenth-century bell pits, the finest Cornish beam engine house on the coalfield and rare coking ovens. Radstock's fine museum contains much of interest on the coalfield. Just a short distance away, the last colliery at Lower Writhlington closed in 1973. Peat dug from the Somerset Levels was another fuel, although it is now associated with the horticultural trade. Oil shale could have provided an important fuel in the 1920s but attempts to extract it failed, leaving behind a curious retort at Kilve.

Clay was dug extensively for brick and tile making. Bridgwater was an important centre for roofing tiles and the Bath brick was also manufactured here from the special silt of the River Parrett. The last brickworks was that of William Thomas & Co. at Wellington, where one of three circular Hoffmann kilns was the largest in Britain when built in 1867. All have gone, but Bridgwater is home to a brick and tile museum. Potteries were less important in Somerset than some other counties; nevertheless, wares from Donyatt had a long life from the eleventh century to 1939.

There are hundreds of corn mill sites along Somerset's abundant streams and rivers. Decline of the small mill was accelerated by the introduction of roller mills and the number of millers fell by over three-quarters in the century down to 1950. Local engineers made iron water-wheels and machinery, and turbines were also installed to improve efficiency. Some mills used auxiliary steam

The Buckingham Mine engine house at Dodington is a reminder of the efforts to exploit copper ore around the Quantock Hills in the early-nineteenth century.

power, or were built for steam from the start. Spillers, the national flour milling giant, had its origins at Bridgwater where the Bridgwater Steam Flour Mills was an early establishment. Some water mills are open to the public today. There are also two preserved tower windmills, both of which used auxiliary steam power before they ceased milling corn in 1910 and 1927. There were post windmills in Somerset since at least 1212, their sites now mostly recognised by place names.

Malting was an important rural industry and the barley malt of Porlock was especially prized. Small village maltings gave way to large malthouses in the later nineteenth century, notably at Oakhill, a small Mendip village where there was also a brewery of some repute. Hancock's Brewery in the small town of Wiveliscombe was one of the most successful in Somerset, with mineral water and cider factories attached. The end came in the 1950s, after a takeover, but the buildings still dominate the town. The old Anglo-Bavarian Brewery, where lager was brewed, is a notable landmark in the town of Shepton Mallet which is best known for the Babycham drink manufactured by Showering Bros from the late 1940s.

Cider was a farm-based activity, equipped with apple crushers and cider presses from local manufacturers, but there were cider factories in the twentieth century. Cheddar cheese is Somerset's best known dairy product, again first made on farms. Daniel Defoe described it as 'the best cheese that England affords, if not, that the whole world affords.' High praise indeed. Commercial dairies and creameries were established in the later nineteenth century alongside railways which took their milk, butter and cheese products to London and other large cities. The St Ivel brand name has its origins in Yeovil, while Unigate originated partly in Wiltshire and Somerset. The nationwide hauliers Wincanton Transport began with Cow & Gate at Wincanton in 1925.

The woollen textile industry was more widespread in Somerset before it became centred on Frome and Wellington in the late-eighteenth century. Its greatest legacy is the Fox Bros' Tonedale Mills at Wellington, a huge complex on a scale that would not be out of place in West Yorkshire. The mills at Frome were more numerous but far smaller. For a time, mills around Exmoor made woollen textiles too. Decline in woollen manufacturing was replaced with other textile industries. Silk spinning and throwing took place at Taunton, Shepton Mallet and Evercreech, and lace became important at Chard. Flax and hemp industries around Crewkerne and Martock

produced canvas, sailcloth, webbing and yarn. 'Coker canvas' was used for the sails of HMS *Victory*. There is still a working horsehair weaving mill at Castle Cary, using looms invented here in the nineteenth century. Shirt and collar manufacturers employed large numbers in Chard, Ilminster and Taunton; at the latter the Van Heusen collar was made. Brushes, from toilet brushes to high-quality shaving brushes, were made at Nimmer Mills from 1875 until 1990, all the while powered by a waterwheel.

Tanning industries used oak bark from Exmoor, which was also exported. There were tanneries and leather dressing works at Glastonbury, Taunton (steam), Yeovil and Milborne Port. Yeovil was the leading producer of leather gloves in the 1890s and the industry still survives in the surrounding district. The shoe factory of C. & J. Clark at Street employed much of the town's population, while sheepskin rugs were another side of the leather industry at Glastonbury.

Somerset's ironfounders and engineers achieved more than just local importance and exported their products nationwide and abroad. Many began by making agricultural tools and implements, such as Dening & Co. of Chard or the Fussell edge tool ironworks at Mells. George Parsons' Parrett Works near Martock was built as a fascinating complex of foundry, engineering works and flax mill. At Frome, Edward Cockey was a notable ironfounder, while the Singer foundry cast famous sculptures, such as the Old Bailey's 'Justice' or the Boadicea monument on the Embankment in London. Foundries and works made steam engines at Taunton and Bridgwater, and iron bridges were made at the latter too. Of local importance were men such as the engineer and millwright John Chidgey of Watchet. John Stringfellow of Chard experimented with a steam-powered model aeroplane that actually flew in 1848. The name Petter is famous for a highly successful range of oil engines manufactured at Yeovil in the first half of the twentieth century. Petters Ltd founded the Westland aircraft works, another name that is known the world over.

Today's visitors to the Wookey Hole tourist attraction can see demonstrations of paper making in part of the old paper mill. This mill was one of many others exploiting the clear water issuing from the Mendip Hills here and at Cheddar. Over in the west, the Wansbrough Mill at Watchet has carried on the tradition of paper making since at least 1750. A third large paper mill at Creech St Michael was noted for its tall chimney-stack of 1875.

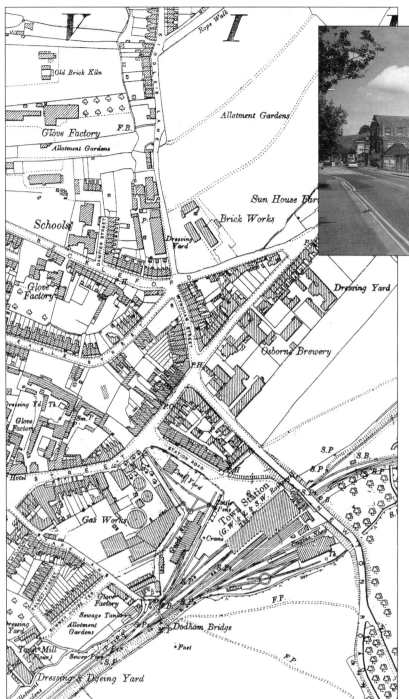

Above: *Loss of industrial heritage: the complete demolition of a glove factory and chimney at Yeovil, 5 June 2003. One building remains.*

Left: *Yeovil's industrial landscape in 1901, from the Ordnance Survey 25-inch map. This small part of the town includes four glove factories, four leather dressing yards, a dressing and dyeing yard, brewery, flour mill, railway station (with goods and engine sheds, cattle pens and coal yard), gasworks, two brickworks, a rope-walk and a sewage works. Petters' engineering works, Aplin & Barrett's creamery and the* Western Gazette *printing office were soon to be added to the scene.*
ORDNANCE SURVEY: CROWN COPYRIGHT RESERVED

Means of transport have always been essential to commerce and industry. It is also worth noting the prehistoric timber trackways discovered across the Levels and moors near Meare. The first true roads date from the Roman period, and the Fosse Way is one of the best known in Britain. It was not until the mid-eighteenth century onwards that Somerset was well provided with turnpike roads, with a sudden flurry of activity in the 1750s creating no less than 11 trusts. The legacy of the turnpike era is seen in toll-houses, milestones, mileposts and bridges, some of them iron. Bridgwater had an early

iron bridge cast at Coalbrookdale that spanned the Parrett from 1797 until 1883 when it was replaced by the present structure.

Water transport included river navigations on the Tone and Parrett, the former described by Defoe in 1724. With the exception of the Dorset & Somerset Canal's branch, already abandoned by 1803, Somerset's canals came late and were soon overtaken by the railways. Aqueducts, boat lifts, inclined planes and tunnels were the order of the day on the Grand Western and Chard Canals. These and other derelict courses hold much of interest to the industrial archaeologist and can be compared with the restored Bridgwater & Taunton Canal of 1827.

The railways immediately captured traffic from the canals. The first was Brunel's broad gauge Bristol & Exeter Railway (1841–44) and the route remains the busiest in the county. Other lines and branches were created in the nineteenth century but the network was devastated by many closures in the 1960s, including the Somerset & Dorset Railway's classic route over the Mendips. Despite this, the full length of the West Somerset Railway and part of the East Somerset Railway have been restored to steam working. There was a brief period when trams ran in Taunton in the early years of the twentieth century. Industrial or mineral railways hold a particular interest. Sidings and tramways served quarries and collieries around the Mendips and there was even a narrow gauge railway exclusively serving the Oakhill Brewery. Of them all, the spectacular West Somerset Mineral Railway employed one of the most impressive inclines in England to climb Brendon Hill.

Bridgwater was Somerset's leading port in the nineteenth century. A floating dock was opened in 1841 and was kept clear from 1844 until 1971 by a steam mud-scraper boat designed by Brunel. The redundant dock retains some original features. For a while Burnham was a railway port on a direct route across the Bristol Channel to South Wales before the opening of the Severn Tunnel. Watchet's busiest time was for exporting iron ore in the 1850s–'80s, but other ships traded here well into the twentieth century. Porlock Weir was also developed with iron ore shipments in mind. Minehead was far more important than Watchet or Porlock in Defoe's time, but had much declined by the nineteenth century. In the Age of Steam, paddle-steamers called at piers at Burnham and Minehead. The only lighthouses on the Somerset coast were a pair of lights at Burnham and one on the Watchet pierhead.

The water supply industry grew out of small private initiatives and larger works financed by the authorities in the second half of the nineteenth century. A striking monument is the pair of water towers at Rockwell Green near Wellington, associated with the nearby Westford pumping station which contains historic machinery. The almost circular Cheddar Reservoir is recognised immediately on any map. The removal of excess water for improving agriculture on the Somerset Levels was tackled

The last days of steam on the Somerset & Dorset Railway: Evercreech Junction station in November 1965. M.J. MESSENGER

by a number of drainage schemes in the early-nineteenth century, all employing steam power for pumping. Westonzoyland's unusual pumping machine of 1861 ran until 1951 and has been preserved in working order.

Gas and electricity utilities were both pioneered in Taunton. Coal gas was first used to light a home in 1816, although it was not until 1833 that the streets were successfully lit. Numerous gas companies were established throughout the county, from Minehead to Milborne Port. The Frome ironfounder Edward Cockey, who was involved in his own town's gasworks, specialised in making gasholders and other equipment. There were many amalgamations and closures before nationalisation in 1949. Many works closed in the 1950s before natural gas was introduced twenty years later. Gas lighting was followed by gas for cooking and heating towards the end of the nineteenth century, by which time electricity was becoming a rival. Taunton had its first electric street lighting in 1886, seven years after football matches here and at Wellington had been floodlit by arc lights, perhaps for the first time in the country. The Newton Electrical Works in Taunton came to be an important supplier of equipment. While Taunton had an early power station, developments elsewhere were more variable, so it was a local inhabitant who gave Wedmore a supply in 1908, long before many neighbouring towns. Despite a national grid in the 1930s, Minehead still generated its own electricity until 1952. Only fifteen years after the end of the Age of Steam, the first nuclear power station was commissioned along the coast at Hinkley Point.

Good examples of company houses for workers and their families are seen at Street, where the Clarks built many terraces in the town. There were houses associated with textile mills, such as at Chard, Crewkerne or Wellington. Housing had to be provided for industrial workers at remote sites outside the towns. There is now little trace of the iron miners' village at Brendon Hill, but a chapel still serves a wider community. Chapels, institutes and reading rooms were frequently donated by employers and are other aspects of workers' welfare which might be considered by the industrial archaeologist.

These then are the main themes covered by this book, yet other industrial activities falling within the scope of industrial archaeology have contributed to making Somerset special. Take, for example, three very different sites around Bridgwater. A saltworks at Dunball extracted brine from a deep bore hole in 1911–22, the large British Cellophane factory was begun at Bridgwater in the

late 1930s, and the Royal Ordnance complex was opened at Puriton soon afterwards. The communications industry includes the Somerton radio station, opened in 1927 by the Marconi company with aerials covering a 400-acre site, and the BBC's Williton radio transmitter of 1933 and its art deco building. Monuments of military activity falling within the Age of Steam range from the Victorian fort at Brean Down to Second World War airfields at Charlton Horethorne, Culmhead, Henstridge, Merryfield, Westonzoyland and Yeovilton, and the pillboxes along the 1940 defensive line between Axmouth and Bridgwater.

A pillbox on the embankment of the Chard Railway near Creech St Michael is evidence of the defensive line hastily erected on an industrial scale in 1940.

Steam power played an important part in Somerset's industrial development. The earliest steam engines were for pumping water to allow deeper working on the collieries, although they were in an area no longer in Somerset. The first Newcomen pumping engine was installed at Paulton Engine Colliery in about 1740. Jonathan Hornblower erected a compound pumping engine in 1782 at Middle Pit, Radstock, which led to a dispute with Boulton & Watt who feared their patent had been infringed. By the early 1800s winding engines were also on the collieries. In 1821 a pumping engine was installed and started by J. Bond at Huish Colliery (ST697540).

Elsewhere, the textile industry used early steam engines, often to supplement water power. A 6hp steam engine may have been installed at James Hoddinott's Milton silk mill as early as 1806 and four years later a 4hp steam engine was noted at Adderwell woollen mills, Frome. By the 1820s there were several steam engines at Frome.

At Shepton Mallet, a woollen mill worked entirely by steam power was offered for sale in 1814. Steam power was not confined to the mines and textile mills. In 1827 a Boulton & Watt beam engine was installed in the Charlton pumping house on the Bridgwater & Taunton Canal. In 1826–27 William Ashman's first railway locomotive in the West of England ran on the Somerset Coal Canal's tramroad to Midford, no longer in Somerset. The first effective steam locomotives were not seen in Somerset until the opening of the Bristol & Exeter Railway to Bridgwater in 1841.

Somerset engineers designed and made steam engines. In 1853 George Parsons patented a steam engine with a cylinder in a steam jacket and displayed a 7hp portable engine 'of very high quality' at the Bath & West Show of 1856. He continued to make these portable engines and in 1863 one was 'commended as a good sensible machine' and rated higher than other leading manufacturers of the day. From 1875 William Sibley & Son made steam engines at the Parrett Iron Works, and oil engines in the early-twentieth century. Other Somerset steam engine

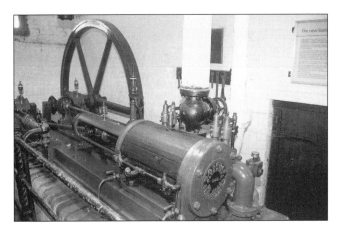

This horizontal engine manufactured by W. & F. Wills of Bridgwater in 1886 is preserved in steaming order by the Westonzoyland Engine Trust. Such engines found many applications during the Age of Steam.

manufacturers included C. Allen & Son and Easton & Waldegrave of Taunton, Bishop Bros of Wellington and W. & F. Wills Ltd of Bridgwater.

Despite their prevalence, there were many cases where steam engines were used to supplement water power and did not supplant it unless absolutely necessary. The large Tonedale Mills had a 30ft by 10ft (9m by 3m) suspension wheel; a turbine was installed in c.1900 and the machine shop was run by a smaller water-wheel. At the same time there were three beam engines and one

Prowse's Mill is a textile mill in a typical rural setting near Wellington.

This beam engine worked at Pearsall's silk mill until 1955 and is now displayed in the Somerset County Museum at Taunton.

COURTESY SOMERSET COUNTY MUSEUM

horizontal engine from the mid-nineteenth century. Sailcoth was manufactured at Tail Mill near Crewkerne, using water-wheels and an internal beam engine. Prowse's Mill at Westford maintained a large high breastshot wheel.

The long tradition of using water power continued into the early-twentieth century. There was sufficient water at some sites to provide power for more than one activity, such as Wallbridge at Frome, where there was a corn mill and textile mill. Rural mill sites were small and numerous. Studies published by the Somerset Industrial Archaeological Society show how the waters of the Tone and Isle were applied to more than just corn mills, with industries such as textiles, tanneries, slate, brush making, edge tools, sawing and fulling all giving an indication of the importance of these rivers. For example, in the first 2¼ miles of the River Isle there were seven mill sites, including corn, fulling, woollen textiles and a brush mill. Several quarries had water-wheels, such as the slate quarries and Newland lime quarry. Vallis Vale had a

turbine and wheel, supplemented by a steam engine when the river was low, as late as 1898.

A beam engine takes pride of place in the Somerset County Museum at Taunton. It was made by Easton & Amos of Southwark in about 1850 and worked for a century in James Pearsall's silk mill in the town. A second engine from the mill is now in the Henry Ford Museum, Dearborn, USA. A third Taunton beam engine, made by Bury, Curtis & Kennedy of Liverpool, was still in E. & W.C. French Ltd's tannery when it was surveyed by SIAS in 1974, but has since been removed. A second-hand Boulton & Watt beam engine was taken from a Frome woollen mill in 1820 to Gifford, Fox & Co.'s lace mill at Chard, where it worked for over a century. This is now believed to be in the USA. Steam was vital in the drainage of the Levels and it is appropriate that an Easton & Amos engine of 1861 is maintained in steaming order by the Westonzoyland Engine Trust alongside other engines recovered from sites in Somerset.

2

FARMING IN THE INDUSTRIAL AGE

The Royal Bath & West of England Agricultural Society was founded in 1777 and the state of agriculture in Somerset was described by John Billingsley in the 1790s when county surveys were being made for the Board of Agriculture. Prosperous times for farmers were cut short as soon as the Napoleonic wars ended, but it was also the labourers who suffered, with poor wages and living conditions.

The nineteenth century saw the invention and manufacturing of a wide variety of agricultural implements and machinery, such as ploughs, rakes, harrows, rollers, threshing machines or chaff cutters, many by engineers who gained a national reputation. Brickyards were also kept busy making pipes for field drains, and the ambitious enclosures and drainage schemes on the Somerset Levels set the county apart from its neighbours. By mid-century the larger landowners and farmers were experimenting with crops and animal breeding and investing in the latest equipment on their farms. Some model farms were powered by steam, while out in the fields traction engines were employed for threshing and ploughing. This application of industrial technology must have greatly disturbed a rural working lifestyle where horses and manpower had ruled for centuries. It was not popular with all, and even the vicar saw fit to complain to the owner of the Nynehead estate about the 'horrible engines cultivating his great fields, smoking and whistling and puffing.'

Steam threshing with a traction engine, believed to be at Moorlinch, c.1900. M. WATTS COLLECTION

The period of high farming failed in the great agricultural depression of the 1870s which was caused by a combination of poor harvests and cheap foreign imports. While many farmers left the land, others specialised in dairying or cheese making and took advantage of the railways to carry their products to distant urban markets. The twentieth century saw the most radical changes in agriculture when tractors began to replace horses despite a depression between the wars. Steam ploughs were utilised occasionally during the Second World War and steam threshing continued in places into the 1950s after which the combine harvester took over.

Farms, estates and woodland industries relied on the power of horses, water and steam in the nineteenth century. Barn machinery could be worked by horse gins, where a horse walked in a circle attached to a timber shaft and overhead gearing. The gin house was usually attached to an existing barn and may survive long after the gearing has been removed. A horse gin at Sweethay Court, Trull (ST 205213) drove a wooden-rollered apple crusher in a barn next to two cider presses. The number of horse gins in Somerset is unknown but a survey has located at least 12 in the single parish of Ash. Most were for cider apple crushing or chaff cutting. Portable gins were towed to anywhere on the farm, and one of four examples recorded was last used to drive butter churns. A horse gear at Church Farm, Ash, was replaced early in the twentieth century by an oil engine supplied by Brown & Winsor of Yeovil. Small engines like this were common providers of power on farms in the twentieth century.

Water-wheels were used for milling, preparing animal feeds, chaff cutting, threshing, sawing, water pumping and, later, working milking machines. The drive was either by gears from the wheel shaft to pulleys and belts, or by a ring drive which engaged with a pinion to turn a lay shaft running to the machinery in the barn. Unlike corn mills, most farm wheels were only worked for short periods and so even the smallest stream could be utilised or dammed to form a millpond.

A survey of 47 sites in the area between Exmoor and the Quantocks revealed 20 surviving farm wheels in 1975. Of

Iron undershot wheel at Milborne Wick Farm. Many farms used water-wheels to work barn machinery during the nineteenth and early-twentieth centuries.

these 16 were overshot wheels and 11 had ring gearing. One was still working a thresher in a barn at Northcombe Farm (SS 917291) near Dulverton. This was an overshot wheel of 18ft (5.5m) diameter made by Robert Page of Dulverton in about 1890. There was a similar wheel, although wider, at Horner Farm near Porlock, while examples of undershot wheels survived at Egrove Farm and Bridge Farm near Williton. The 14ft (4.27m) diameter wheel at the latter (ST 076408) was made locally in 1890 by J. Chidgey of Watchet, who made a similar wheel

at Kentsford Farm. The problem of water supply at remote farms was overcome in some unusual ways. Gupworthy Farm utilised the water from a mine adit, while Great Bradley Farm was fed by a long leat from a reservoir formed on a small stream high up on the hills near Dulverton.

At West Buckland, Gerbeston Manor (ST 162194) had a water-wheel at 'Machine Barn' (a threshing machine?) in the 1830s. When surveyed by SIAS in 1996, the barn contained gearing, shafting and pulleys to drive an oat crusher, kibbler, grist mill and a combined bench saw, planer and router. There was also evidence for an oil engine and generator, but the prime motive power was a 10ft 6in by 4ft (3.2m by 1.2m) iron overshot wheel made by Ford Bros of Wellington in 1898, very similar to one from the same firm at Hopkins Farm, Bishops Lydeard. The Gerbeston wheel has been retained but the machinery transferred to the Hestercombe estate workshop.

The Gerbeston wheel was clearly a replacement but other farms were installing turbines at the end of the nineteenth century. In 1893 a 21hp 'British Empire' turbine was installed by Joseph Armfield of Ringwood at Hinton Farm Mill (ST 574206) on the Yeo near Mudford. It worked until the Second World War when its last function

Hinton Farm Mill near Mudford was powered by a large water-wheel (now a turbine) beneath the floor and fed by an underground leat. The barn stands some distance from the River Yeo and the millstone is the only clue to its purpose.

was to drive a milking machine pump. The turbine is 20ft (6.1m) below ground level at the bottom of the former stone-built wheelpit. The original fourteenth-century mill was prone to flooding and so the present mill was built in about 1768 on higher ground, necessitating a 1000ft (305m) tunnel to bring the water to a 20ft by 6ft (6.1m by 1.83m) breastshot water-wheel. This timber wheel and its iron successor drove three pairs of millstones and machinery including a thresher, sawmill and water pump.

A turbine made by Gilbert Gilkes of Kendal was installed in 1882–83 inside a small house at a weir on the River Tone at Hornshay Farm, Nynehead. Machinery in a barn was driven by a 185ft (56.4m) shaft supported on brick pillars to keep it clear of floods. When the estate was sold in the early 1940s, a new turbine was installed to generate electricity. Although the electric mains came to the farm in 1968, the turbine continued to provide lighting until 1981. An estate barn at Dodhill Manor had a Gilkes turbine of the 1890s for working a grist mill, sawbench, water pump and, again, electricity generation.

Small water-wheels pumped water to farms and houses, although hydraulic rams became widespread during the nineteenth century. Using a simple mechanism these pumps used the volume and fall of a stream to raise a lesser quantity of water to where it was required. Hydraulic rams proved reliable and efficient until the introduction of mains water, yet some are still in use today. A few wind engines were erected on farms to pump water in the later nineteenth and early-twentieth centuries.

An up-to-date farm complex was developed at Drayton (ST 452159) in 1859–60 by William Blake. It was built in two parts, with dairying, piggeries and sheepfolds on one side of a lane and a more industrial complex on the other. Here a steam engine provided power via line shafting for two pairs of millstones, two apple crushers (for two cider presses), a chaff cutter, thresher, flax and seed roller and scutching machines. A granary over the wagon and cart shed was supported by six iron columns cast by George Parsons of the nearby Parrett Works. When the site was divided in 1932, this part became Flaxdrayton Farm. The schedule included a steam engine (Parsons), boiler (Foster), kibbling mill (Turner) and threshing machine (Tasker). The steam engine and boiler were retained until the 1950s. A serious fire in 1993 destroyed many of the buildings, although the granary has been restored incorporating the cast-iron columns. The 56ft (1.7m) chimney-stack remains a landmark.

Steam power was used at a model farm of a similar date at Cutsey, Trull (ST 188205), where the buildings were planned on a slope so that the livestock could be fed by gravity. The Home Farm at St Audries, West Quantoxhead, was laid out on a new site by 1855. Two ponds supplied water for a 20ft (6.1m) diameter overshot water-wheel for driving barn machinery including a threshing machine, corn mill, chaff cutter, hoist, cider mill and press. A nearby private gasworks was built for the estate (see chapter 20).

Mechanisation enabled estate sawmills to replace the old sawpits. Circular saws and vertical reciprocating saws were in use by the early-nineteenth century and in 1830 the horizontal reciprocating saw was found to be ideal for small rural workshops and sawmills. The timber was fixed to a horizontal bed and a rack and pinion moved it towards the saw blade, whose slow action gave a much smoother cut than a circular saw. It could also cut bends and crooks for boat building. The band-saw was introduced in about 1860 although it had been invented some fifty years earlier. Smaller estates continued to use sawpits while others hired portable steam engines working mobile reciprocating saws.

A steam engine was installed in a new planned farm complex at Drayton near South Petherton in 1859–60. The chimney remains.

The estate sawmill at Simonsbath (ST 771391) was restored in 2003 by the Exmoor National Park Authority. It has a complete sequence of buildings and evidence for three phases of power. A water-wheel of perhaps 30ft (9.1m) diameter was installed around 1855–65 and was replaced in 1897–98 by a turbine made by H.P. Vacher of Winchester and fitted by Garnish & Lemon of Barnstaple. It drove two sawbenches, a threshing machine, chaff cutter and other barn machinery, and from about 1905 it drove a dynamo to supply part of the village with electricity. After the terrible Exmoor storm of August 1952 destroyed the weir on the River Barle, a diesel engine was put in the next year. Both turbine and engine survive, as do a racksaw (probably locally made in the 1860s) and a table sawbench made by Sam Worssam in the second half of the nineteenth century.

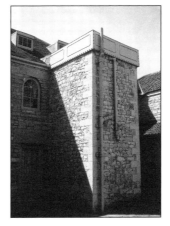 

Above left: *A water tank at Kelway & Son's Nurseries, Langport.*

Above right: *A traditional withy boiler is seen here near Westonzoyland in 1989. It is still in use but is incorporated into a building, and the leaning brick chimney has been supported.*

The extensive buildings at Kelway & Son's Nurseries near Langport have been converted to other uses.

The nursery is an aspect of archaeology that has received little attention, yet Somerset had a world-famous one founded by James Kelway in 1850 at Huish Episcopi near Langport. He became renowned for propagating gladioli so that by 1878 he was winning at international exhibitions. His son William gained similar fame for hybridising paeonies. By 1899 Kelway & Son's Royal Nurseries covered 200 acres (81ha) and included four dwellings and other buildings. The nursery moved a short distance away in 1991 and the listed buildings have been restored to other uses including a hotel and council offices grouped around a courtyard (ST 426276).

The growing of withies (willows) began in the early-nineteenth century in the wake of the drainage schemes on the Somerset Levels. Special boats navigated the drainage rhynes carrying the bundles ('bolts') of harvested withies. In 1932 some 1600 acres (647ha) were given over to withy growing on the moors of North Curry and Stoke St Gregory. Many of the inhabitants were involved in harvesting and processing the withies, as well as making baskets and artists' charcoal. The old method of stripping the bark by hand was superseded by a French-designed machine which first required the withies to be boiled. Cut in autumn and winter, the withy bundles were immersed in boiling water for up to eight hours and became stained by the bark's tannin. The withy boiler has a long iron tank set in brickwork with a firebox and a chimney at one end. About 5cwt (254kg) of coal was required for each firing, when metal sheets were placed over the open top to retain the heat. Some were made by cutting in half redundant boilers from the steam pumping stations of the Levels. Initial surveys in the 1970s recorded 11 boilers still in use out of a total of 27 sites. Coal, oil and wood were the fuels. A number survive, some still in use and, for example, one can be seen easily from the lane at Stanmoor Bridge (ST 358301).

Oare weed was gathered from the shore between Minehead and Kilve from at least the late-sixteenth century. It was burnt to produce kelp which was sent off to be used in glass bottle making. Kelp was shipped from Watchet in 1797, but a century later the oare weed was only collected by farmers for manuring their land.

3

SOMERSET STONE

A tour of Somerset's towns and villages gives a clear indication of the great variety of local building stones available in the past. The sedimentary limestones and sandstones are of all colours and quality, such as the grey lias limestone of central Somerset, the golden Ham Hill and oolitic limestones of the south, or the Old Red Sandstone (Devonian) and New Red Sandstone (Triassic) of the Brendons, Quantocks and Vale of Taunton Deane. Hundreds of humble quarry pits were opened for local needs, then forgotten ever since. Only the most prestigious buildings, such as Somerset's famous churches, could afford the expense of transporting the best stones from longer distances. Small outcrops of special stones were exploited, such as Draycott Marble, a Dolomitic breccia or conglomerate capable of taking a polish. Bryscombe Quarry (ST 477511) was the main place, where the stone was sawn and polished for tombstones and other decorative work from at least 1860 until 1939. The tough Draycott stone was also used for lintels and gateposts in the neighbourhood. Yeovil or Marston Marble was a limestone quarried on a limited scale for ornamental polishing. Chert was quarried from small pits in the Greensand of the Blackdown Hills and it was even worked underground at Snowdon Hill, Chard (ST 314090). This flinty material was knapped for building stone or used for road making. Pits were opened in sands and gravels wherever they occured. During the Age of Steam improved transport facilities opened up stone markets and encouraged the development of new and larger quarries equipped with machinery.

Ham Hill (ST 478168) overlooks the stone villages of Norton Sub Hamdon and Stoke Sub Hamdon. Ham stone is a Jurassic limestone at the top of Upper Lias, and has been prized as an attractive freestone since Roman times. Alec Clifton-Taylor called it 'one of England's most seductive stones', and its natural orange-brown

Steam derrick working at the Ham Hill quarries, April 1922. The introduction of steam power in the late-nineteenth century permitted deeper working of these freestone quarries. BRITISH GEOLOGICAL SURVEY (NERC COPYRIGHT RESERVED)

colour and textural interest, enriches the villages around the hill and buildings further afield. The Normans began quarrying in earnest for carved work in churches, abbeys and castles in the region. It was often used for windows, doorways and pillars where other stones such as the blue lias were used for walling. Later buildings include Montacute House, which is a fine advertisement for the stone in the Elizabethan period.

There was a revival in the second half of the nineteenth when Joseph Staple owned the Norton or Ham Hill quarries. His son-in-law Charles Trask took over from about 1865 until his death in 1907. In 1893 the Ham Hill Stone Co. (Trask, Staple and Hand) employed 150 men (70 masons, 25 quarrymen, 55 sawyers, hauliers, odds, etc), and other quarriers were Mrs Elizabeth Williams, employing 30 men and W. Bishop with six men. The main quarries were about 90ft (27m) deep, but a considerable overburden had to be removed to reach the freestone beds. The quarrymen made use of natural joints but sometimes had to pick out vertical channels to isolate a block before driving in horizontal wedges to lift it from its

bed. The quarries had at least 13 cranes, mostly hand-worked. Trask's stone, however, was lifted by steam cranes from the quarries and run on tramlines to the masons' sheds where steam-powered machinery included saw frames, planers and moulders. The trade was mainly in dressed stone, some being sent as far as London. By the 1930s pneumatic drills were replacing the traditional hand-channelling in the quarries, but the industry declined after the Second World War. There was a revival in the later twentieth century, with stone sold for buildings and restoration work.

The main Norton stone works and a smaller quarry are still operating, but footpaths in the Ham Hill Country Park provide easy public access through a strange landscape of disused quarries and overgrown spoil tips. The exposed stone faces have evidence of the quarrying method, with clear marks of the quarrymen's picks. The large Deep Quarry (ST 481615), abandoned soon after the 1880s, has three high faces showing natural cross-bedding, vertical joints and the quarrymen's pick marks. A nearby kiln burnt stone to make lime (see chapter 4).

Quarrymen picking out channels in the traditional way at the Ham Hill stone quarries in April 1922.

A vertical saw at the Norton Stone Works, Ham Hill, in April 1922. The stone slab on the carriage is being moved forwards slowly as sawing progresses.

BRITISH GEOLOGICAL SURVEY (NERC COPYRIGHT RESERVED)

Tooling marks on an old face in Deep Quarry at Ham Hill, with a scale 200 mm long. June 2000.

Centuries of quarrying have left this unusual landscape of overgrown workings and tips at Ham Hill. June 2000.

Another important freestone worked in medieval times was the pale oolitic limestone from Doulting, east of Shepton Mallet, where St Andrew's Quarry (ST 647435) supplied stone for building Glastonbury Abbey and Wells Cathedral. In the 1890s Frederick Witcombe was working here but the main activity was a little to the north in Chelynch Wood where Charles Trask & Sons had quarries using seven cranes. Quarrying was by picking a vertical line of close holes for inserting 'chips and wedges' which were hammered home to split the stone. By 1902 the Chelynch quarries were working on both sides of the lane and were served by branches of a tramway running south to the Doulting Stone Works beside the East Somerset Railway. A large masons' shed with steam-powered machinery including two saw frames and two stone planers was described here in 1893 when Trask & Sons employed 40 quarrymen and about 100 masons, stone drawers, boys, etc. Their Bramble Ditch Quarry (ST 647424) produced a softer stone and had the only steam crane at Doulting, but was abandoned by 1902. Trasks became the Ham Hill & Doulting Stone Co. in

The Doulting Stone Works was once served by an overhead traveller crane, but all now lies derelict. February 2001.

1896 and continued until at least 1939, by which date A. Gane & Sons were also at Doulting.

The quarries at work today employ mechanised saws to extract the stone. The historic St Andrew's Quarry has been infilled, but there are numerous overgrown spoil heaps and a small quarry face in Chelynch Wood (ST 650438). Traces of the Trask tramway and parts of the old stone works also survive.

Blue lias limestone has been worked extensively around Somerton, Keinton Mandeville, Charlton Mackrell and Street. This grey stone is seen in many houses of central Somerset, where Ham stone is often used for window and doorway dressings. It has also found a wide market for paving and kerb stones. William Marshall witnessed the quarrying and polishing of blue lias as he travelled from Langport and Somerton to Shepton Mallet in September 1794, noting:

Large limestone flags … Marble quarries on either side
of the road. Many men at work; and teams waiting.
Mostly raised in large slabs, six or eight inches thick,
and several feet in dimensions.

He saw men polishing the harder stone, hence his reference to 'marble'. There are no true marbles in Somerset but it is a term commonly given to polishable limestones.

Forty-nine quarrymen were recorded at Keinton Mandeville in 1831 and by 1898 the Hard Stone Firms Ltd was the largest employer with 60 men in nine quarries (including Coombe and Harepitts) here and at

A view over Station Quarry, Charlton Mackrell, July 1992.
The thin even beds of blue lias limestone are removed in the
shallow quarry to leave a low face characteristic of the
neighbourhood.

Charlton, with a further 30 men in two quarries at Street. The workable limestone is found close to the surface in up to 16 horizontal beds just a few inches thick. Clay partings allowed the stone beds to be prised up with large bars, before being lifted out with a crane. Slabs up to 14ft (4.27m) square were raised but had to be split with plugs and feathers to the required size. The thin even beds made the stone ideal for building, paving, kerbs, channels, chimney pieces and headstones, while thicker beds found at Street were useful for steps, sills and lintels. The blue lias quarries were generally shallow, and once restored to farmland a low quarry face was left along the boundaries as the only evidence. Other quarries are active in the district today.

To improve the markets, the Keinton quarriers planned a standard gauge tramway alongside the road with the intention of joining with the Great Western Railway near Castle Cary. This was overtaken by the GWR's new Castle Cary to Langport link in 1906. In 1898 a traction engine was hauling 16 tons of stone in two trucks to the railway, returning with corn, coal, road metalling and other materials.

Outcrops of metamorphic Devonian slates in west Somerset provided a material less durable than Cornish or Welsh slates, but they were of local importance especially in the second half of the nineteenth century. There were three main quarries in addition to numerous small local ones on Exmoor, the Brendons and the south Quantocks. Roofing slates from Treborough were used for Dunster Castle in 1425, and Oakhampton Quarry was recorded in 1608. Despite the introduction of machinery in the nineteenth century, roofing slates were still split by hand until all the quarries had closed by 1939. Large spoil tips are a feature of these quarries, for one ton of finished slate might produce 20 tons of waste.

The Treborough Quarries (ST 015368) were developed on the edge of the Brendon Hills from 1850 by William Pritchard who came from Caernarvonshire, the centre of the North Wales slate industry. The stone was blasted with gunpowder and the quarried slate was trammed through a tunnel to a water-powered dressing mill. A second quarry was begun in 1863 and workings in this steeply dipping slate may have extended underground. Pritchard died in 1882 and was buried in Treborough churchyard along with other slate workers. His firm carried on until 1889. Treborough Quarry was reworked in 1894–1910 and 1914–35, when a stationary steam engine was installed. A 'Blondin' crane (aerial ropeway)

Working at Tracebridge slate quarry in the 1930s. Note the slabby nature of the quarry face and the stone ready for lifting to the surface in the aerial ropeway skip.

C. TILLEY COLLECTION

lifted stone from a depth of 300ft (91m). As well as roofing slates, the quarry also produced slabs for cisterns, floors, hearths, shelving, steps, sills, staddle stones, chimney tops and garden edging. Limestone was also quarried here. Since abandonment, the main quarry has been infilled but the dressing floors, wheelpit, tunnel and the extensive tips survive in woodland.

Oakhampton Quarry (ST 086301) was worked in the early-seventeenth century, but it was not until the 1870s that the Wiveliscombe Slate Quarry Co. started on a commercial scale. This coincided with the opening of the nearby Devon & Somerset Railway, with the potential of transport to markets further from the immediate area. Blue and purple slates were quarried, for roofing, mantelpieces, flooring, sills, hearthstones and water and beer cisterns. The quarry reached a depth of 300ft (91m) and had two inclines worked by an 8hp steam engine. Closure came in about 1914. There are remains here and at other quarries in nearby Combe Wood, worked on and off between 1841 and 1929.

Slate was worked at Tracebridge Quarry (ST 067212) where the River Tone passes through a narrow gorge on the border with Devon. Bryant Bros employed 12 men here in 1896. The stone was trammed out through an adit tunnel to a dressing mill next to the river where a low breastshot water-wheel powered stone dressing equipment, four saws and a planer. When quarrying went deeper in the early-twentieth century, the stone was raised by an aerial crane to supply a new mill opposite the quarry entrance. The Tracebridge Quarry Ltd employed up to 25 men before final closure in 1939 after an accident. The

waste tips were removed for wartime airfield construction and the quarry is now overgrown, with the original dressing mill and wheelpit mostly in ruins.

Roadstone and aggregates are by far the most dominant quarry products in Somerset and England today. Mendip's Carboniferous limestone is the main supplier and active workings include Battscombe and Callow Hill near Cheddar, but the largest are the 'super-quarries' of Merehead and Whatley near Frome which send millions of tons of crushed stone by rail to the South East of England. Such modern quarries bear little resemblance to those of 1950 at the end of the Age of Steam, in terms of size and the machinery employed.

Roadstone quarries have been worked all over Somerset, but their scale increased dramatically from the late-nineteenth century to meet the demands of road makers and the building industry. The more numerous early quarries were generally small and were worked in benches by hand with some drilling and blasting with gunpowder and high explosives after the 1890s. Machine drilling did not become widespread until the twentieth century and the broken rock was trammed on narrow gauge lines from the quarry face to the crushing and screening plant. Mechanical excavators became common as quarries increased in size from the 1930s onwards and quarry tramways and sidings remained significant until motor lorries took over most transport forty years later. Abandoned roadstone quarries can be dangerous places, having steep faces and being flooded to a great depth. Smaller quarries are sometimes more accessible and safer to visit. Their archaeology may include shot holes for blasting in the face and the concrete foundations for storage bins, crushing and screening plant, since most salvageable equipment has been removed. A smithy for tool sharpening and undertaking repair work was also an essential part of most quarries.

Frome is close to an area of extensive roadstone quarrying at the eastern end of the Mendip limestone. Vallis Vale has older and smaller quarries where the Somerset Quarry Co. worked from 1894, producing 'Mendip Mountain Limestone'. Tramways ran from the quarries to a crushing plant at Hapsford where the stone breakers and an incline were worked by a water-wheel and Gilkes turbine, supplemented by a 10hp portable steam engine made by Brown & May of Devizes. Some of the quarries continued working into the mid-twentieth century, but all are now silent. They are mostly overgrown but two quarries have clean faces worth investigating (ST 757487 and ST 755492).

A small abandoned roadstone quarry face at Vallis Vale exposing a classic 'unconformity' where younger limestones overlie dipping Carboniferous limestones, with 90 million years missing between. This is of special interest to geologists, but the industrial archaeologist will look for traces of quarrymen's bore holes for blasting. February 2001.

Jaw-type stone crushers of all sizes were once used in roadstone quarries where they could be worked by a portable steam engine. Concrete foundation bases for these and other plant may survive in old quarries.

Quarries at Vobster were opened in a folded outcrop of Carboniferous limestone by the Westbury Iron Co. in 1869 and eventually stone from the main quarry was drawn on a double tramway through a 230ft (70m) tunnel to the stone breakers, screens and storage bins. From here a branch railway ran to Mells Road station where an asphalt plant was opened in 1887. Eleven years later asphalt was being sent to South Wales and London, and roadstone went to Somerset, Wiltshire, Berkshire, Oxford and Sussex; gravel had also been supplied to Windsor Park. John Wainwright & Co. were here, followed by Roads Reconstruction Ltd, which incorporated many quarry companies in 1934 and became ARC in 1967.

While some quarries sold their stone as 'Mendip Mountain Limestone', so-called 'Mendip granite' quarries were opened near Stoke St Michael in small exposures of older

Silurian andesite, an igneous rock with hard-wearing properties and ideal for roads. John Wainwright & Co. Ltd have been at Moons Hill Quarry (ST 664462) since at least 1902, and were also involved at limestone quarries around Windsor Hill near Shepton Mallet, Wells, Cheddar and Vobster in the early-twentieth century. The Mendip Granite and Asphalt Co. Ltd worked an igneous quarry at Downhead at the turn of the century. A tramway linked these quarries to a works and exchange sidings at West Cranmore station on the East Somerset Railway.

Outside the Mendips, hard limestones and sandstones were also exploited by private firms and councils around Exmoor and the Brendon Hills, but most especially along the west side of the Quantock Hills at West Quantoxhead, Bicknoller, Halsway and Triscombe.

4

LIME BURNING

When limestone (calcium carbonate) is burnt at 900°C, carbon dioxide is released to leave behind quicklime (calcium oxide) which reacts violently with water to form slaked or hydrated lime. Lime has been used for building mortar since Roman times. References to limekilns in the medieval period include work on Taunton Castle in 1207–08, but it was not until the eighteenth century that there was a rapid growth in the number of kilns to produce lime for agriculture. This largely rural industry had declined by 1900 as a result of agricultural depressions, competition from large commercial lime burners, and the introduction of Portland cement for building. Some kilns continued to be built in the twentieth century, culminating in a large gas-fired rotary kiln at Battscombe Quarry near Cheddar, burning lime for the steel and chemical industries, while a far smaller kiln has been producing hydraulic lime from the blue lias at Tout Quarry, Charlton Adam.

Relatively few lime burners or merchants are recorded in trade directories but this is misleading because many limekilns were on farms, estates or a part of stone quarrying businesses. Agricultural lime was the most important use and became widespread on farms in the late-eighteenth century. In 1798 John Billingsley called lime

the grand manure of this district, by which the improvements of cultivation are in a great measure brought about, kilns for burning it are numerous, and generally thought well constructed.

A common kiln, built for about £10, could produce 480 bushels of lime per week which was enough to 'manure' three acres. In 1797 lime cost 14d–16d per quarter.

Farmers carted the lump lime from the kiln and allowed it to slake in the corner of a field before being harrowed and ploughed in. This soluble form of calcium neutralises soil acidity to encourage the action of bacteria which render fertilisers and other nutrients available for plant growth. It also improves the texture of soil. Today, ground limestone is the most usual agricultural 'lime' dressing which, although less soluble, is far cheaper and easier to handle.

Lime was slaked and mixed with sand for building mortar. Markets fell once Portland cement became available in the second half of the nineteenth century, although lime continued to be sold to the trade in small quantities. Certain limes were used for stucco work and plaster, lime ash was used for laying hard cottage floors, and there was whitewash. Victorian water suppliers used lime for softening water, while it was also used for purifying gas and sewage.

Surviving limekilns are difficult to date but most probably belong to the early- to mid-nineteenth century. They were usually the draw type, which could burn for weeks if a continuous supply of lime was required. A typical limekiln was sited at a quarry and built into a bank so the pot could be loaded from the top and discharged from below. Free-standing kilns required a loading ramp. Local stone was used for the thick insulating walls, although details might be finished in brick. The kiln pot was circular, with sides tapering towards the base. It was usually lined with header-bonded bricks, many of which show signs of vitrification from the heat. Some in west Somerset were lined with stone, perhaps reflecting the cost of transporting bricks into that area. The draw arch is the most striking feature of a limekiln, giving access to the draw hole at the base of

Pack donkeys delivering limestone to the Warren limekiln at Watchet, late-nineteenth century. This method of delivering stone and culm and taking away the lime would have been commonplace a century before. SOMERSET STUDIES LIBRARY

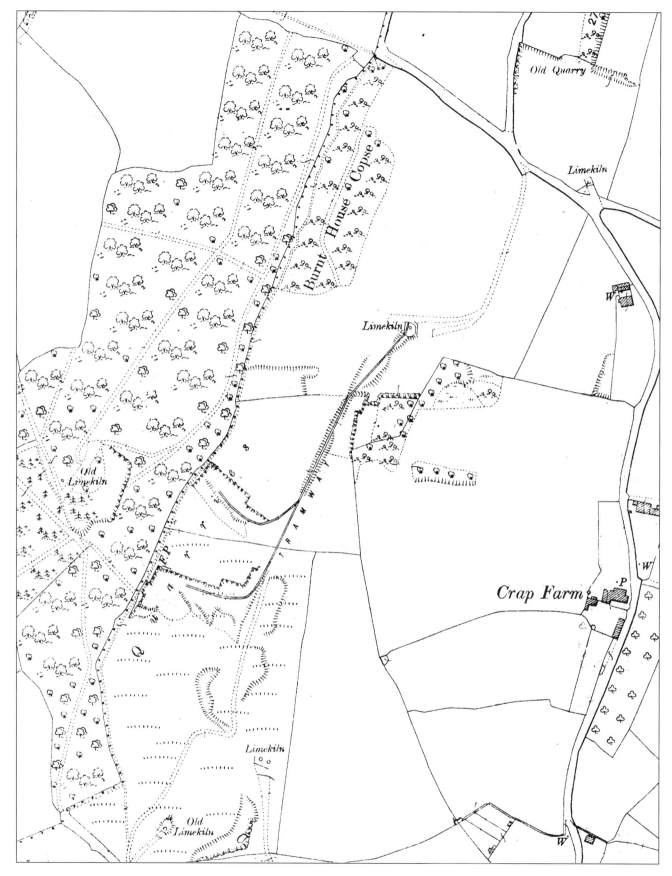

An area of working and abandoned lime burning at Thurlbear Wood near Stoke St Mary, shown on the Ordnance Survey 25-inch map of 1901. Note the tramway leading from the shallow quarries to the larger kiln which has access from the nearest lane.

the pot. Sometimes there may be two or even three arches as in kilns at Castle Hill near Wiveliscombe. The draw hole provided draught and the means of extracting the burnt lime. Small poking holes above it were for inserting an iron bar to test or dislodge the charge.

Brushwood, furze, timber and even peat were available for fuel, but Welsh culm, a form of anthracite, was preferred from the late-eighteenth century. Broken limestone was delivered by cart or barrow to the kiln head and tipped into the pot for burning. The stone and fuel were loaded in the proportions of four to one. As burnt lime was taken from the draw hole, more stone and fuel were added at the top. It might take three or four days to burn the lime and controlling the burning was an art. The draught could be regulated through an iron draw hole door, if fitted, and the poking holes. The kiln top was usually left open. If there was no sheltered access to the draw hole it was usual to attach a shed to protect the burnt lime from the weather when was being handled or stored. The lime burner had to be in attendance at critical hours and sometimes a special shelter was provided, as at Warren Bay and Glenthorne.

It has been suggested that there may be around 1000 limekiln sites in Somerset. The parish Tithe Maps of around 1840 provide the first useful information, sometimes marking the actual kiln or giving a field name to indicate its presence. More reliable, however, are the first and second edition 25-inch Ordnance Survey maps of the 1880s and 1900s which include most sites, although by this time many were already disused. Most kilns were single, but there were also banks of two or more. A few limekilns have been restored, including one at Bishopswood Meadows (Somerset Wildlife Trust) in the Blackdown Hills and another conserved as a millennium project at South Petherton, but more deserve some form of recognition or preservation.

The kilns were widely distributed on the limestones of the county, with just a few exceptions. About a third were on the Carboniferous limestone of Mendip. Here, for example, the parish of Priddy had at least 70 limekilns, many of them farmers' kilns related to agricultural improvements in the nineteenth century. They stood alone in the fields and burnt stones cleared from the surface and, it would seem, even taken from walls. Only six of these small kilns survive in a recognisable form. The remains of limekilns can be seen at Vallis Vale (ST 754492) near Frome, where two were recorded burning stone from the roadstone quarries in the 1890s. These are

all in great contrast to twentieth-century commercial kilns in the Mendip quarries at Battscombe, Callow Hill or Gurney Slade.

One of the old limekilns at Vallis Vale is revealed in February 2001. During the summer abandoned structures like this become almost totally lost beneath vegetation.

Bank of two limekilns at Tengore Lane near Long Sutton, March 1994. This picture also shows the building quality of the local blue lias stone.

Quarry waste from the lias limestone was also an important source of lime. A bank of twin kilns (ST 454266) in a shallow quarry between Tengore and Limepits Lanes near Long Sutton has a loading ramp on each side. The culm fuel was barged up the Parrett Navigation to Load Bridge before being brought here by road. A document refers to a limekiln in the vicinity in 1754. The tradition continues, as in recent years hydraulic lime has been produced in a modern kiln at Tout Quarry, Charlton Adam.

In the Ham Hill quarries a small limekiln (ST 481164) was in existence in the 1880s and produced lime from the quarry waste. This kiln has been repaired at some time with fragments of sawn Portland stone, presumably from the nearby stone works. Although only part of the draw arch survives, the draw hole, a poking hole and the brick-lined pot are intact.

The Permo-Triassic sandstones contain calcareous stones and there is a close relationship between the outcropping Budleigh Salterton Pebble Beds and limekilns around Milverton and Ash Priors, where the limestone pebbles from these conglomerate beds were selected for burning and the rest used for road making. A kiln in a wood at Northway (ST 138294) is one of the few 'listed' limekilns in Somerset and there are other old kilns nearby around Ash Priors. An impressive group of three kilns at Castle Hill (ST 096285) obtained cheaper fuel after the opening of the Devon & Somerset Railway to Wiveliscombe in 1871 although the railway also brought competition from bigger lime producers. At Milverton there was a railway siding to a bank of three kilns built in 1872 and which worked until about 1912. The site was demolished when the Milverton bypass was built along the disused railway course.

Locally significant kilns were sited on the rare outcrops of Devonian limestone in west Somerset, where lime was in great demand for improving the acid soils of Exmoor and the Brendon Hills. There was a limeworks at Newland Quarry (SS 825385) near Exford since 1800. Two deep quarries were developed and a 23ft (7m) diameter water-wheel worked pumps and winding gear by about 1880. A complex arrangement of tunnels directed water to and from the wheel which was connected to the pump via a flat rod to a T-bob at a shaft. There were two banks of limekilns, of two and three kilns each. Isaac Taylor worked here but leased the quarry to John Westcott by 1891. The west quarry had been abandoned in the 1880s and the remaining quarry was suddenly flooded in 1914

Limekiln at Castle Hill near Wiveliscombe. The arrangement of additional draw holes or poking holes is unusual.

Bank of two large buttressed limekilns also at Castle Hill. The three form part of one of the finest groups in Somerset.

The limekiln at Bossington beach was supplied from boats landing on the shore. This view shows one of the two draw arches.

The remains of the pot of the Bossington beach limekiln. The Exmoor coast is beyond.

A pair of ruined limekilns at East Quantoxhead, just one of many former sites along the Somerset coast.   May 1976.

and the site closed a few years later. The T-bob house survives at the edge of the quarry. Limestone on the Brendon Hills was quarried for burning at Nurcott near Luxborough until the 1920s. An incline from Nurcott Quarry (SS 965388) was worked by a water-wheel, and its pit survives along with traces of limekilns. Limestone was also quarried near the Treborough slate quarries and there is an impressive pair of buttressed kilns with three draw arches beside the lane (ST 017369).

Limekilns were built on the coast, for example around Watchet, where local limestone, perhaps including stone collected from the beach, was burnt with culm shipped over from South Wales. Hydraulic lime, which has the property of setting under water, was obtained from the blue lias at Watchet. In 1756 John Smeaton employed a reputable merchant to hire a vessel and forward this lime, rammed into 80 cider casks, to his Eddystone Lighthouse workyard at Plymouth. Among the coastal sites are kilns at Lilstock (ST 173453), Kilve (ST 144444) and Warren Bay (ST 057433), this last being a line of three kilns, each of a different date and style. A bank of three limekilns at Doniford (ST 088430) has an access ramp to the top. Further west, along the Exmoor coast, both limestone and fuel from Wales were landed on the beach in front of the kilns. A limekiln on Bossington Beach (SS 891483) is free-standing, with two draw arches, while another at remote Glenthorne (SS 800495) also has two draw arches and lime burners' accommodation behind a wall along the beach.

Some kilns did not depend on a local limestone source but were located where the lime was needed by taking advantage of available transport facilities. Limekilns at Firepool in Taunton, for example, were fed by the Bridgwater & Taunton Canal (ST 231254), while a pair of kilns high up on the summit of Brendon Hill (ST 020342) obtained limestone and fuel by means of the West Somerset Mineral Railway.

Plaster of Paris was made from gypsum quarried from the cliffs at Warren Bay near Watchet and there was a small cement works at Goodings Mill, Washford, from the 1850s until about 1906. Hydraulic cement was made at Pylle, where the Somerset Lime & Cement Works (ST 608387) had a siding from the Somerset & Dorset Railway. The largest cement works was at Dunball near Bridgwater. The Down End Cement Works was established by John Board & Co. in 1844 and products from the Polden Lias were shown at the Great Exhibition in 1851. The firm was expanded in the later nineteenth century by William Savage Akerman who developed a true Portland cement. The cement factory was well placed, with sidings alongside the Bristol & Exeter Railway, but in the 1890s Board & Co. moved to a works on the other side of the line. This site disappeared beneath the M5 motorway works but part of the Down End site (ST 314413) still contains a bank of six kilns.

5

MINING FOR METALS

Metal mining was mostly confined to the uplands in west and east Somerset. The presence of Roman lead miners on Mendip is well known, but slag, occasional coins and radiocarbon dating have provided increasing evidence for Iron Age, Roman and medieval iron working on Exmoor, the Brendons and the Blackdown Hills. Mineralisation on Exmoor and the Brendon Hills is associated with the folded Devonian slates and sandstones. On Exmoor, the Roman Lode (SS 753382) is a long openwork trench with prospecting pits across a hillside near Cornham Ford. It could be Roman, but most of the early earthworks here may date from the sixteenth century. A water-powered smithy at Horner Wood (SS 897439) was worked in the fifteenth to seventeenth centuries, using local iron. On the Brendons, nineteenth-century miners encountered early openwork trenches but they have been infilled. Over 130 extraction pits at Colton Pits (ST 053348) may be medieval or earlier. Nodular iron deposits were worked on the Blackdowns from at least the Roman period.

The principal nineteenth-century iron mining developments took place on the Brendons where the ore is siderite (iron carbonate). The lode, which weathers to haematite near the surface, is not continuous and the ore is found in pockets. Its potential was discovered in the 1840s and the Brendon Hills Mining Co. was formed in 1852 and began work at Raleigh's Cross. The Ebbw Vale Co. took over, and their Brendon Hills Iron Ore Co. mined 4000 tons of ore in 1855. The first workings were from adits until shafts were sunk. The Brendon Hills became a significant source of non-phosphatic iron ore required for the new Bessemer steel-making process but its exploitation was only made possible by building the West Somerset Mineral Railway for carrying ores to Watchet for shipment to the furnaces in South Wales. Morgan Morgans was the mines captain and railway engineer until 1867 and under his guidance

production rose to 36,000 tons in 1864. Output was affected by a steel recession but picked up again in the 1870s so that 46,894 tons were mined in 1877. Thereafter, decline was rapid because of competition from Spanish ores and the introduction of the new Gilchrist-Thomas steel-making process which could use any ores. Only 10,081 tons were produced in 1883 when the Brendon mines were abandoned and the mining communities at Brendon Hill and Gupworthy declined virtually overnight.

The most powerful steam engines on the hill were at the large Raleigh's Cross Mine (ST 025342). In 1865 it had a 50in beam engine for pumping and a horizontal winding engine. The shaft was 820ft (250m) deep when the mine closed. The buildings were demolished in 1907 and a few mounds in a field are all that remain today. In contrast, Burrow Farm Mine (ST 009345) has the only surviving engine house, which would not look out of place in Cornwall (Cornish miners were involved in its building). It contained a 25in cylinder rotary beam engine for pumping and winding from a nearby shaft. It was built in about 1880 but was only to be in operation for three years. The waste dump is also part of the iron mining industrial archaeology. A similar engine house at Kennisham Hill (ST 963361) was built in 1873 for pumping and winding, but this was demolished in 1978. Carnarvon Pit (ST 021342) had a horizontal winding engine and portable pumping engine. Gupworthy Pit (SS 967353) had steam winding engines at the new and old pits. Langham Hill (SS 977356) had a 40in rotary beam engine for pumping and winding in 1866 and the shaft reached 700ft (213m) by

Pictured: *Burrow Farm Mine has the sole surviving engine house on the Brendon Hills. A pumping and winding beam engine was erected here in a final working of the mine in c.1880–83.*

Above: *Kennisham Hill engine house in a ruinous state in 1976, two years before it was demolished. It was built for a pumping and winding engine in 1873.*

Left: *The Burrow Farm engine house, showing the low bob wall upon which the beam was pivoted.*

1874. Langham was also at the head of an aerial ropeway from Kennisham Hill adit. This was worked by a portable steam engine of a type used on several of the mines, and the foundations have been excavated in recent years. Nearby, a horse whim worked an incline from Bearland Wood Mine. A ventilating chimney of this mine stands in Chargot Wood (SS 974358).

The Somerset Mineral Syndicate attempted to reopen some mines in 1907–10, with adits driven at Timwood and West Colton. The latter (ST 050351) was connected by a narrow gauge tramway to the top of the refurbished WSMR incline. The ore was found to crumble in the blast furnaces, so the Watchet Briquetting Syndicate first converted it into briquettes in a kiln at Washford station (ST 048411).

The Brendon Hills Iron Ore Co. also mined the western extension of the Brendon iron lodes at Eisen Hill (SS 906369 and SS 915369), where high ground allowed deep workings without the need for pumping. The ore had to be carted either to the railhead at Gupworthy or down steep roads to the coast for shipment. Eisen Hill could never have been worked to its full potential without a mineral railway, and this was true of the smaller mines further west. Exmoor's iron mines were on a much smaller scale and none had a permanent steam engine for pumping or winding.

John Knight of Simonsbath had acquired mineral rights on Exmoor in the hope of finding copper, but it was his son Sir Frederic Knight who did most to promote iron mining in the 1850s. The mines came to little despite his projected mineral line from Simonsbath to Porlock Weir, for which the Dowlais Iron Works agreed in 1855 to supply the rails. Knight leased mines to the Dowlais Co. in 1855–58 and they excavated openworks at Cornham Ford (SS 749387) in 1855–56. Leases were also taken up briefly in the late 1850s by Schneider & Hannay of Lancashire and the Plymouth Iron Co. of Methyr Tydfil.

Wheal Eliza (SS 785381) was one of the larger mines around Simonsbath. It was never successful when opened for copper in 1846–49, but was worked again for iron by Schneider & Hannay in 1856–59. A shaft, adit, waste dumps and ruined miners' cottages survive, while across the River Barle a leat leads to the site of a pumping wheel. Picked Stones (SS 798377) was among the smaller sites investigated by the Plymouth Iron Co. in 1857–59. The Exmoor Mining Syndicate was here in 1912–14 and built a tramway to the nearest road so that ore could be carried to Dulverton station. The more promising Blackland Iron Mine (SS 841368) by Pennycombe Water was worked in 1875–81 by the Exford Iron Co. Again, transport was never going to be easy had the mine become a success and there were plans for a 9-mile narrow gauge tramway to Dulverton and a proposed aerial ropeway to

Dulverton station in 1895. In 1907 the Withypool Mining Co. employed a traction engine to haul ore to Minehead and in 1908–10 the Somerset Mineral Syndicate built a 436-yard (400 m) narrow gauge incline up the steep valley side to the Withypool road. There were further investigations in 1937 and 1942. The site has a waste dump, two adits and the tramway course.

The lead mining and smelting industries on the Mendip Hills lasted from Roman times to the first decade of the twentieth century. Galena (lead sulphide) is found emplaced in fissures in the Carboniferous limestone, where it was at first relatively easy to extract. Evidence for Roman lead mining comes from the discovery of inscribed lead ingots, including five from Green Ore dated to AD69–79 and displayed in the museums at Wells (four) and Taunton. Although activity at Charterhouse was long suggested by a settlement and fortlet close to workings or rakes on Ubley Warren, it was not until 1993 that archaeologists positively dated a shallow rake to the early-Roman period.

Mendip was divided into four Liberties (Chewton, Harptree, Wells and West) in medieval times when the

The site of Wheal Eliza on both sides of the River Barle, near Simonsbath. Note the leat following the far bank leading to the position of a pumping water-wheel to the left of the footbridge. The mine shaft is on the extreme left.

lead industry had its own laws and customs enforced by special courts, as was common in similar English mining districts. There was more activity in the mid-sixteenth century, particularly during Elizabeth I's reign, but by 1670 the mines were declining because of drainage problems with increased depth. Centuries of activity are represented by 'gruffy ground', the name given to the grassed-over areas of old lead workings, shafts, pits, mounds of spoil and thousands of tons of slag.

The nineteenth century saw the final phase of the Mendip lead industry when most attention was turned to the re-smelting of ancient slags still containing economic quantities of lead which could be processed by improved smelting techniques. The three main smelting sites were at Charterhouse, Priddy and East Harptree. There was some mining activity at various locations but of only limited success. In September 1812, the *Bristol Mercury*

The ancient lead workings known as Charterhouse Rakes.

New Shaft was sunk by the Mendip Hills Mining Co. in search of lead in the 1840s, leaving a tip of waste rock spilling into the ancient open working of Ubley Rakes.

BRUCE HOWARD

mentioned two 'Fire Engines', presumably for pumping, on the Wells Mining Co.'s 'rich and promising' lead mine at Chewton Mendip. Over 200 tons of lead ore had been raised, although ominously the engine shaft had fallen in.

The Charterhouse and Ubley Rakes are open excavations on the hillside across the valley southeast of Charterhouse. Now partly within a nature reserve, these rocky excavations may date back to medieval and perhaps even Roman times. In 1844–49 the Mendip Hills Mining Co. was active here, employing Cornish miners to sink a number of shafts among the old rakes. Barwell's Shaft (ST 507554) in Charterhouse Rakes had a horse whim for winding and the round platform still survives. Nearby are the ruins of the mine manager's Bleak House, and workers' tenements. The square-sectioned Stainsby's Shaft (ST 505555) was sunk to a depth of 354ft (108m) before underground work ceased with only traces of lead ore discovered.

The Roman slags heaped about at Charterhouse were smelted by Dr Benjamin Somers from 1824 to 1848, apparently to great profit. The Mendip Hills Mining Co. established a works in Velvet Bottom in 1848 to smelt the old slag and washings (slimes) which they excavated in the valley and trammed to the site. This material was concentrated in round buddles using water brought a mile in a wooden launder which was vandalised when the inhabitants of Cheddar discovered the waste tailings were polluting their water supply. A series of dams across Velvet Bottom collected the tailings which are now grown over with grass. The company later had to buy up a local farm because the smelting works fumes were contaminating the land. The Cornish lead smelters Treffry & Co. took over in 1861 and built a new smelter at Blackmoor (ST 507560) which worked until 1878. It was abandoned seven years later and remains the most impressive lead works site, with lines of parallel flues for condensing the fumes into a lead-rich soot. There are mounds of black glassy slag and reservoirs here provided water for dressing processes.

The Romans obtained silver from the lead (perhaps their main reason for coming here) and in the nineteenth century a small plant was constructed at Charterhouse to extract silver by the Pattinson process. In 1864, 2660 ounces of Mendip silver were recorded but there are no records after 1879. The old Pattinson plant was destroyed in the late 1960s, although the line of the small flue marks the site (ST 506556).

A line of round buddles and the course of a tramway in the 'gruffy ground' of Velvet Bottom, Charterhouse. August 2001.

The St Cuthbert's lead works near Priddy c.1900. Smoke appears to be coming from at least one chimney, which dates this picture to before closure in 1908. The works has been almost completely demolished and it is difficult to imagine the scale of this site. M.J. MESSENGER COLLECTION

The Blackmoor lead smelter flues at Charterhouse. August 1992.

Ruined walls at the St Cuthbert's lead works site. August 1992.

The second important lead site is at the Priddy Mineries where the remains of the St Cuthbert's smelting works (ST 545505) lie in a shallow valley near Priddy. The Cornishman Nicholas Ennor came here in 1857 and concentrated lead slag in buddles before smelting it. This activity led to a notable lawsuit in 1860 after the Wookey Hole paper mill received his lead tailings in its stream, the result being that over 20 catchpits were installed to prevent the pollution. In 1862–69 the St Cuthbert's Lead Smelting Co. (managed by Horatio Nelson Hornblower of Cornwall) developed furnaces which did not require the slag to be concentrated before smelting and a beam engine provided the blast. The smelter was rebuilt in 1881 and 650 tons of lead were produced in 1889, but falling lead prices led to its closure in 1908 and thus the end of the lead industry on Mendip. Fragments of masonry and some flues remain, but there is far less at the smaller Chewton lead works (ST 546511) except for black slag and the line of the flue. In the gruffy ground just to the north are buddle pits, while the dammed Waldegrave

Pool is a reminder of how precious water was for their operation.

The only smelter chimney remaining on Mendip is at Smitham Hill, where the East Harptree lead works (ST 555546) operated in 1867–75, again utilising old slag. The chimney is in the Cornish style, in stone with the upper part finished in brick.

Calamine (zinc carbonate) was mined on Mendip at Shipham and Rowberrow, where there is gruffy ground and a chimney for an oven to process the ore (ST 445574). The zinc supplied the brass industry in Bristol in the mid-eighteenth century. The pits were shallow and winding was by a hand windlass, although an old locomotive was adapted as a stationary steam engine at the deepest mine in the centre of Shipham village. Mining had finished by 1853 but there was prospecting in 1869–70. Calamine was also mined at East Harptree in the late-eighteenth century.

The 1820 beam engine house at Glebe Shaft of the Buckingham Mine, Dodington, is a remarkable survivor. It is seen here in May 1976.

The only surviving chimney on Mendip is at the East Harptree smelting works. The top is finished in brick, in typical Cornish style, and has been conserved. November 1981.

Copper ore was mined from the Devonian strata around the flanks of the Quantocks, where the Buckingham Mine at Dodington was the largest and most successful working. There had been mining here earlier in the eighteenth century before the Buckingham Mine was begun in 1786. Cornishmen were in charge, with William Jenkin of Redruth acting as agent to the Marquis of Buckingham, and Samuel and Matthew Grose involved with the mining. Shafts were sunk and levels driven, and copper ore was shipped from Combwich on the Parrett to smelting works at Swansea.

The mine closed in 1801 but was reopened in 1817 when a 46in cylinder Boulton & Watt beam engine was installed at Beech Grove (ST 172405) for pumping the deeper workings. This was moved in 1820 to a new engine house at Glebe Shaft (ST 175401) where good ore had been found. The mine closed in 1821 and the engine was sold the following year, advertised as 'about 52 horse power, with cast-iron bob about 12 tons, parallel motion, etc, two wrought-iron boilers each 20ft long and 5ft diameter'. The two engine houses are unusual survivors and the one at Glebe Shaft is the oldest intact beam engine house on a mine in South West England, and is therefore one of Somerset's significant industrial landmarks. The mine's counting house or office is a private residence (ST 174399).

There were brief copper trials at Raswell Farm (ST 212317) over on the south side of the Quantocks in the 1840s and '50s when a small steam engine was installed. The last attempt was by the grandly named Broomfield Consols Copper & Silver-Lead Mining Co. Copper was also mined on Exmoor, but the main sites were further west into Devonshire.

Some ironstone was mined or quarried from pits on Mendip, mostly in the form of ochre for smelting or making paints. The ochre mine at Axbridge (ST 431551) was worked until the 1920s and had a tramway and incline. Other miscellaneous Somerset minerals included small quantities of manganese from sites on the Brendons and Mendip Hills, while veins of barite were worked in a small way by openworks and in the face of a limestone quarry near Cannington before about 1920.

6

COAL MINING AND OTHER FUELS

Radstock Museum, housed in a superb late-Victorian covered market building, is the best starting point for any tour of the Somerset coalfield. Radstock was at the heart of the coal industry and although it now lies in Bath and North East Somerset, it is close enough to the present county border to be considered here. Collieries at Clandown, Paulton, Timsbury and Pensford are to the north, so just the southern part of the coalfield lies in modern Somerset. The Lower and Upper Coal Measures of the Radstock basin were difficult to work because the seams are generally thin and many are steeply folded or faulted.

The Romans may have burnt coal at the temple of Minerva in Bath, which is just along the Fosse Way, but mining was first recorded from the fifteenth century onwards. The earliest workings were along outcropping coal seams, such as around Coleford and Nettlebridge to the south of Radstock, but in time shallow shafts were worked by a windlass. These were of the bell pit type and the larger ones had a horse gin (whim) for winding. Drainage became an increasing problem with depth, and water-wheels were used for pumping from the seventeenth century. Greater depths and more coal could be reached by the use of steam power. The first Newcomen beam engine for pumping was erected by 1745 at Paulton Engine Colliery, while the first rotary engine for winding was at Old Pit, Radstock, in 1794. Horizontal steam engines for winding were installed from the mid-nineteenth century.

The development of the coalfield relied on turnpike roads for local transport, but canals and railways carried the coal to further markets. An important role was played by the Somerset Coal Canal, which joined with the Kennet & Avon Canal, but the Dorset & Somerset Canal failed even to make a complete connection with Frome. A railway was not opened to Radstock until 1854 and the lack of good transport continued to impede the coalfield

until a network of railway branches and colliery tramways was established. Annual output reached 1,250,000 tons in the early-twentieth century when the smaller and older pits were being closed and some new ones were opened.

There were only 12 collieries at the time of nationalisation in 1947, but within ten years these had been reduced to five. Steam power was not replaced by electric winding until 1963 at Kilmersdon and 1966 at Lower Writhlington. These two collieries near Radstock struggled on until 1973 when they were the last on the whole coalfield to close.

It has been said that Somerset has one of the best-preserved coal-mining landscapes in England, largely because in this rural area many of the relatively small older sites have escaped the mass demolition and redevelopment witnessed on most other coalfields. Even so, photographs taken of the collieries in the 1950s and '60s show how much has since vanished. As well as pumping and winding engines, the headframe above the shaft, workshops and offices, the surface of a typical late-nineteenth-century colliery also had screens for sorting the coal. Washeries and pit-head baths appeared in the twentieth century at the larger collieries. It is easily forgotten that spoil heaps ('batches') were major features of the colliery landscape. Although some sites no longer have standing structures, they are likely to contain significant remains of buried archaeology.

Elements demonstrating different mining technologies survive at the surface of colliery sites in the landscape at Coleford and in the Nettlebridge valley. Traces of early shaft mounds in a field at the edge of the mining village

Pictured: *A small field containing early shaft mounds near Coleford, not dramatic but of archaeological significance. January 2001.*

of Coleford (ST 696493) may date from the seventeenth and eighteenth centuries. These were bell pits, where a depression marking the shaft is surrounded by a ring of spoil. They were sunk to no great depth and workings would have extended only a short way once a coal seam was encountered. Larger and probably later earthworks in a wood in the valley just to the south east (ST 699491) have evidence of pits, horse gin platforms, leats and a wheelpit. The water-wheel was for pumping and these deeper coal pits were connected below ground. Where fields have been restored to cultivation, the old colliery sites may show up as a black spread in the plough soil. These early workings contrast with the nineteenth-century collieries.

The arched remains of the rare Guibal fan house at Mackintosh Colliery, near Coleford. January 2001.

Newbury Colliery (ST 696498) was sunk in 1858 by the Westbury Iron Co. which erected coking ovens here and built a railway to the main line at Mells. The mine closed in 1927 and since the 1950s there has been a reconstituted stone factory on the site. Surviving features include the pumping beam engine house which is one of the most impressive buildings on the coalfield. It was built to a high standard in limestone, with attention paid to the window arches and quoins. Massive gritstone blocks on the bob wall supported the beam for the 65in cylinder engine made by Harveys of Hayle in Cornwall. The shaft immediately in front has been capped. Set at right angles

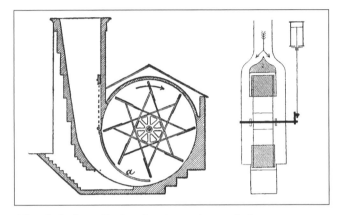

The Guibal ventilation fan, in section and plan.

The Cornish beam engine house at Newbury Colliery, with the winding house to the left. January 2001.

The overgrown coke ovens at Vobster Breach Colliery are important survivals of the English coalfields. January 2001.

The horizontal winding engine house on the Mells Colliery site. January 2001.

is the brick-built winding engine house of the 1920s, with repair workshops beyond. Newbury was connected underground with Mackintosh Colliery (ST 6912497), sunk in 1867, and a tramway ran between the two at the surface. There was a steam winding engine here but its foundations were destroyed when the shaft was capped in 1995. Mackintosh served as the upcast shaft and a steam-driven Guibal Fan was installed to improve the ventilation. Part of the curved brick structure of the fan house is of great interest, but the other buildings have been demolished.

Despite its late date, Vobster Colliery (ST 704489) used a water-wheel for pumping and the course of a leat still leads to the site. It was worked for around fifteen years from 1860 with Vobster Breach Colliery (ST 697488). Both mines had horizontal steam winding engines. Vobster Breach is potentially one of the best-preserved mid-nineteenth century colliery sites of its type, although the engine house, heapstead (shaft), workshops and other structures are ruinous and overgrown. The large spoil tip, typical of all collieries, is equally part of its archaeology. The coal was suitable for making coke and 77 arched coking ovens are a rare survival and possibly the only examples of their type in England. The ovens are in two banks, one single and the other double, and the arches are lined inside with refractory bricks. The ovens were front loaded and closed with an iron door. The course of a horse-drawn tramway crosses a field towards Vobster Colliery from where it climbed to the Newbury railway at Vobster Cross. Coke and coal were sent to the Westbury ironworks in Wiltshire and it is likely that a downturn in that industry in the 1870s caused Vobster Breach to close.

Away to the east, Mells Colliery (ST 712500) worked in 1863–81 and 1909–43. Its site has been turned over to industrial use, but survivals include the stone-built heapstead around the shaft and a brick winding engine house in good condition. This first contained a horizontal steam engine before replacement by an electric winder in the 1930s. Mells Colliery had sidings from the Newbury railway branch which ran alongside. Something of an outlier from the main coalfield, Oxley's Colliery (ST 744508) was sunk to a depth of 420ft (128m) in the late-nineteenth century, but without success. A brick chimney-stack emerging from a copse marks the site in a field to the west of Buckland Dinham.

A group of early colliery sites around Nettlebridge has records dating back to the fifteenth century. Stratton Common (ST 653490) had early pits, now recognised as mounds or marks in the plough soil. Most workings had probably ceased by 1800, when larger mines were being financed and sunk. Pitcote Colliery (ST 655494) was worked in the mid-eighteenth century down to about 1824. The owner Capt. Knatchbull was being rather optimistic when he planned in the 1780s to erect a 'fire engine' to make his mine 'one of the Compleatest Coal Works in all the Country,' and it is unclear whether it was installed. There was certainly a steam engine at nearby Barlake Colliery (ST 661494) in 1820. The mine may have closed ten years later and the site has long lain abandoned and forgotten. It could be that the mounds here contain evidence of the early engine house and other structures. A lane descends from these collieries to the site of the terminus of the unfinished Dorset & Somerset Canal at Edford.

The lonely chimney of Oxley's Colliery marks a failed attempt to mine coal near Buckland Dinham. January 2001.

Moorewood Colliery (ST 642495) lay in the valley bottom and was worked briefly from the 1860s to 1876 by the Westbury Iron Co. It was reopened in 1909 and a tramway was built to sidings on the Somerset & Dorset Railway. The mine closed in 1932 and the horizontal winding engine house still stands although a house has been built on the site.

New Rock Colliery (ST 646506) was sunk in 1819 and by the 1880s had pumping and winding engine houses at two shafts 1200ft (366m) deep. A power house for generating electricity was built in 1904. New Rock is important in this story because it was the scene of the last major investment on the Somerset coalfield. Although steep, the coal seams are thicker than normal and the National Coal Board worked hard to exploit the potential millions of tons of reserves here. New Rock was linked underground with a new 'Mendip Colliery' which was developed at the 1834ft (559m) shaft of the disused Strap Pit. An electric winder was transferred from South Wales and put in a purpose-built winding house. A steam winder worked at New Rock until 1966 when it was replaced by electricity but despite the investment, labour shortages and difficulties in the workings caused the mine to close in 1968. New Rock, now an industrial estate, has the offices, power house and a tip.

Outside the coalfield, prospecting pits were dug on Chard Common in about 1797 and of course nothing was found. Despite this, drilling took place in 1826–27 near the Ship Inn and £3000 was spent boring down to 379ft (115.5m) before it was realised there would be no coal.

Oil shale was a potential Somerset fuel. An unusual brick structure surmounted by an iron shaft stands near the car park near the shore at Kilve (ST 144443). This was part of a small experimental oil shale retort built in the early 1920s. Surrounding structures and pipes have been removed but the retort is a reminder of what could have been if this quiet corner between the Quantock Hills and the sea had witnessed a twentieth-century oil boom.

Most of Britain's oil requirements were imported from the USA in the second half of the nineteenth century. However, oil shale was mined and successfully retorted on a large scale in West Lothian, Scotland. Less successful were enterprises nearer to home, to work the Kimmeridge shale of Dorset for its oil and gas content. Demand for oil increased dramatically during the Great War and potential resources were investigated in south Dorset. Meanwhile, John Berry, a mining engineer who had been gold prospecting in South Africa, had discovered oil shale in the cliffs and beach at Kilve in 1914. It was not until 1920 that any serious attempt was made to investigate this find under the guidance of Dr W. Forbes-Leslie, an expert on oil. The Aqueous Works Boring Co. Ltd drilled a 9in (228mm) exploratory borehole near Kilve Priory to a depth of 1016ft (310m), and the discoveries were said to indicate that the shale contained sulphur-free lubricating oil.

Promotion in 1923 was by the Williton Syndicate Ltd, and Shalime Ltd was to be formed to produce petrol, fuel oil, paraffin and lubricating oil, as well as manufacture cement from the limestone and shale residue. It was estimated that in 10 square miles there were 200 million tons of lubricating oil in the shale beds, which were claimed to be the thickest in the world, and that each ton of shale could yield 40 gallons (182 litres) of oil. But in order to develop this great resource a railway branch from Bridgwater would be needed and moves were put in hand to promote it. Two refineries were planned at Kilve and Combwich, where a contract was made for 72 retorts, and 500 workers' houses would be required.

The experimental retort at Kilve was working in 1924 in the charge of John Black, who had been manager of the Oak Bank Oil Co. in Scotland. It was 35ft (10.7m) high, half that of the normal Scottish retorts. The lower sections were firebrick, with a cast-iron upper section and a feeding hopper. The retort was charged with broken shale every forty minutes, using 2 tons in twenty-four hours. Shale was used as the fuel. The fractions (spirit, kerosene, gas oil and lubricating oil) given off upon heating were passed through condensers and scrubbers and the resulting crude oil was run off into barrels. This oil was apparently stored in the building alongside to await further refining. However, by the end of the year it was found that the oil did indeed contain sulphur, the yield was only 5–10 gallons per ton, and more costly mining rather than opencast quarrying would be necessary because the overburden was far greater than anticipated. And so ended Somerset's 'oil bonanza'. There was limited interest later, when oil shale was found at two sites near Stogursey in 1938 and 1946, the latter when there was an idea that the shale could be used in manufacturing plastics.

Peat from the Somerset Levels, especially to the north and south of Meare, was locally important as a fuel and in this sense is considered to be a 'mineral'. It was cut regularly in the medieval period and the traditional hand turfing with special tools continued down to about 1960. The cut turves were stacked in 'winrows' and then beehive-shaped 'ruckles' to dry over about twelve weeks before being carried away by cart or boat. Most peat was sold locally as a fuel but in the nineteenth century some was carried by rail as far as Bristol or Exeter. Some was cut for horticulture in the 1880s but it was not until the 1960s that this fast became the main market. As a result the old labour-intensive methods were replaced by the first cutting machine in 1963. The large Eclipse Peat Co., which became part of Fisons in 1970, had a narrow gauge railway system to carry the peat to the processing works.

This weighbridge house of c.1820 stood at the entrance of Huish Colliery near Radstock. January 2001.

The remains of the experimental oil shale retort at Kilve. May 1976.

Peat cutting by hand in the 1930s, with turves drying in 'ruckles'.   SOMERSET STUDIES LIBRARY

Rows of traditional peat ruckles are seen behind the narrow gauge tramway of the Eclipse Peat Co. in 1965.

M.J. MESSENGER

7
CLAY INDUSTRIES

The Somerset Brick & Tile Museum at Bridgwater (ST 300376) is a valuable survival of an industry where so much has completely vanished. It incorporates the sole remaining conical kiln of Barham Brothers' brickyard site, now appropriately surrounded by builders' merchants. Displays and artefacts show how the common brick is just one part of a wide range of products, and visitors can learn of the history and techniques of this once thriving industry.

The availability of good building stone in Somerset may be the reason for the relatively late arrival of brick making in the seventeenth century. Clay was dug close to building projects, prepared and made into bricks before

Right: The conical kiln and chimney at the Somerset Brick & Tile Museum, Bridgwater.

Below: Barham Brothers' brick and tile works with its conical kilns is seen here eleven years after its closure in 1965. The old riverside quay on the Parrett is rotting away and the derelict Bridgwater site awaits redevelopment.

firing in clamp kilns which could be crude and wasteful. There were no permanent buildings or kilns, which is supported by the fairly inconclusive results when Taunton's early Southfield brickyard site was excavated in 1977–78. The late-eighteenth century saw the establishment of more permanent brickyards with purpose-built kilns which produced bricks of a better and more reliable quality. Brick making was still a seasonal activity. A duty on bricks in 1784–1850 does not seem to have unduly impeded the industry.

The main period of activity was during the nineteenth and first half of the twentieth century. Brick and tile yards were established wherever there was suitable clay but there were concentrations in Bridgwater, Burnham, Taunton and Yeovil, with others more dispersed. Bridgwater was the main production centre for roofing tiles and was also home to the Bath brick industry. Trade in bricks, tiles and pottery goods declined in the 1930s and by 1939 there were only 15 firms operating in Somerset. Six were around Bridgwater, with branches at Combwich and Burnham, and the others were at Bishop's Hull, Crewkerne, Glastonbury, Highbridge, Evercreech Junction, Minehead and Wellington.

There were closures after the war when poorly paid workers were tempted away by new industries. Somerset's last brickworks, at Wellington, finally closed in 1996. Many brickyards were demolished soon after closure and became industrial estates or other developments. The clay pits were filled as rubbish tips, although those that remain flooded give an idea of their scale, for example around Bridgwater and Combwich.

Clay beds were dug from pits by hand during the winter and allowed to weather in a heap. The clay was next mixed in a pug mill turned by hand or horse power. Summer was the time for making bricks by hand. After being rolled in sand, a 'clot' of clay was thrown into a wooden mould and a man could produce up to 800 bricks a day and even more if he had an assistant. These 'green' bricks were dried in open air 'hacks' or long open-sided drying sheds. From the mid-nineteenth century, steam power was used at the larger works to drive the pug mills and new machines for producing extruded wire-cut bricks. In the early-twentieth century oil or gas engines were in use at the smaller brickyards.

Firing took place in intermittent updraught or downdraught kilns, or continuous types. Loading and unloading by hand was a laborious business and firing took about three days with as much time for the bricks to cool before they could be taken out. The larger Hoffmann kiln could be used continuously, with its chambers being fired in rotation, with some chambers burning, others cooling, unloading or loading. This type needed the regular output from a large brickyard to keep it going, so the intermittent kilns were better suited to the smaller works.

By the mid-nineteenth century the brick and tile yards best placed to meet the increasing demand from mass markets were those with access to good transport. Bridgwater had many advantages. The alluvial clays were highly suitable, many of the brickyards were next to the navigable River Parrett and the railway and new docks became available from the 1840s. Yards were enlarged and new ones built at Bridgwater, Chilton Trinity, Combwich and Puriton to the north, and Dunwear and North Petherton to the south. Large quantities of bricks, roofing tiles and Bath bricks were exported from the port of Bridgwater. Other products included architectural mouldings, roof finials, garden ornaments and drain-pipes. There were also perforated bricks and special perforated malt kiln tiles. The latter were manufactured by John Sealy & Co. of Hamp and Dunwear, just south of Bridgwater. Sealy's products were shown at the Great Exhibition in 1851 and examples of malt kiln tiles have been found as far away as Anglesey, Baltimore (USA) and Quebec. H.J. & C. Major Ltd took over the business in the 1860s and built a circular Hoffmann kiln to increase output. The Hamp yard closed between the wars but the Dunwear works closed in 1956, along with the Colley Lane Patent Tile & Pottery Works (ST 307366). A horizontal steam engine made by W. & F. Wills of Bridgwater in 1886, and reputedly used by Majors, was saved and is preserved (in steam) at Westonzoyland.

Barham Brothers and John Board were among the largest brick and tile producers, while also manufacturing cement and lime. Barhams were renowned for the quality of their roofing tiles and occupied a large site on the east bank of the Parrett from 1857 until 1965. The abandoned kilns and sheds lay derelict for some years before the whole site was redeveloped as an industrial estate. The remaining conical kiln is a notable monument incorporated into the Somerset Brick & Tile Museum. It was originally an updraught kiln before efficiency was improved by conversion to a downdraught type, hence the chimney set in the side. Very few examples of this type of kiln survive nationally.

John Browne, who patented the Bath brick and made use of the old Chandos glass cone (see p. 47), had a number of brick and tile works at Bridgwater. Colthurst, Symons & Co. Ltd were established in 1857. This important firm, with works at Combwich, Burnham and Dunball, sold hand-made tiles until the end. William Symons is said to have designed the Double Roman pattern of tile.

Brick and tile making was subjected to the periodic booms and recessions of the building industry, and those works with higher transport costs were the first to suffer.

A ridge tile extruding machine for a brickworks, made locally by W. & F. Wills Ltd of Bridgwater. Early-twentieth century.   I. & M. MILES COLLECTION

Looking up: clay products in the form of bricks, roof tiles, finials and chimney pots in a Bristol Road terrace, Bridgwater.

Decline set in at the time of the Great War and there was little incentive for investment. One major exception in the inter-war period was the Chilton Tile Factory at Chilton Trinity (ST 299393), built in 1929 and extended in 1933. This new works was set up by John Browne & Co. (Somerset Trading Co. Ltd) to counteract cheap imports of mass-produced tiles from the Continent. It was fully automated and had an unusual zigzag kiln that recycled the waste heat for drying. Up to 5 million tiles were produced annually. The Chilton Tile Factory closed in 1968.

Outside the Bridgwater area, some brickworks were established beside railways which brought coal fuel and took away the products. Such was Somerset's largest brickworks at Poole near Wellington (ST 150217), which was also the last to close. William Thomas & Co. Ltd was established in 1842 and dug clay from a large deposit of Keuper Marl alongside the Bristol & Exeter Railway, to which the brickworks was connected by a siding. Thomas created a Sick Benefit Club for his employees by 1860. In 1867 the largest circular Hoffmann kiln in Britain was built at Poole, with 12 chambers and a tall central chimney. Two similar kilns were added and there were also six pottery kilns. By 1890 Poole was the major brick-works in the West Country, with 150 men employed making bricks, tiles, field drain pipes and pottery. The dark red bricks were formed by a wire-cutting machine and were in such demand for government and railway works that 20 railway trucks were often sent off daily from the siding.

Steam power for the brick-making machinery and hauling clay from the pit was replaced in 1935 by a Ruston & Hornsby diesel engine. After the Second World War there was a great demand for building materials, and Poole produced 7,965,000 bricks in 1950. The three continuous Hoffmann kilns were in use until the 1960s, but were demolished between 1965 and 1978. An automated brick-making plant and a tunnel kiln were installed but these were troubled times and the firm was sold in 1968. Subsequent owners included the Steetley Brick Co., Redland Bricks and Ibstock, who closed the works in 1996. Although the magnificent Hoffman kilns have gone, the manager's house and some other early buildings survive here in an industrial estate, with the clay pit being used for waste disposal.

William Moss started a brickworks at Bishop's Hull in the early 1870s, with a 10hp steam engine to work the plant. The yard was bought by William Thomas of Wellington in 1903, amalgamated with neighbouring Cornish's yard in 1915 and continued as the Taunton Brick & Tile Co. Ltd until closure in 1962. The site was immediately demolished and an industrial estate built here. Survivals in 1939 included the Glastonbury Brick, Tile & Pottery Co., at Glastonbury, the Maiden Beech Brick, Pipe, Tile & Pottery Works at Crewkerne, and the Somerset Brick & Tile Co. Ltd at Evercreech Junction, this last with a siding from the Somerset & Dorset Railway.

Bricks, tiles and pottery were made around the edge of Exmoor. Near Minehead, the Victoria Brick & Tile Works was set up at Alcombe in 1897 by John Marley (later, J.B. Marley & Son). This large brickworks had a Hoffmann kiln and 60,000 bricks could be produced weekly, many of them shipped to Ireland, Cornwall and around the coast. A small yard at the Warren made coarse kitchenware, bricks, tiles and ridge tiles from 1759 until 1919, while along the coast John Ridler had a brick and tile works at Porlock Weir in 1840–88. A small rural brick kiln at Blue Anchor (ST 032435) is a rare survival in Somerset and is Grade II listed. Converted to a shed, the general form survives with fire hole arches along the sides. Robert Henson, the proprietor of the Blue Anchor Hotel, was recorded here in the 1860s. Coal was landed on the beach opposite.

The unique Bath bricks, or scouring bricks, deserve a special mention. The name may derive from their resem-blance to the texture of Bath stone, and they were manufactured in at least ten brickworks beside the River Parrett for a mile above and below Bridgwater's Town Bridge. The bricks were formed from the very fine sandy mud deposited by the Parrett, the best locality being where the river and tidal flow met. Special platforms or 'slime batches' were made beside the river and up to 12ft (3.66m) could be collected every year. After being baked in square or bottle-shaped updraught kilns, the bricks were rubbed off into their final shape. Women were employed to do this until the 1920s. Purchasers reduced the bricks to a powder for polishing, scouring, cleaning cutlery, brass and tinwork. Water was added but soap was not always necessary. Brick and tile makers were closely associated with the industry. The first patent was granted to John Browne and William Champion in 1823. Edward Sealy was another early manufacturer, Barham Brothers and Colthurst, Symons were involved, and the Parrett Bath Brick Co. was begun later in 1886. Such was the importance of the Bath brick industry that a plan to improve the Parrett

A Bath brick manufactured by the Somerset Trading Co., formerly John Browne of Bridgwater.

COURTESY SOMERSET BRICK & TILE MUSEUM

drainage in the 1890s was vigorously opposed because slime batches would have been endangered. In 1859 some 8 million bricks were being made annually, and mostly exported to France, America, the Middle East and China. Output had increased to an average 24 million bricks by the end of the century but the industry collapsed during the Great War when other cleaning agents became available. Some over-fired Bath bricks were built into Bridgwater garden walls in the 1930s. Other scouring bricks were made at Huntspill and Highbridge in the mid-nineteenth century.

As well as bricks and tiles, most brickyards manufactured a variety of pottery goods ranging from roof finials and architectural mouldings to sea kale and rhubarb pots. An interesting site is in Northgate, Bridgwater (ST 298374). This was the Chandos Glass Cone, built and run none too successfully as a glassworks by the first Duke of Chandos in 1725–34. By the 1820s it was being used as a pottery and twenty years later it was incorporated into John Browne's brickyards when three small updraught kilns were built inside, one specialising in glazing. Earthenware vessels, baking dishes, cream pans, sea kale and rhubarb pots, chimney pots, and roof finials were made here. The brick-built cone is estimated to have been 110ft (33 metres) high and therefore one of the tallest in Britain, but it was demolished in 1943. The surviving lower courses have been on display since their excavation in 1976–77.

The preserved foundations of the Chandos glass cone of 1725 at Northgate, Bridgwater. The glass cone was later used as a pottery within a brickworks.

The well known Donyatt pottery was made at a number of potteries and kilns around the village near Horton just west of Ilminster from the late-eleventh century until 1939. Donyatt supplied Taunton with nearly all its domestic and dairy wares in the seventeenth century but this declined rapidly from the eighteenth century onwards. Evidence of kilns and the pottery has been excavated but some standing structures have survived, such as a round thatched stone shed for a pug mill at Whitney Bottom Farm (ST 323138), or workshops and drying sheds at the Old Pottery Garage (ST 325145). Elsewhere, in 1759 the coarse kitchenware requirements of the Luttrell estate were made in a small kiln which is now in the grounds of the Luttrell Arms Hotel at Dunster. A potter from Donyatt worked here at one time.

8

CORN MILLING

Water-powered corn mills became well established during Saxon times so that by 1086 Domesday Book recorded 370 mills in the historic county of Somerset, and only Norfolk and Lincolnshire returned a greater number. Somerset's abundant streams were already the source of power that would affect local economies for close on a thousand years. Hundreds of water-mills were located on streams and rivers within towns and villages or deep in the countryside. Successful sites were refurbished many times so that most mill buildings today date from the eighteenth and nineteenth centuries.

From the early-nineteenth century cast iron began to replace timber for water-wheels, sluices and milling machinery, often manufactured in the county. These and other technological improvements, including turbines, introduced in the wake of the Industrial Revolution enabled some mills to stave off outside competition from larger steam-powered roller mills a while longer. Others down-graded to animal feed, or introduced small roller plant to supplement stones, as in the case of Clapton Mill.

Millers listed in *Kelly's* trade directories fell from 226 in 1866 to 174 in 1902, declining further to 71 in 1927 and just 47 by the outbreak of the Second World War. After the conflict some mills continued until the 1960s or a little later, often relying on animal feed milling. Today, there are no commercial working water-mills, since the last at Clapton Mill near Crewkerne ceased in 1971. There are restored mills in various forms open to the public at Allerford, Bishops Lydeard, Bruton, Burcott, Combe Sydenham, Dunster and Williton.

A typical corn or grist mill working in the second half of the nineteenth century had three floors, with grain bins at the top and two or three pairs of stones on the first floor. The internal or external wheelpit contained an undershot, breastshot or overshot wheel according to the head of water available. Power was typically transmitted from the wheel shaft (axle) by the pit wheel, wallower, upright shaft, great spur wheel and stone nuts to drive the millstones. Most early wooden gearing was replaced by

The recently restored iron water-wheel and wooden launder at Bishops Lydeard Mill.

The pit wheel and wallower at Bishops Lydeard Mill.

Gearing arrangement at Piles Mill, Allerford.

Wooden tuns enclose the two pairs of millstones at Piles Mill. Note the 'crane' for lifting off the runner stone for dressing.

cast-iron wheels with hardwood cogs. Other equipment could be worked, such as a hoist for raising grain sacks to the bin floor. Outside hoists were sometimes given protection by a weather-boarded 'lucam', a feature seen on other industrial buildings such as breweries or warehouses. Elevators could be used for moving grain within the mill.

Grain was ground between the closely set runner and bed stones, fed into the centre of the stones and discharged as meal at the outside. Millstones of around 3ft 6in (1.07m) to 4ft (1.2m) in diameter were made of sandstone conglomerate from around Monmouth but the 'peaks' of Millstone Grit from Derbyshire became more common. The best millstones were the French burr-stones, imported throughout the nineteenth century from the Paris basin. These hard millstones are easily recognised because they were made in segments and held with iron hoops. Composition millstones of emery and cement, which needed less dressing, were developed as a cheaper alternative for preparing animal feeds.

The usual arrangement was to have at least two pairs of millstones so that one set could be kept running while periodically the other was laboriously dressed by hand.

The heavy stones were mounted on a strong wooden hurst frame that was integral to the mill. Later hurst frames were made of cast iron. After grinding, the meal was sifted to separate the broken husks or bran, using rotating machines, such as a bolter which forced fine flour out through a cloth sleeve, or a wire machine which separated different grades of flour at the same time.

The miller controlled the water flow to the wheel by hatches or sluices. Water was taken directly from a weir on a river, or via a leat from a weir further upstream. Mills on smaller streams had a millpond large enough to conserve water for a day's working, while also increasing the head. At Clapton Mill (ST 414063), the water came from more than one supply, with the wheel worked as an overshot by water brought from Clapton Brook by a long leat ending with an iron launder on piers, while water from the River Axe turned the wheel as a breastshot.

Some large iron water-wheels were installed by Somerset ironfounders and engineers. There are examples of wheels by Sibley & Son, 12ft diameter by 12ft wide (3.66m by 3.66m) at Hambridge Mill (ST 396222), William Sparrow at Madey Mill, Martock (ST 467191), the Somerset Wheel & Waggon Co. at Knole Mill, Long

The handsome Thorney Mill stands beside a weir and half-lock on the River Parrett. The large water-wheel alongside the building is sheltered by a tiled roof.

The site of Gants Mill near Bruton dates back to Domesday times and there have been many alterations. As well as corn milling, it has seen fulling, woollen textiles and silk throwing. A turbine was installed in 1888.

Sutton (ST 483251), and Edward Pearce of Taunton at Rowlands Mill (ST 344162). Wheels were also supplied from outside the county. For example, in 1870 Bodley Bros of Exeter supplied the 18ft by 6ft (5.5m by 1.83m) overshot wheel at Hornsbury Mill (ST 332108) near Chard, while Thorney Mill (ST 428227) has a large 14ft by 14ft (4.27m by 4.27m) breastshot wheel of 1866 by Coombs of Beaminster, Dorset. Charles Coombs also made a 15ft by 6ft (4.57m by 1.8m) overshot wheel for Court Mill (ST 312106), Combe St Nicholas.

While some of Somerset's water-mill sites have disappeared (for example, the only reminder of Taunton's Town Mills is a millstone set in a wall by a weir in Goodlands Gardens), others stand derelict or have found alternative industrial or commercial uses. There are also mills that have been converted to private housing, many retaining their wheels and machinery.

A few water-mills are open to the public at certain times, and three of these produce flour. Burcott Mill (ST 521456), near Wells, is a stone-built nineteenth-century watermill with two pairs of stones. The water-wheel and machinery are dated 1864. Gants Mill (ST 674342) near Bruton, which has a long and interesting history, is also open. West Somerset has more working mills. Combe Sydenham Mill (ST 073367) at Monksilver has an overshot wheel and produces wholemeal flour, while the late-seventeenth-century Dunster Mill (ST 991433) has twin overshot wheels, each originally driving two pairs of stones. Having fallen derelict the mill was restored to working order in 1979. Non-working mills are Piles Mill (SS 905465) at Allerford and Orchard Mill (ST 073405) at Williton, which has a 16ft (4.88m) overshot wheel and now houses the Bakelite Museum.

The introduction of roller milling began to severely affect traditional stone milling, both water and wind, from the 1880s onwards. Not only did roller mills process greater quantities of grain, but steam power released milling from remote river or hilltop sites. Large steam roller mills were built in the ports, where grain was imported, or close to those centres of population which were the main markets for flour. Such locations also benefited from access to railways for moving grain and flour products. The advent of motor lorries in the early-twentieth century, with their greater range, was another factor in the decline of small rural mills.

Water turbines became increasingly popular from the last quarter of the nineteenth century as a way of competing against the new steam mills, being more efficient and requiring little maintenance. Turbines could dispense with heavy gearing by using pulleys and belts instead. Their size was well suited to the small rural corn mills and several were supplied from the 1880s by Joseph J. Armfield of Ringwood in Hampshire. The 'British Empire' turbine was the most popular and came in a variety of sizes. A 20in (508mm) turbine was installed at Gants Mill in 1888 to replace an iron overshot wheel. The mill, which has four pairs of stones, still grinds small quantities of animal feed. This was a Domesday site, later serving as a fulling mill and a silk textile mill before reverting to corn milling in 1840. Turbines made by Gilbert Gilkes of Kendal were also installed in Somerset. Washford Mill had its water-wheel replaced in 1898 by a 22hp Gilkes turbine. Flour milling ceased in 1935, but animal feed continued for many more years. The large water-wheel at Thorney Mill, though, was retained when a second-hand Gilkes & Gordon turbine was added. Pen Mill at Yeovil (ST 571161) had a turbine installed in the pit of a large 16ft by 8ft (4.88m by 2.44m) breastshot wheel.

Dunster's twin wooden water-wheels, seen in May 1976 before the mill was restored to working order.

Higher Mill is a typical village corn mill at Croscombe. A little way downstream, a wheel pit and a steam engine chimney survive at Middle Mill.

Some mills tried small, possibly portable, steam engines to supplement their water-wheel before installing a turbine, such as at Washford Mill in 1881 and Gants Mill in 1883. In 1890, Town Mills at Taunton was using an auxiliary steam engine despite having three 12ft (3.66 m) diameter water-wheels. By 1903 a 25hp turbine was installed here. A chimney may be the clue that a water-mill had auxiliary steam power, and Croscombe Middle Mill (ST 590443), Ham Mills (ST 289253) on an island in the River Tone, and Somerton Mill (ST 498285) are examples. Newport Mill (ST 316237) at North Curry was refurbished as late as 1928 and its steam engine had a direct drive to the water-wheel by a pinion and ring gear. By the twentieth century water power was also supplemented by oil, gas or diesel engines. At Clapton Mill, for example, a Ruston & Hornsby diesel engine replaced an earlier engine in 1931. This worked until the mill closed in 1991, along with the 21ft by 8ft (6.4m by 2.44m) water-wheel and a set of roller mills by Joseph Armfield of Ringwood.

The steam engine enabled new mills to be built at any location where water was not available. The late-nineteenth-century Othery Steam Mill (ST 384314) worked until 1944. Its chimney has since gone and the building converted to a residence. Chaingate Mill on Magdalene Street, Glastonbury, had four pairs of stones worked by a small 6hp beam engine bought second-hand

William Stoate & Sons' steam-powered roller mill at Watchet, c.1900. Paper bags were made here after the mill burnt down in 1911.

Bowerings animal feed mill is the last industrial activity still taking place at Bridgwater Dock.

from a Cheddar paper mill in 1865. This engine, possibly made in about 1820, was still working in 1927 when Herbert England was the miller. A bakery was attached to this small steam mill.

Chilton Street Mill (ST 298379) at Bridgwater may have begun as a tide mill but in 1845 it was extended and a 16–20hp steam engine was installed to work four pairs of stones. This 'Bridgwater Steam Flour Mills' had an output of 300–400 sacks per week. It was leased until 1854 by Joel Spiller and Samuel Browne who had set up in business as corn and flour merchants in 1840 just when the Bridgwater Dock was being completed. Spiller was to become a national name in flour milling, working other Bridgwater mills before 1860 when the business headquarters was moved across the Bristol Channel to Cardiff where a large milling plant had been built close to the docks, into which foreign grain was imported.

A water-wheel at William Stoate's large Town Mills at Watchet (ST 070432) worked ten pairs of stones until 1885 when the whole operation was converted to a steam-powered roller mill. Hard grain best suited to roller milling was imported through the harbour and flour was shipped out to Ireland, South Wales and Bristol, although this trade was severely hampered when the piers were destroyed in the great storm of 1898. A

turbine was installed in 1903 but after the mill burnt down in 1911, William Stoate & Sons moved away to Bristol and the site became a paper bag mill.

Wind was another source of power for corn milling and Somerset is fortunate in having two preserved windmills, as well as a number of stone towers. There are just over a hundred known sites, mostly on high ground like the Polden Hills, flat moorland or the island-like hills of the Levels where they were well placed to catch the wind. The first record of a windmill was at Seavington St Michael in 1212. The earliest types were wooden post mills, built around a central post supported by quarterbars and crosstrees anchored in a mound. These have long since gone, save perhaps the mound. Interestingly, excavations during the construction of the M5 motorway in 1971 revealed medieval pottery and parts of a mill's quarterbars and crosstrees within a mound near Bridgwater. Evidence may be found in documents, early maps and place names such as the common 'Windmill Hill', while there are carvings of post mills on sixteenth-century bench ends in the churches at Bishops Lydeard and North Cadbury. Post mills continued into the nineteenth century when there are reports of them being blown over in gales. Shapwick Mill, for example, survived until it was blown over in 1836 and the miller was killed. It was replaced soon afterwards by a stone tower mill on a different site.

Stembridge Windmill at High Ham is maintained by the National Trust. Autumn 1976.

The thatched cap of Stembridge Windmill is now unique in Somerset. July 1985.

Tower mills were built from at least the early-seventeenth century. These had a stone tower with a cap and sails that turned into the wind. The four common or plain sails were fitted on stocks attached to a wind shaft bearing a large brake wheel to engage with a wallower and upright shaft. Machinery inside the mill was the same as a water-mill except that the power to the millstones was transmitted from above. However, several mills only had a single pair of stones driven direct from the brake wheel. The Somerset towers were generally short although, for example, the Pibsbury windmill at Huish Episcopi was much taller. This particular mill was built in about 1800 and ceased working in 1897. After part of the tower blew down, the rest was demolished to build a house in 1921. Windmilling was already in decline by the mid-nineteenth century so that by 1900 only seven windmills remained at work, and four of these were backed up with auxiliary power. The last windmill, Ashton Mill, stopped in 1927 and is one of Somerset's two preserved examples.

Stembridge Windmill (ST 433305) at High Ham is now unique in having a thatched cap with gables. The 26ft (7.9 m) lias stone tower stands on a raised platform and tapers towards the top. It was built in about 1822 when John Sherrin was the miller. The cap was turned with an endless chain until the gearing on the curb jammed in 1897–98, after which a small steam engine provided the power until the mill ceased working in 1910. There was also a bakehouse here next to the tower. Stembridge Windmill is now owned by the National Trust who restored it in 1971. Not all the machinery is complete, but there is enough to see how it worked.

Ashton Windmill (ST 414504) at Chapel Allerton stands on the Isle of Wedmore in the Somerset Levels, not far from the Mendip range. The parallel-sided tower was built in about 1770, seemingly on an earlier windmill mound. John Stevens was the owner from 1887 to 1938, and when he 'modernised' the mill in about 1900 he

The attractive Ashton Windmill near Chapel Allerton.

Ashton Windmill was the last windmill to work in Somerset. It stopped work in 1927 and has been restored since.

The Walton Windmill tower stands high up on a ridge at the east end of the Polden Hills. It has been converted to a house.

replaced two sails with spring sails, reclad the thatched cap in corrugated iron, strengthened the tower with three iron hoops, installed machinery taken from Moorlinch tower mill and made other changes. Like Stembridge Mill, a portable steam engine was brought here in 1894 to provide auxiliary power. The windmill stopped work in 1927, the last in Somerset. It was restored in 1958 and given to Bristol City Museum but is now maintained by Sedgemoor District Council.

Not far away is the similar tower of Stone Allerton Windmill (ST 406515), built on a mound. It dates from about 1760 and ceased working at the end of the nineteenth century. The tower and miller's cottage were built into a new house in 1911. Other windmill towers can be seen in Somerset. Watchfield Mill (ST 348470) near Highbridge survives as a fine stone tower. It worked throughout the nineteenth century and ceased at the time of the Great War, by which time a steam engine was supplying auxiliary power. Walton Windmill (ST 462352) is the only tower remaining on the Polden Hills, having been converted to a house in 1926. There was a post mill on Walton Hill in 1342 and a tower mill was built in about 1740, but this one dates from the 1790s. It last worked in 1906 when Charles Phillips was described as a 'windmiller, baker and grocer.' The miller's house and bakery survive near the 30ft (9.1m) high tower. The Shapwick tower mill which replaced the nearby post mill blown down in 1836 was short-lived as it burnt down in 1856. Now only a few courses of the base of the tower survive (ST 425374).

9

BREWING AND MALTING

Malt for brewing was selected from the finest local barley, for which the Porlock Vale had the very highest reputation. Malting took place in small rural malthouses and it was not until the second half of the nineteenth century that purpose-built malthouses were erected at the larger breweries. There were 92 maltsters listed in Pigot & Co.'s *National and Commercial Directory* for 1830 and just one, at Frome, was also a brewer. It was not unusual to combine the occupations of maltster and miller, and there were probably farmers who also had a small malt kiln. Maltsters had declined to 73 in 1866 and later trade directories by Kelly & Co. show a dramatic fall to just 17 by 1902. This was brought about by a rise in large commercial operations (mostly at the breweries) at the expense of the smaller maltsters. Maltings were closed in the 1920s, often having been taken over, so that just four maltsters were listed by 1939.

The usual arrangement was to have storage for the incoming barley at one end of the main malting floors and the kiln at the far end. Further storage was necessary for the malted barley. After selection the finest barley grain was first 'steeped' in a water cistern and, until a malt tax was repealed in 1880, the steeped grain was next 'couched' to calculate the excise duty. It was then spread over the malting floor and allowed to germinate to render the starch soluble in water and release enzymes for converting it to sugar. The grain on the floor was raked, turned and watered periodically to ensure even germination. The skill of the maltster was to recognise the critical point to stop germination, when small shoots and rootlets had appeared. This green malt was next kilned to give it colour and flavour, stored to mature and then bagged. Nothing was wasted, as the dried rootlets and shoots were sold for animal feed. The kiln floor had perforated tiles, and the fuel could be charcoal, coke or anthracite. Externally, the kiln has a characteristic tapering roofline with a vent. Floor maltings have low ceilings and small windows, making them difficult to convert to other uses, but there have been successes.

A good example of one of the rural Porlock malthouses is a neat stone building under a slate roof at Lynch (SS 900476). John Clarke, who was also a miller, was here in 1830. Another rural malthouse is at Ford (ST 094289) near Wiveliscombe, and a larger one in this area at Halse (ST 140280) was unusual in having two kilns, one at the south end and the other on the east side, giving it a cruciform plan. Both had perforated Ham stone tiled floors. Barley grain was stored on the top floor, and steeped next to the kilns before being spread on the malting floor. There is a datestone of 1768 although John and Richard Hancock were not recorded as maltsters here until 1790. Malting had ceased by the Second World War when the building was used for corn drying. The malthouse has been converted to a residence, but the kilns survive.

Although converted to housing, the small malthouse at Lynch near Porlock is recognised by its kiln roof. The malthouse and the mill opposite were run by John Clarke in 1830.

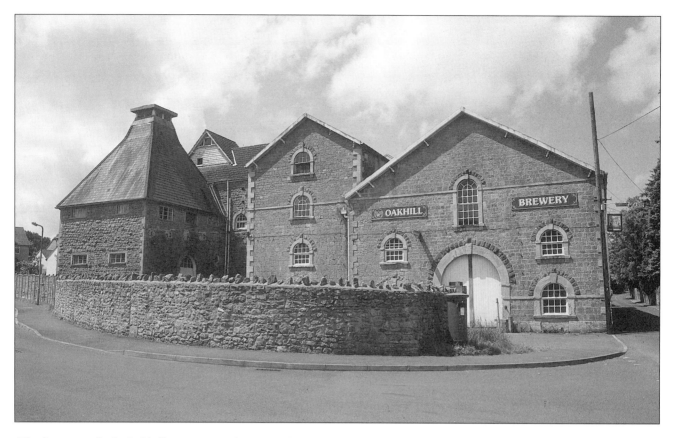

The fine stone-built Oakhill Brewery Maltings. A distinctive malt kiln is on the left while a small brewery has reoccupied part of the once extensive premises.

From the later nineteenth century, brewers found it expedient to have their own malting floors on-site. One of the largest was at the Oakhill Brewery (ST 632473), where two floor malthouses were built in the mid-nineteenth century and 1890 to supply malt to the brewery and others in Shepton Mallet and Bristol. They were rebuilt with six floors and kilns after a fire in 1926 and, modernised with the installation of 'Saladin boxes' in 1961, continued malting until Christmas 1986. Oakhill, therefore, witnessed the last malting in the whole of Somerset. Parts of the stone-built maltings are now occupied by the Oakhill Brewery, a much smaller operation than its predecessor. A fine example of a late-nineteenth-century brewery malthouse in polychrome brick survives at North Street, Crewkerne (ST 442105). It was designed by the Weymouth architect G.R. Crickmay and had its kilns in the centre rather than at the end. The Crewkerne United Brewery was taken over by Arnold & Hancock of Wiveliscombe and closed in 1938, but malting continued until 1949. Norton Brewery at Norton Fitzwarren was also taken over and closed in the 1920s, but the red-brick floor malting and its two kilns survive (ST 197258). There are converted maltings in other towns, such as Frome (Lamb Brewery, ST 776478),

Shepton Mallet (Anglo-Bavarian Brewery, ST 616438, and Charlton Brewery, ST 631432) and Taunton (Canon Street, ST 230248, and Castle Street, ST 225246). The village of Holcombe has a large stone brewery malthouse, where malting ceased in 1930 (ST 673498).

In the early-nineteenth century most inns had a small brewhouse at the back for their own requirements, although occasionally beer was carried further afield. This must be the reason why only 19 brewers were listed in Somerset in 1830. Thereafter, the century saw the building of small breweries in villages and towns, with the capacity to serve a wider district. Large architect-designed breweries appeared in the second half of the century as transport facilities improved, first with the railways opening up the markets and then with steam and motor road vehicles. The twentieth century was a period of consolidation when the larger brewers gradually bought out and closed their smaller neighbours while keeping the tied houses as outlets for their own beers.

In 1866 there were 43 brewers listed in Somerset, but numbers had fallen to 32 by 1902, reducing further to 13 by 1927–39 as a result of takeovers and closures. Brewing

The North Street malthouse at Crewkerne was designed by the Weymouth architect G.R. Crickmay, whose other works included maltings at Weymouth and Oakhill and the Dorchester Brewery.

Polychrome brickwork on the North Street maltings, Crewkerne.

The brick maltings in Canon Street, Taunton, were built in 1907 and acquired by Starkey, Knight & Ford in 1923. They have been since converted to other uses.

finished at Burnham, Taunton and Wiveliscombe by 1960, and the brewery at Rode closed in 1962. Later revival saw a new generation of small real-ale brewers, such as the Oakhill Brewery and Exmoor Ales at Wiveliscombe.

Victorian breweries were among the most distinctive and handsome of all industrial buildings and were designed to contain all the brewing processes. As today, successful brewing depended on the skill and experience of the brewer as well as the type and quality of raw materials. Malt barley, which gives beer its character, was passed through roller mills to crack the husks and mixed with hot water (liquor) in the mash tun where soluble starch was converted to malt sugar. After perhaps two hours of mashing, with revolving rakes, the porridge-like mixture was washed out with a hot-water spray and the sugary liquid (wort) drained through slotted base plates into the copper. Here the wort was mixed with sugar and hops. Different varieties of hops give the beer its bitter flavour and aroma, while also sterilising the wort and giving the beer its keeping quality. After boiling in the copper, the wort passed through the hop back where spent hops were filtered out and then it was cooled to room temperature by passing through a heat exchanger, and run into fermenting vessels. This is where the brewer added yeast of a particular strain to change the malt sugar to alcohol and carbon dioxide. After about four days of fermentation, depending on the temperature, the beer was then settled in tanks in the conditioning room. Draught beer was run down by gravity to the racking cellar for filling casks. Beer for bottling had further fermentation before cooling in the 'cold room'.

Little was wasted. Spent grains and hops were sold to farmers as cattle feed. The yeasty head was skimmed off the top of the fermenting brew and passed through a yeast press, part being kept for future brews and the surplus sold as a feedstuff. Energy was saved by using the warm water from the heat exchanger for new brewing liquor.

Most breweries had their own well to provide a guaranteed water supply of consistent quality for brewing liquor, although water for the breweries at Wiveliscombe and Stogumber came from springs. By the late-nineteenth century a busy brewery would also have a cooperage for making and repairing barrels, a washing plant, bottling plant and a transport department with stables and drays.

Hancock's Brewery was well known throughout the nineteenth and much of the twentieth centuries and its red-brick tower still dominates the town of Wiveliscombe (ST 083279). Its history provides a good example of how the brewery industry developed and declined in Somerset. William Hancock built a brewery and malthouse here at Golden Hill in 1807. This was enlarged in 1830 and by 1875 it was dubbed the 'largest brewery in the West of England', no doubt benefiting from the recently opened railway to the town. William Hancock & Sons Ltd was formed in 1896 and in the following year the brewery was extended again when the tower was built. The 100 employees were producing over 20,000 barrels of beer annually at this time to supply the company's 85 public houses. An aerated water factory was set up at the brewery in 1901 and a cider factory was added in 1917.

There followed a period of takeovers, starting in 1919 with the Tiverton Old Brewery and its public houses. In

1927 Hancocks amalgamated with S.W. Arnold & Sons of Taunton, the firm later becoming known as Arnold & Hancock Ltd. Stephen William Arnold had established a brewery in 1876 at Rowbarton, Taunton, and in 1897 bought the West Somerset Brewery in St James Street. Arnold Ltd acquired and closed William Hewett & Co.'s brewery and malting at Norton Fitzwarren and developed a trade with North Devon before joining with Hancocks. The Wiveliscombe maltings supplied both breweries until 1938, the year that the Crewkerne Brewery was bought and malt was supplied from there. All went

Right: William Hancock & Sons' brick brewery tower of 1897 at Wiveliscombe.

Below: Wiveliscombe's brewery still dominates the town despite closing in 1959.

well until Arnold & Hancock were acquired in 1955 by Ushers' Wiltshire Brewery of Trowbridge, who shut down the brewery at Taunton and the maltings at Wiveliscombe. Great hardship was felt locally when the Wiveliscombe Brewery was closed in 1959. It became a food-processing factory and then lay derelict before being divided into industrial units. The delight is that the small Exmoor Ales brewery has been established here. Meanwhile, the Taunton premises became offices and a depot for Watneys (who had in turn taken over Ushers) but the site was redeveloped. The only physical evidence left is the brewer's house (ST 228249) next to the Brewhouse Theatre.

The Anglo-Bavarian Brewery (ST 616437) at Shepton Mallet is the most impressive brewery building in Somerset. It was built in 1872 to produce light ale and India Pale Ale, but turned to lager when Garton Hill & Co. took over in the late-nineteenth century. At one time 500 were employed, but brewing declined after 1918 and the brewery closed in the 1930s. The complex has survived as the Anglo Trading Estate and still includes the tall stone-built brewery with a decorative brick chimney, as well as three-storeyed maltings and the weigh house at the entrance.

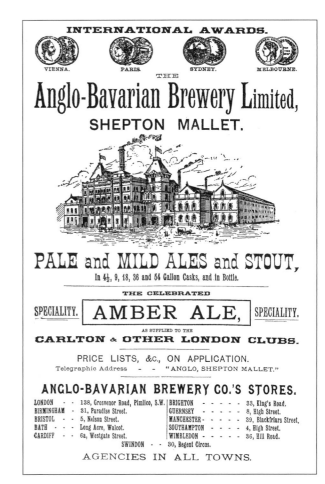

The Anglo-Bavarian Brewery at Shepton Mallet is one of the finest industrial buildings in Somerset. The brewhouse, maltings and other buildings have been turned over to other uses. Inset: An architectural flourish on a corner of the brewery.

Shepton Mallet was something of a brewing centre, with two breweries on the eastern outskirts. The Charlton Brewery (ST 631432) was begun in 1844 in a disused woollen mill and closed in 1961. The maltings have been

The unusual little brewery building at Hambridge in 1975.

D. WARREN

converted to commercial use and survive. The nearby Kilver Street Brewery (ST 627436) worked from 1860 until 1949 when Showering Bros began producing Babycham sparkling perry here, names that became closely connected with Shepton Mallet.

Fewer brewery buildings have survived than maltings, as in the case of the once large Oakhill Brewery just north of Shepton. The brewery had been founded in 1767 and it was increased in size when a public company was formed in 1889. An 'invalid stout' was a speciality and there were depots in Bath, Bristol and Cardiff. This brewery ran its own private steam railway to the main line at Binegar in the first years of the twentieth century. Oakhill Brewery burnt down in 1915 but was rebuilt and taken over by Bristol United Breweries, eventually coming into the hands of Georges and then Courages who continued to use the maltings.

A much smaller rural brewery survives as an eye-catching building just north of Hambridge village (ST 397223). There was a brewery here from about 1840 until 1935. The first brewers were the Lang family, who had a mill at the rear, and the last was Henry Matthew & Co. Although the rest of Hambridge Brewery has been

Stogumber Brewery in 1908, with a bridge joining the brewhouse to a malt kiln on the left. Tom Salter stands with the horse Gipsy harnessed to a delivery cart.

I. & M. MILES COLLECTION

STOGUMBER CELEBRATED PALE ALES.

HIGHLY RECOMMENDED BY THE FACULTY.

Brewed SOLELY from Malt, Hops, and the Medicinal Water of Harry Hill's Well.
STRONGLY RECOMMENDED TO INVALIDS AS RENOVATING AND DELICIOUS.

FOR TESTIMONIALS AND PRICES OF ALES AND MALT APPLY TO

SCUTT BROTHERS,

BREWERS AND MALTSTERS,

THE BREWERY, STOGUMBER, near TAUNTON.

demolished, the remaining stone building has a bellcote and overhanging timber-clad upper floors, all now converted to commercial use.

Stogumber Brewery (ST 096372) was established by George Elers in about 1840. By 1894 Scutt Bros were brewers and maltsters here, when the 'celebrated' pale ale was 'brewed solely from malt, hops and the Medicinal Waters of Harry Hill's Well. Strongly recommended to invalids as renovating and delicious.' The water was considered important and was piped 100yd (91m) to a reservoir from the well. As with other breweries in the late-nineteenth century, Scutt Bros also had a mineral and aerated water factory making ginger beer,

The brick building of the Cross Keys Brewery is a notable contrast in the stone village of Rode.

lemonade, orange champagne, kola champagne, potash water, soda water, pineapple and ginger ale. The brewery closed in 1912 and the buildings were demolished in 1973.

The Cross Keys Brewery (ST 804538) was set up at Rode by Henry Fussell alongside the Cross Keys Inn and after his son took over it became known as Sydney Fussell & Sons Ltd. A new brewhouse was built in 1904 and extended in 1935. Brewing ceased in 1962 when the firm was bought by Bass and bottling continued until 1968. The main brewery buildings and their two chimneys are in brick and contrast with the mellow stone houses over which they stand. They were under conversion for housing in 2003.

Other Somerset brewery names included Starkey, Knight & Ford Ltd at the Northgate Brewery in Bridgwater and Holt Brothers Ltd at Burnham Brewery. The latter had a small horizontal steam engine which worked until closure in 1960. It was made by J. Culverwell & Co. of Bridgwater in about 1860 and is now preserved by the Westonzoyland Engine Trust. Such engines would have been common in most breweries.

WITCOMB BROS.,
Strong Beer, Pale Ale,
STOUT & PORTER
— BREWERS. —

PRICE LIST ON APPLICATION.

LIMINGTON ✚ BREWERY,
ILCHESTER.

10
CIDER AND CREAM

Cider is more popularly associated with Somerset than beer. Cider was made on farms for centuries, for the farmer's own personal use or his labourers', and it came to be sold outside the region too. In 1894 there were 24,000 acres of cider apple orchards in Somerset, but this had more than halved by 1950. Many farms had a cider house or 'wring house'. The two main pieces of equipment used by the farm cider makers were the apple mill and the press. Apples were crushed by an edge runner mill turned by a horse, but smaller wooden framed apple mills were more convenient to use by turning a handle. The resulting 'pomace' was piled on the large wooden press in layers with straw and screwed down to squeeze out the juice, which was then allowed to ferment in a clean wooden cask or vat. Wood was used in the equipment to prevent tainting and contamination by metalwork.

Cider-making equipment was made by local agricultural engineers and founders. For example, artefacts at the Somerset Rural Life Museum in Glastonbury include apple mills, each with two granite rollers, manufactured by Wightman & Dening of Chard and Alfred Day of Mark. Pressing was also done by specialist cider makers who travelled around the countryside with their own equipment combining the mill and press on one portable vehicle.

Cider factories were not established until the early-twentieth century. The one started in 1911 at Norton Fitzwarren (ST 196257) became the Taunton Cider Co. Ltd in 1921, a famous brand name throughout the rest of the century despite changes in ownership. A cider factory of 1917 at the Wiveliscombe Brewery was noted in chapter 9. The Sunshine Cider Mills was run by B. Rogers in a disused butter factory at Chaffcombe (ST 340103) near Chard from 1940 until 1967. The apple crushers were made locally by Dening & Co., and a Petter diesel provided the power and generated electricity. Water was pumped from a deep well for washing the apples and for heating in the old factory's boiler to wash the vats, barrels and bottles. Another cider factory was established in a former creamery at Marston Magna (ST 599224). Perry, made from pear juice was developed by Showering Bros at Shepton Mallet in the 1940s and their 'Babycham' became a nationwide drink. The large Showerings operation is now owned by Matthew Clark plc, along with Taunton Cider. Farm cider is still made in Somerset today, including at R.J. Sheppy & Son's Cider Centre at Three Bridges Farm near Wellington where equipment is displayed in a museum.

The world-famous name of Cheddar cheese is a reminder of Somerset's dairying industry. In the 1720s Daniel Defoe described the making of cheeses weighing a hundredweight or more at Cheddar, where the townsfolk grazed their cows on a specially rich grassland:

The milk of all the town cows, is brought together every day into a common room, where the persons appointed, or trusted for the management, measure every man's quantity, and set it down in a book; when the quantities are adjusted, the milk is all put together, and every meal's milk makes one cheese, and no more; so that the cheese is bigger, or less, as the cows yield more, or less, milk. By this method, the goodness of the cheese is preserved, and, without all dispute, it is the best cheese that England affords, if not, that the whole world affords.

Dairying was at first a farm industry, but by the end of the nineteenth century a fully developed railway network enabled fresh milk, cheese and butter to be carried to distant cities within hours. Throughout the dairy farming areas of Somerset, dairies, creameries, butter factories and milk distribution depots were established alongside railways, to which they were often connected by a siding.

Pictured: *A stone cider mill or apple crusher at R.J. Sheppy & Son's Three Bridges Farm near Wellington. A horse harnessed to the end of the axle walked in a circle to turn the edge runner stone for pulping the cider apples.*

The firms or co-operatives were of local origin and, like the breweries, they were gradually amalgamated and taken over by bigger groups, finally resulting in closure. This important rural industry has been neglected in the past and is deserving of more historical research. Many creameries were built around the turn of the century, often in red brick. Aplin & Barrett's Western Counties Creameries Ltd was established in 1888 and nine years later a large creamery was built in Newton Road, Yeovil. Since 1901 their trade name 'St Ivel' has been a national brand. The St Ivel company closed their factory at Yeovil in 1976.

There was a cluster of creameries on the railways to the northeast of Yeovil in the early-twentieth century. Beside the Castle Cary to Yeovil line was the Sparkford Vale Co-operative Dairy Society Ltd's milk depot (ST 605263), now the Haynes Group printing works, and in about 1900 Aplin & Barrett built the Marston Magna Creamery (later a cider factory). By the 1920s they had a small creamery and cheese factory at Keinton Mandeville station (ST 564304)

A small creamery and milk depot was built C. & G. Prideaux beside Castle Cary station. This was a common location for many similar dairies which used the railway network to carry their fresh products.

C. & G. Prideaux's creamery and milk depot at Castle Cary station, Ansford.

where the new Castle Cary to Langport link crossed the Fosse Way. A small milk depot, complete with its chimney, still stands beside Castle Cary station at Ansford (ST 635335). This was built in 1910 by C. & G. Prideaux, whose main creamery at Evercreech (ST 648390) was transferred to Unigate in 1959 and is still operational.

Wiltshire United Dairies built a factory in 1909 at Bason Bridge (ST 347458) with a siding on the Somerset & Dorset Railway. Although the station closed in 1966, the railway was kept open for the milk traffic until 1972. The factory closed in 1987. In the same area, Highbridge was well known for its cheese markets, and the West of England Creamery here was a branch of the Chippenham Cheese Factory Ltd. A spin-off from the Highbridge dairy industry was the bacon factory (ST 317469) built in 1890, where the pigs were fattened on the whey by-product of cheese making.

The West Surrey Central Dairy Co. Ltd was at Wincanton in the 1920s, with a milk depot and sidings on the Somerset & Dorset Railway, becoming Cow & Gate in 1933. Infant foods were made here and the tall chimney with 'Cow & Gate' written down the side was a landmark for many years. Cow & Gate merged with United Dairies in the early 1950s to become Unigate Ltd. The factory has closed but the subsidiary Wincanton Transport & Engineering Ltd, which was created in 1925, survives as a familiar nationwide organisation. Other railside creameries and depots included Nestle & Anglo Swiss Condensed Milk Co.'s milk depot at Thorney (ST 428231) on the Durston to Yeovil branch.

The Horlicks factory (ST 346152) at Hort Bridge, Ilminster, had its origins with the Ilminster & District Farmers Co-operative Society Ltd. Kraft Dairies Ltd were recorded here in 1939. The Somerset, Dorset & Devon Dairy Co. Ltd built the Model Dairy Factory at Chaffcombe near Chard, which later became the Sunshine Cider Factory as noted above. It was opened in about 1896 for making butter and the finished butter was stored in two special square rooms with stone floors kept cool by water pumped from a well. A water-wheel (by W. Sparrow of Martock) is still there. The factory was one of the first premises in the area to be lit by electricity. After a takeover by Salters & Stokes Creamery of Chard Junction (on the railway!) it was closed in about 1930 when the latter was itself taken over by Wiltshire United Dairies of Trowbridge. United Dairies was acquiring depots and dairies throughout the region at this time. Large creameries operating today at Frome, Evercreech and Chard Junction, all rely on road transport.

11
TEXTILES

A variety of textile industries have left their legacy across the county. Woollen manufacturing was carried on at a number of centres, traditionally at Taunton, Frome, Shepton Mallet and Chard. By the nineteenth century, the textile industry had diversified, with woollens centred on Frome and Wellington, silk at Taunton, Shepton Mallet and Evercreech, lace at Chard, canvas, twine and webbing around Crewkerne and Martock, horsehair at Castle Cary, and shirts and collars at Chard and Taunton.

The West of England woollen textile industry reached into Somerset from west Wiltshire and Gloucestershire and in 1724 Daniel Defoe commented on the woollen textile industry based around a fast-expanding Frome. This town, Bruton, Castle Cary, Shepton Mallet and Wincanton were engaged in the making of

fine Spanish medley cloth, being the mix'd colours and cloths, with which all the gentlemen and persons of any fashion in England, are cloth'd, and vast quantities of which are exported to all parts of Europe.

This trade supported great numbers of poor families and made many rich ones. The clothiers farmed out the work of spinning and weaving and marketed the finished cloth and the houses they built on the profits are seen today in Frome and Shepton Mallet. 'Serges, druggets, etc and several other kinds of stuff' were made in Taunton where 1100 hand-looms were fully employed. Despite this evidence of a vibrant commerce, Defoe noted with some disgust the prevalence of beggars in nearby Wellington.

By the 1790s, John Billingsley reported that the woollen industry of Taunton had moved to Wellington. He noted some gentlemen in Taunton had joined with patentees with the secret of making cloth without spinning or weaving, 'samples they have exhibited gave flattering hopes of success.' The plan was quickly abandoned. Taunton had no more than 12 looms by 1821. Twelve Somerset woollen manufacturers were listed in 1866, reducing to eight in 1902 and the three left in 1939 were Alfred H. Tucker Ltd and Houstons Ltd at Frome, and Fox Brothers & Co. Ltd at Wellington.

In Billingsley's time, over a third of the population in the Frome district was employed in the woollen industry and cloth manufacturing was also significant in Shepton Mallet. Gig machines were introduced in the 1760s, against much opposition from those who saw machinery as a threat to employment. Shepton Mallet was the first place in the West Country to have the spinning jenny in 1776, which caused such disorder that the military had to be called in. A mob of workers destroyed jennies at Frome in 1781. Billingsley saw the inevitable march of progress with machinery for carding and spinning, which 'must and will be universally introduced, otherwise these districts, where it is not used, must be sacrificed to those where it is.' However, he was also aware that machinery could cause unemployment if the current low export trade was to continue.

All textile sites relied on water for power and for processing the wool and cloth, in scouring, fulling or dyeing. This dependence was not new, as for centuries water-powered fulling or tucking mills had pounded cloth to thicken the fabric and remove excess grease. Early references to fulling mills include Taunton in 1219, Bishop's Hull in 1246, Dunster in 1259 and Gants Mill, Bruton, in 1290. By the early-nineteenth century there were horse-driven workshops, and one for sale at Frome in 1813 could produce 12 to 15 pieces per week, which was comparable to the output of some water mills. Spinning was mechanised first but hand weaving continued until power looms were introduced in the mid-nineteenth century. In 1838 four woollen mills in Frome accounted for five steam engines and two water-wheels. Water, however, was still significant in this part of Somerset where 28 textile mills (including eight silk) had 16 steam engines and 33 water-wheels, providing a total of 276hp and 303hp respectively.

There may have been a steam engine at South Parade Mill in Frome as early as 1807 and the Adderwell woollen mills had a 4hp steam engine in 1810. Sheppards were the dominant Frome woollen manufacturers and had at least one steam engine by 1814, increasing to four engines supplementing water power at Spring Garden Mill and two other factories by 1833. The firm closed in the late

The dyehouse of 1887 at Wallbridge Mill, Frome.

1870s and the bell from Spring Garden is in Frome Museum. Wallbridge Mill (ST 786478) was the last new factory to be built at Frome and was the last to close. There was a fulling mill here on the river in at least 1727 but steam power was used in the nineteenth century. Alfred H. Tucker Ltd was here from 1868 until the end in 1965. As well as spinning and weaving, the Frome area also had fulling mills and dyehouses (Wallbridge Mill has a fine dyehouse dated 1887), and there were circular wool drying stoves, the most obvious now surviving as the Tourist Information Centre in Justice Lane (ST 778482).

Shepton Mallet was no longer a woollen town by the early-nineteenth century and its Kilver Street and Darshill mills became silk factories by the 1830s. The woollen industry used a large number of teazels set in 'handles' for raising the nap of the finished cloth. This was a wet process and the teazels were dried in special ventilated handle houses, with a good example at Darshill (ST 604439).

The handle house at Darshill near Shepton Mallet, where 'handles' of teazels for raising the nap of cloth were dried.

Tonedale Mills (ST 128213) at Wellington is one of the great industrial monuments of Somerset. The rise of Wellington as a textile centre stemmed from the Were family's Tone fulling mills of 1754. Their grandson Thomas Fox first employed outworkers for spinning and weaving and then in 1790 took over the Tonedale flour mill and converted it to a woollen factory in 1801–03. Water from the Westford Brook and Rockwell Green Stream was stored in two reservoirs known as the Basins (ST 129208) and fed by a leat to the water-powered mill. In 1797 Fox bought Coldharbour Mill at Uffculme, Devon, which carried on the business after Tonedale Mills burnt down shortly after his death in 1821. The new Tonedale Mills was built two years later in stone and brick with brick-vaulted ceilings and floors as a fire-proofing measure. It was well placed close to the Bristol & Exeter Railway which opened through Wellington in 1843. Steam power was introduced in 1840 and the first power looms arrived in 1853 at a time when the dyeing processes were improved. The finishing and dyeing works were beside the River Tone (ST 126218).

Fox Brothers & Co. Ltd, as the business became known, was successful in producing fine-quality flannels. The spiral puttee was first made at Tonedale in 1896 and became popular for activities such as riding or exploration, and large orders were despatched to the British army. The firm also invented a process for making khaki-coloured cloth, which was much in demand by the War Office. Although machinery was old and in poor condition by the end of the Second World War, Fox Brothers gained a reputation for making lightweight flannels particularly for the American market. In the 1950s the Pollitt & Wigzell 'Iron Duke' horizontal steam engine of 1897 was still providing power through shafting, although there were now motors driven by electricity generated by a pair of Crossley gas engines, later converted to diesel. As well as the workers engaged in wool sorting, scouring, combing, carding, spinning, weaving, finishing and dyeing, there was a staff of fitters, turners, blacksmiths and mechanics to maintain the large factory. Modernisation in the 1960s included the installation of fast Sulzer shuttleless looms. Tonedale is now given over to other uses, but the firm survives in name at different premises and still specialises in high-quality West Country cloths.

Many hundreds were employed at the firm's peak. In 1800 Fox established a self-supporting shop for his workers, to alleviate the distress caused by high prices of the time. In 1863 the firm later started a profit sharing

Fox Brothers' magnificent Tonedale Mills stands almost in open countryside on the edge of Wellington.

Tonedale Mills from the west.

A wall crane at Tonedale Mills.

Textile workers at Fox Brothers & Co.'s Tonedale Mills, Wellington, c.1900.

WELLINGTON MUSEUM

A brick-built factory with tower at Elworthy Brothers' Westford Mills. The long combined leat and millpond emphasises the importance of water power.

scheme and in 1874 introduced an old-age pension, sickness insurance and medical care for its workers. Dining rooms, recreation rooms and a sports ground were also provided.

There were other textile mills upstream at Westford (ST 120203), where Thomas Elworthy's worsted mill was rebuilt after a fire in 1821. Prowse's Mill (ST 113199) was taken over in 1866 and around 400 were employed at one time. Elworthy Brothers & Co. Ltd made tweeds, fine dress serges, saddle serges, bandages, worsteds and other yarns before closure in 1934. The disused mills are due for conversion.

Two woollen mills near Chard were worked by the Brown family on the upper reaches of the River Isle. Wadeford Woollen Mill (ST 308105) was worked with two water-wheels from 1847 by William Brown. This mill is said to have woven material for greatcoats in the Great War before closing. It was a fulling mill site, as was Pudleigh Mill (ST 317108) where a new woollen mill was built in 1843–45 with a steam engine. Frederick Brown closed the mill during a strike in the early 1900s. Samuel Brown, woollen cloth manufacturer, briefly held Nimmer Mills in the 1840s.

The Yarn Market at Dunster is a reminder that woollen textiles were important in Exmoor's economy. It was built in 1601 by the Luttrells and cloth was shipped from Minehead until the end of the eighteenth century. A woollen mill in Chapel Street, Dulverton, produced serges and blankets before the 1830s when it turned to silk throwing and making crêpe for about forty years. The mill had a large breastshot water-wheel and became a laundry by the early 1900s. Just over the county border in Devon, Heasley Mill (SS 738322) had two overshot wheels and made a serge known as 'long ells' for the East India Co.'s trade with China until 1834, thereafter making a cheap cloth until about 1861.

The decline of woollen textiles at Shepton Mallet and Taunton was matched by a rise in the silk industry which took over the empty mills. Imports of finished silk goods were banned in 1776 which encouraged manufacturers to seek rural sites with water power and cheap labour. The heyday of the industry was short and decline set in as import restrictions were lifted between 1826 and 1860. Imported raw silk was brought to the mills where water-powered machinery was used for silk throwing. The throwsters used an 'engine' to wind skeins of silk onto bobbins before being twisted, or thrown. As well as spinning, the first silk weaving took place at Taunton in 1780 and by 1820 there were 1000 looms in the district with 500 persons employed in the throwing mills, although the trade was depressed ten years later. By 1866 the silk industry was said to have 'nearly departed' with just one throwing factory left. Silk spinning, however, continued in Taunton at James Pearsall & Co.'s East and Tancred Street Mills until well into the twentieth century. One of Pearsalls' beam engines, which worked until 1955, is displayed at the Somerset County Museum.

Thompson & Le Gros were established in 1840 at Merchants Barton in Frome, and employed 400 at the peak of production here and at Shepton Mallet. In the latter town Thomas Kemp & Sons had silk mills at Bowlish, Draycott and Darshill in 1872. It is said that the velvet coronation robes for Queen Victoria and King Edward VII came from Shepton Mallet. The Kemps also owned a silk-weaving factory in Shapway Lane, Evercreech (ST 648389), where velvets were made until about 1919. Across the road another silk factory was run by John Sharrer Ward of Bruton until he was bankrupted in 1852. Outside Evercreech, Albion or Milton Silk Mill (ST 659377) was developed for silk throwing by James Hoddinott and leased to George Cox in 1788. Girl employees were accommodated at the site. In 1813, the leasehold was taken by Theophilus Percival (of Gants Mill) and Samuel Saxon when the four-storey mill had a 14ft by 6ft (4.3m by 1.88m) water-wheel and a 6hp Boulton & Watt steam engine. The mill was sold in 1838 to Thomas Matthews (producer of webbing and horse-hair seating at Castle Cary) for making silk thread. By 1861 flax spinning was taking place but two years later it was offered for sale with a water-wheel, 24hp steam engine and eight workers' cottages. It had been demolished by 1887.

Gants Mill (ST 674342) near Bruton is an example of an historic corn mill and fulling mill site, adapted for textiles. The east wing was built in 1740 by the Berkeley family as a new woollen factory which operated until 1773. In 1812 Theophilus Percival bought the mill and added a four-storey west wing for silk throwing. Up to 200 were employed here but it was for sale in 1830 after Percival was bankrupted. Gants Mill returned to corn milling ten years later and is still in working order. In 1769 George Ward inherited a silk mill in Quaperlake Street, Bruton, which passed to his son John Sharrer Ward in 1790. After closure in the 1850s, horse-hair seats were made here before it became a bacon factory in 1900.

The four-storey west wing at Gants Mill, Bruton, was built in 1812 by Theophilus Percival for silk throwing.

John Sharrer Ward's silk mill in Quaperlake Street, Bruton. June 1992.

Lace making came to Chard after 1819 when manufacturers moved here from labour troubles of Nottingham and took over empty woollen mills in the district. Steam power was often installed. Wheatley & Co. took a large weaving mill in Old Town, although this burnt down in 1825 and was rebuilt. Boden & Co. took over from Wheatley & Riste in 1888. Other lace factories were established and by 1830 some 1500 people were said to be engaged in the industry. J.B. Gifford was at Blacklands Mill at Forton, until it burnt down in 1848 and lace production moved to Holyrood Mill. Chard lace was plain net or bobbin net lace. The industry suffered from peaks and troughs in the trade and even Chard was not without industrial disputes; there was unrest in the 1840s and a fourteen-month lockout in 1878–80. Mosquito nets were made at the Chard factories in both world wars. Two notable lace mills stand in Chard, although both have lost their chimneys. Gifford Fox & Co.'s Holyrood Mill (ST 322084), which closed in 1964, is five storeys high and has been converted to the Chard Library with

Gifford Fox & Co.'s Holyrood Lace Mill at Chard closed in 1964 and has since lost its chimney.

Boden & Co.'s factory was the second large lace mill in Chard.

Powered machinery in Boden's lace factory, Chard, c.1900.

CHARD MUSEUM

council offices above. Its Boulton & Watt steam engine is now thought to be in the USA. The equally impressive Boden's Lace Factory is nearby at the end of Mill Lane (ST 324085) and has an archway entrance of 1901.

To the south, lace was made at Cuff & Co.'s Perry Street factory (ST336049) until the 1840s when J.B. Payne started manufacturing bobbin net lace-making machinery. John C. Small & Tidmas Ltd was established in 1895, with another factory in Nottingham. The Derby factory in Barnstaple was bought in 1926. The firm was taken over by Swiss Net of Zurich in 1984 and is still at work. In 1892 the Chard Lace Co. was started at Rose Mill, Ilminster, another redundant fulling and woollen mill (ST 344150). This firm also made machinery and two Armfield turbines were installed to generate electricity. Lace-making machinery was made at Shepton Mallet for Jardine & Co.'s lace factories in the north of England. This mill (ST 627436) was built in 1890 but there had been a woollen mill here before.

Canvas, sailcoth, webbing and twine industries around Crewkerne, Martock and Merriott were originally based on locally grown flax and hemp. 'Coker canvas' was renowned and the Coker Sailcloth Co. of North Street, Crewkerne, is said to have made the sails for HMS *Victory*. The old building burnt down in 1997. At Martock, Yeo Bros & Paull have been tent makers since 1864 and continue in business although they have moved to a modern works. Sailcloth and twine were made at Tail Mill (ST 449123) near Merriott, a complex of buildings originally sited here for water power.

George Parsons was a tenant farmer with a flax mill and engineering works at West Lambrook until it burnt down in February 1854 after a chimney spark ignited a store of flax. As a result he built the Parrett Works (ST 446186) outside Martock as an innovative fireproof flax mill, alongside an engineering works and a rope-walk. Two great water-wheels provided the power. The largest, in the main building, is a breastshot wheel measuring 16ft by 9ft (4.9m by 2.74m), with a ring gear drive. It is a suspension wheel with ventilated buckets and 'George Parsons West Lambrook 1854' is cast on the shrouds. In another building, the second breastshot wheel measures 12ft by 9ft (3.66m by 2.74m) and also has a ring drive. The main four-storey Ham stone building presents an impressive façade, complete with bellcote and iron-framed windows. Inside, the iron column of the spiral staircase was designed as a water pipe to serve hydrants on all the floors. 'Coker canvas' sailcloth was supplied to the Royal Navy in 1862, and the West of England Engineering & Coker Canvas Co. was formed in 1865. A power loom shed was built and around 200 were employed until the firm was liquidated in 1869. The textile side of the works was taken on by George

Above: *The covered rope-walk behind the Parrett Works in March 1994.*

Left: *George Parsons' fireproof flax mill at the Parrett Works. The main front had a clock and bell.*

Below: *Flax and hemp yarn were spun using steam power at Dowlish Ford Mills near Ilminster, from 1840 until the Second World War. The engine house is in the centre.*

Hedgecombe Smith for making rope, twine, cord and Napier matting, and lasted until 1941. The rope-walk survives behind the works.

Dowlish Ford Mills (ST 358133) had seen woollen and silk manufacturing until 1840 when Samuel Hutchings began spinning flax and hemp yarn using steam power. H. Shepherd & Co. were here by 1866 and the factory expanded to employ 240 at its peak. There was a 200hp horizontal condensing engine made by Hick Hargreaves of Bolton, with three Lancashire boilers. The factory spun yarn in 1936 for the carpets of the new Cunard liner *Queen Mary*, but the site was given over to making cables during the Second World War. It has been a shoe factory for Clarks of Street since 1965. The site still impresses, with the millpond, engine house and a long weaving shed.

A rope or twine walk at West Coker (ST 512137), which closed in 1968, is said to be the only example in the country to retain its machinery. Israel Rendell was a twine maker here at Millbrook in 1830 until bought out by John Dawe in 1877. He built a covered rope-walk, with machinery supplied in 1899 by William Sibley of the Parrett Works. A small steam engine, then an oil-gas engine and electric motors supplied the power until closure. There is a second covered walk in the village (ST 521133).

Webbing was made at Crewkerne, where Samuel Sparks and Bartholomew Gidley established Viney Bridge Mills in 1789 for manufacturing linen and woollen girth webbing. It made webbing continuously to the end of the twentieth century, although it passed through several owners. Thomas Matthews was here in the mid-nineteenth century and Arthur Hart dates from the 1880s. After the Second World War Arthur Hart & Son Ltd and Richard Hayward & Co. Ltd of the Coker Works in North Street combined with Joseph Gundry Ltd of Bridport in Dorset to form Crewkerne Textiles Ltd and continued to make webbing and canvas at each of their works. All operations moved to Viney Bridge Mills when the Coker Works was closed. Two hundred years after its formation webbing is still made under the name of Arthur Hart Webbing. Water power was first used at Viney Bridge, with a beam engine installed later in a specially built house. A second steam engine was added in the 1890s. Robert Bird & Co. were webbing makers in 1894 when hand looms were still used alongside machine looms. Their products included girth and body belts,

Rope-making equipment inside John Dawe's rope or twine walk at West Coker in 1980.

D. WARREN

The chapel-like window of the engine house at Viney Bridge Mills, Crewkerne, August 2002.

sashes, reins, upholsterers' web, seamless web tubing for covering ropes or rails, belting for engines, a thin web for binding cheeses and webbing for 'poncho' belts made for the South American market.

John Boyd Textiles Ltd's factory in Castle Cary is one of the few horsehair weaving mills in the world. The town is closely associated with this industry and by 1815 Thomas Matthews was employing home weavers to make a horsehair fabric with a cotton or linen warp. John Boyd, a Scotsman, established a business in 1837 and built the three-storey Ansford Factory for hand looms in 1851 behind his Ochiltree House in Upper High Street (ST 644325). The short length of the horsehair restricts the width of the weave and, although expensive, horsehair fabrics are exceptionally hard wearing and therefore became popular for chair seating. Hand looms were used until a new machine loom was patented by Boyd in 1872, using a 'picker' to select one hair at a time for the shuttle. Around 120 looms were in use at peak times and some of these are still working today. Traditionally, the horse tails are first hackled to separate the hairs before being clamped at the side of the loom.

Boyd was listed as a manufacturer of hair seating and curled hair in 1866, while T.S. Donne & Sons were flax

John Boyd's three-storey Ansford horsehair factory of c.1851 at Castle Cary.

Higher Flax Mills and the old rope-walk, Castle Cary. The main mill in the background was erected in 1870 by T.S. Donne & Sons and webbing, rope and twine were made here using water and then steam power. June 2002. B. DEAVIN

John Boyd & Co. now occupy part of the Higher Flax Mills at Castle Cary, where horsehair weaving takes place using specialist power looms patented in 1872. This loom is seen working in June 2002. B. DEAVIN

spinners and hair seating warp manufacturers. In 1797 Charles Donne began making sailcloth and girth webbing at Ansford, later moving to nearby Torbay. This factory suffered several fires, the last in 1857 when 50 workers lost their jobs. In 1870 Donne & Sons built the Higher Flax Mills (ST 635323) and a large millpond provided water for a wheel which powered the factory by shafting. This was in turn replaced by a steam engine. Donnes made

webbing, rope and twine until closure in the 1980s. Meanwhile, John Boyd Textiles moved to Higher Flax Mills in 1956 and still occupy a smaller and perhaps older building than the main mill. A rope-walk survives at the site. Although Castle Cary was the main centre, the Ward silk factory at Bruton became a horsehair seating manufactory for a while and Samuel Laycock & Sons had similar factories at Hortbridge Mill, Ilminster, and North Street, Crewkerne, in the late-nineteenth and early-twentieth centuries.

Chard, Ilminster and Taunton were home to shirt and collar manufacturing. It grew in the mid-nineteenth century but was at the mercy of fashions so that in 1901 the trade was 'dull' when 915 women and 148 men were employed. At Chard, the Snowdon Collar Works had been John Stringfellow's workshop for making bobbins and bobbin carriages for lace-making machines since 1833, but John Thompson began making shirt collars here in 1866 and advertised for 'respectable young women and girls' to work in his factory. There were 300 employed in 1875 when the factory had expanded. It had a long lantern light in the roof of the main machine room. Soft rainwater used in the process was collected in a storage tank. James Cook & Co. were in occupation from the 1880s until the 1930s and L.S. & O.J. Sussman made shirts here after the Second World War until 1996. The factory has been demolished for housing. The West of England Collar Manufacturing Co. was a rival firm at Old Town Mills from the late-nineteenth century to about 1930.

Shirts and collars were also made at Ilminster. Frederick Day from London opened a collar factory in Ditton Street in 1862 and F.F. Day Foley was the only firm left by 1935. Shirts were made from 1957 but closure came in 2001 after the firm was taken over by Frederick Theak Ltd. The Ditton Street premises were converted to flats. In Taunton, Robert Moody's factory in Viney Street saw the manufacturing of the Van Heusen collar (a famous American name) from 1922 when John Manning Van Heusen came here.

An unusual industry using fibres should also be mentioned here. Nimmer Mills (ST 322108) near Chard became a brush-making factory in 1875 for Coates & Co., toilet brush manufacturers of Axminster and London. Many types of brushes were made and world-famous shaving brushes were made here when the firm joined with Messrs Simpsons in the 1930s. A 16ft (4.8m) water-wheel provided the power, with an ancillary oil engine, until the mill closed in 1990.

12

LEATHER INDUSTRIES

Leather-based industries were important in Somerset by the start of the nineteenth century, involving tanners, curriers, leather dressers, fellmongers, glove makers, rug makers, and boot and shoe manufacturers. The preparation and processing of animal skins were not pleasant activities and were a serious cause of water pollution. Tanning was the process whereby the skins were impregnated with tannic acid to make leather. The animal skins were first soaked in lime pits so the outer layers could be scraped off, then placed into a mixture of excreta in mastering pits before being washed. The skins were then placed in tanning pits for up to a year, being turned daily with a tanner's hook. Taken from the tanning vats, the leather was finished in the curriers' department where it was soaked, rubbed with a stretcher, 'dubbed' with cod oil or tallow and finally waxed and polished. 'Tawing' was a quicker process used on softer skins such as calf, which were put in a cylinder with alum and other mixtures. A good water supply was essential for all the processes and a site near a source of tannin was also advantageous. Bark from specially coppiced oak trees was ground in a mill with edge runner stones and soaked in leaching pits until there was a strong concentrate of tannin.

The early tanneries acquired animal skins from the neighbourhood but a great many came to be imported as these had more suitable properties, for example for glove making. Most tanneries were small and widely scattered before the second half of the nineteenth century. Water power was used, with steam engines in the larger tanneries. Two large tanneries at Glastonbury took water from a disused millstream from the River Brue. Bailey's tannery in Beckery Road (ST 488384) was built in 1868 of lias stone, with a handsome brick chimney. Clark, Son & Morland's neighbouring sheepskin rug factory was developed from Jacob's tan yard at Northover after 1870.

An impressive building (ST 561162) in Eastland Road, Yeovil, dates from 1853. It is stone-built, with the upper floor retaining its wooden louvres (this was for drying skins). This was William Bide's tannery, later occupied by the leather dressers Perrin Leather Co. Ltd. John Pittard & Son were established in 1847, although Pittard senior had been tanning at Lower Middle Street since at least 1820. The main tannery was off Sherborne Road (ST 563161) and this successful firm survives today in a modern premises at Pen Mill, dressing high-quality leather for gloves and other products. J. Clark & Sons had a tannery and leather dressing works at Milborne Port (ST 675190) until recent years. E. & W.C. French Ltd had a tannery in Tancred Street at Taunton, where a beam engine still survived in 1974.

Part of the disused tannery site in the heart of Milborne Port.

This tannery of 1853 is a landmark in Eastland Road, Yeovil. The upper floor retains its wooden louvres but the whole building poses problems for redevelopment or conversion plans.

A tannery at Porlock (SS 885467) was worked by Thomas Pearce & Sons in 1840–1939. The buildings have now found other uses. Fast-flowing water and a supply of oak bark must be the reason for small tanneries established on the edge of the Quantock Hills. A 25ft (7.6m) overshot water-wheel appears to carve its way through a tiled roof of the buildings at John Hayman's former tannery at Holford (ST 151405). The iron wheel was made in 1892 by James Culverwell of Bridgwater. A timber-clad bark house at Nether Stowey is now a private residence. There was a tannery at Broadway near Ilminster from 1550 until about 1870. When offered for sale in 1844, it comprised

a tan yard, three drying sheds, bark house, store house, two mill houses… the yard which has been worked until a recent period contains 34 handlers, 16 trows, 11 latches, 3 masterings, 1 soak and 4 lime pits… bark is plentiful in the neighbourhood… the yard is situate two miles from the Chard Canal.

Holford's old tannery, where this large water-wheel was made in 1892 by J. Culverwell of Bridgwater. June 1976.

Shoe making is closely associated with the world-famous name of Clarks of Street. The origins of the firm began with the Quaker Cyrus Clark who had a tannery in 1825. His younger brother James joined him as a partner in 1833 and began making shoes. Street became the centre for shoe and boot making and 600 outworkers were employed in the 1850s. The factory site was developed under the management of William Stephens Clark in the last quarter of the century, by the end of which C. & J. Clark Ltd were employing some 1200 workers. A few outworkers remained until 1941. In the factory, machinery was employed in the 'clicking room' where the uppers were cut out by presses with dies, although some work was carried out using a hand knife. In the making-room the soles (cut from oak-tanned ox hide) and heels were stitched to the uppers. The shoes were finished and polished up and put into cardboard boxes made on the premises.

The only Clarks shoe factory left in Somerset is now at Dowlish Ford near Ilminster and much of the Street factory has been turned over to the Clarks Village Outlet Shopping Centre. The site is dominated by a tall brick chimney and some original buildings remain. Part of the premises facing the High Street contains the Clarks Factory Museum (ST 485368) which tells the story of this important industry. It is housed in Cyrus Clark's original tannery. A clock tower of 1887 is apparently based on one in Switzerland, and behind is a handsome water tower built at the time of Queen Victoria's 1897 Jubilee.

Glastonbury became a centre for sheepskin rug making. In the late 1820s Cyrus Clark made rugs from sheepskins at Street when his brother James began making slippers. Skins were first prepared at Bowlingreen Mill where a tan yard was built, but in 1870 John Morland joined the Clarks and the rug-making factory was moved to Northover, Glastonbury. The skins were first washed, rinsed, squeezed through a machine and combed. They were then stretched and dried on wooden frames in the open air or in a heated room if the weather was unfavourable. They were then dyed, with around 40 shades available. Clark, Son & Morland's extensive rug factory now awaits redevelopment alongside the tannery in Beckery Road.

Leather glove making was important particularly around Yeovil where Daniel Defoe had described this as the main manufacture in the 1720s. There were said to be over 4000 people employed and probably a good number of home outworkers too by the 1890s when Yeovil overtook

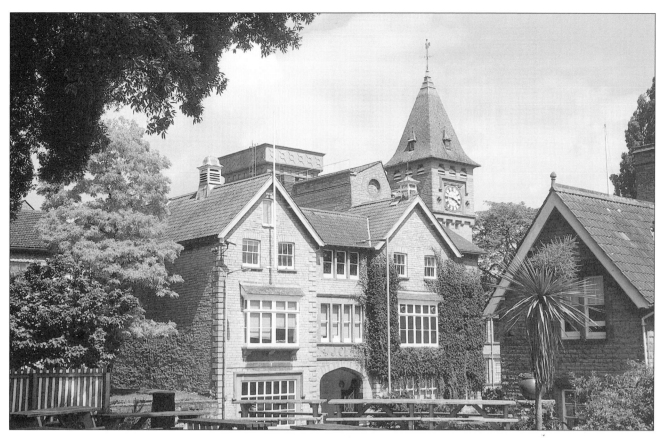

C. & J. Clark's shoe factory at Street. The clock tower dates from 1887.

The High Street frontage of C. & J. Clark's shoe factory.

The water tower was added to C. & J. Clark's shoe factory in 1897. A carving in Ham stone beneath the tank depicts the tower on Glastonbury Tor, once a trademark of the firm.

The extensive tannery and sheepskin rug factory complex at Glastonbury awaits redevelopment in 2003.

A former glove factory in the village of Martock, July 1995. Glove making is still thriving in nearby Stoke sub Hamdon.

Worcester as England's leading glove producer. The best leather for gloving was imported. Sewing machines introduced in the late-nineteenth century greatly changed the nature of glove making, moving the industry into factories. Increasing competition from imported gloves, changing fashions and the popularity of fabric gloves from the 1950s saw the rapid decline of the industry but the remaining firms survived by specialising in high-quality gloves. The last of the many glove factories in Yeovil closed in 1989.

The industry survives, however, in the outlying villages such as Stoke sub Hamdon where Southcombe Brothers were established in 1847 and are still in business in Cole Lane (ST 472175). Silas Dyke & Sons had a traditional leather-dressing factory and gloving factoryin North Street, Milborne Port (ST 676188) from the mid-nineteenth century until the 1980s. Thomas Taylor moved from Stoke sub Hamdon to a gloving factory in Richmond Road, Taunton, in the late-nineteenth century and employed around 300 outworkers, but the firm is no longer in business.

13

FOUNDERS AND ENGINEERS

From the early-nineteenth century Somerset had smithies, foundries and engineering works, mainly catering for the agricultural industry but some diversifying into other products. There were also wagon works of some significance. Most rural sites remained small, while others grew like the Fussell family's edge-tool enterprise near Mells. Important foundries in the towns included Dening of Chard, Cockey and Singer of Frome, Allen of Taunton and Hennet of Bridgwater. On the engineering side, Petter of Yeovil manufactured oil engines in the early-twentieth century and branched into the Westland aviation business.

Right: *Down's foundry building at Beards Yard, Langport, is an example of industrial activity in a small town. 1987.*

D. WARREN

Below: *Where it all began. Some engineering firms developed from the business of the humble blacksmith or wheelwright. This reconstructed wheelwright's shop is at Bishops Lydeard Mill.*

The Mells ironworks date from 1744 when James Fussell was granted a lease to erect 'a good, firm and substantial Mill or Mills for grinding edge tools and forging iron plates'. In 1791 the Fussells were supplying agricultural implements locally as well as exporting them to Europe and America. The scythes were said to owe their temper to the lime-rich water found at Mells. By 1871 there were six works at constricted sites on three streams which

provided the power, with James Fussell, Sons & Co. at Mells Lower Works, Great Elm, Railford and Chantry Works (scythes, hooks, etc), John Fussell & Co. at the Mells Upper Works (spades, shovels, edge-tools), Isaac Fussell & Co. at Nunney (spade, shovel, drainage tools and edge-tools) and William A. Fussell at Rock House (spades, shovels, garden furniture, melon and cucumber frames, hot-house stoves, etc). A downturn in the fortunes of English agriculture in the 1870s affected the business. James, Isaac & John Fussell Ltd was formed in 1882 but bankruptcy came in 1894. The works were closed but the goodwill was acquired by Isaac Nash of Worcestershire.

Derelict for nearly a century, the Lower Works (ST 738489) in the narrow Wadbury valley of the Mells stream was excavated in 1974. Nine water-wheels had powered forges, hammers and grindstones here until the 1860s when a steam engine was installed. Among the ruins, the excavators revealed an 11ft (3.35m) diameter iron water-wheel still in place, a furnace, a row of small hand forges in a paved building and a network of culverts beneath the site. A second water-wheel was discovered at the Great Elm site late in 1999.

Cast products bearing their founders' names include all kinds of agricultural implements and machines, street furniture such as mileposts, lampposts and drain covers, and even bridges. Typical products of a rural foundry might also be the cheese presses, cider presses, apple mills, railings and signposts made by Albert and Henry Day at Mark. Their foundry was established in 1841 and closed in 1950. In the same village James Wensley manufactured a variety of wagons, carts, drays, lorries, floats and timber carriages in the late-nineteenth century. The body of his patent manure cart could be raised or lowered when travelling, to keep it level when going up or down hill.

At one end of the scale there were small rural workshops, such as Elias Nethercott's 'foundry' and sawmill established in about 1860 at Roadwater (ST 031381). Railway keys, trunnions and sleepers were made for the West Somerset Mineral Railway. A water-wheel powered bellows, lathes, drills and a pit saw and was still used alongside two portable steam engines in 1933. Nethercotts, who also undertook steam threshing contracts and building work, closed in 1976. Samuel Rowsell, a carpenter and agricultural machinist, set up his Buckland St Mary Rake & Gate Manufactory by 1851 and in the following decade exhibited rakes and 'American' hay-collectors at the Bath & West and the

Royal Agricultural Society of England shows, both then held at different annual sites. His improved gates had 'excellent fastenings and hangings' and one was awarded a £1 prize by the West of England Society at Yeovil in 1856. By 1876 Levi Dicks, carpenter and builder, was here when a small steam engine made by C. Allen & Son of Taunton was installed for sawing. Finally the 'rakery' was used from the late 1890s until the 1930s by James Board, a carpenter and undertaker.

Millwrighting was another side of the engineering business, designing and installing wheels, sometimes with castings ordered from the foundries. Available work gradually declined as oil engines and electricity took over from water power. Millwrights who made water-wheels for farms included W.H. Pool & Sons of Chipstable (1847–1956), William Govier, recorded at Lopen near Ilminster in 1869–75 (a wheel survives at Somerton Randle Mill, ST 498285), Charles Philips & Son of Bridgetown, Dulverton, makers of surviving wheels at Gupworthy Farm (SS 970349) and Surridge Farm (SS 976271), and John Chidgey & Sons of Watchet.

John Chidgey & Sons were established in 1856 at Mount Pleasant, Watchet, and moved to South Road in the 1880s. After the firm closed in 1936 the site was used by Bill Norman for automobile engineering and car hire until 1976. The Somerset Industrial Archaeological Society surveyed this typical small engineering works when it still had the machine shop and pattern loft, foundry and smithy, carpenters' shop, store and cart shed, arranged around a narrow courtyard. Much of the equipment was complete in the buildings and it was saved for the Somerset Rural Life Museum. The day books, now in the Somerset Record Office, record a variety of work including the supply of iron water-wheels to Dunster Castle (1882), Bridge Farm (1890), Roebuck Farm (1896) and Washford Cement Works (1902). The larger castings, however, were made for Chidgeys by Bodley Bros of Exeter.

The Parrett Works (ST 446186) is a fascinating industrial complex with a handsome Italianate stone chimney in the countryside near Martock. George Parsons had a flax mill at West Lambrook where he began making agricultural machines in the 1840s but after its destruction by fire, he built a new flax mill and engineering works at Cary's Mill in 1855, naming it the Parrett Works. Here were manufactured steam engines, traction engines, threshing machines, water-wheels, flax spinning and power looms. The second part of the works made rope, twine and

The Italianate chimney at the Parrett Iron Works.

engines, sawing machines, quarry cranes, flax machines, twine-twisting machines, Parsons' patent wheels and carts and wagons. Two important engineers came out of the Parrett Works. William Sparrow was the manager before he left in 1868 to set up the Somerset Wheel & Waggon Works (later W. Sparrow Ltd, agricultural engineers) at nearby Bower Hinton and parts of this site survive today (ST 457178). Benjamin Jacobs left the Parrett Works in 1894 for the Nautilus Stove Works in Yeovil and later became the chief engineer for Petter & Co.

At Chard, John Wightman was established as an iron and brass founder in Holyrood Street in 1828. Charles Dening joined him in 1842 and their agricultural machinery was marketed at home and abroad. The successful Dening & Co. was formed in 1866 and moved in 1880 to a larger site at Crimchard where a steam engine provided the power until about 1900 when it was replaced by a gas engine. The Dening family remained in control until 1937. There was expansion during the Second World War when the Somerset Works was built in Tapstone Lane. The workforce rose to 998 in 1948 when 'Somerset' grass mowers were among the agricultural machines being made. However, the firm was wound up in 1951 after losing a major export order to Argentina. It was acquired by the Beyer Peacock Group of Manchester and production under the Dening name continued until 1965. Over the years Dening & Co.'s range of products included corn kibblers, chaff cutters, turnip cutters, seed drills, hay rakes, ploughs, harrows, rollers, apple mills, cider presses, sawbenches, pug mills for brickworks, cast-iron grave markers, lampposts, water troughs and railings. Chard Museum has exhibits and a Dening sawbench is in working order as far away as the National

sailcloth, as described in chapter 11. The firm was liquidated in 1869 and divided into two. William Sibley's West of England Engineering Co., millwrights, founders and makers of oil engines, were here from 1875 until 1928. In 1894 Sibley & Son were advertised as 'millwrights and mill furnishers, engineers and ironfounders', manufacturing water-wheels and all types of mill machinery, steam

Trust's Sheringham estate in Norfolk. Nearer home, an iron milepost by Wightman stands beside the A359 at Galhampton near Castle Cary.

Chard was home to John Stringfellow, the pioneer of powered flight. In 1833 he turned the old Friends' Meeting House into workshops for making lace bobbins and bobbin carriages and extended the premises in the 1840s. It later became the Snowdon Collar Works. Stringfellow is best know for his inventiveness and experiments with a steam-powered model aeroplane which actually flew in 1848 and was far ahead of its time. It is unclear whether the indoor experimental flights took place in these workshops or in the attic of the Holyrood lace mill. Joseph Hawker had a foundry at Town Mill from about 1851 until 1876. He manufactured stationary and portable steam engines for agricultural purposes, fire engines and pumps, milling equipment and water-wheels Of special interest was his 1872 patent for a tracked road locomotive, the precursor of the caterpillar tractor. It is uncertain if one was ever built but, like Stringfellow's aeroplane, it had to wait until the early-twentieth century to come into its own.

Also in Chard, John Hockey had a small works in Tapstone Lane for making agricultural machinery and in 1892 opened a net lace factory at Rose Mills, Ilminster. John Smith's foundry in Combe Street became the Phoenix Works (ST 317093) in 1891 when the Phoenix Engineering Co. Ltd was founded to make pumps and tar boilers for the road-making industry.

Frome was another important engineering centre. Edward Cockey & Sons, originally bell-founders, were well established by the 1860s as engineers and ironfounders, when they employed 250 hands. Steam engines, boilers and iron roofs were among their products, and the cast-iron pillars for the Dorset County Museum's Victorian gallery were made in 1883. However, gasworks apparatus and gasholders with patent regulating valves were specialities and Cockeys furnished gasworks all over England. They were also involved in the management of the Frome gasworks. John Webb Singer started making church ornaments at Frome in the 1850s and then expanded into statuary by opening a new foundry in 1888. Bronze statues were cast from models made by leading sculptors, such as statues of Queen Victoria erected from Carlisle to Wellington in New Zealand, King Alfred at Winchester (1901), the Boadicea statue on the Embankment at Westminster (1902) and Justice on top of the Old Bailey (1906). Singer & Co. Ltd recruited women

John Hockey, maker of agricultural machinery at Chard, displays a portable elevator, c.1900.

in the Great War to make racks for cordite, aeroplane parts and brass for fuse bodies, shell and cartridge cases. By 1918 there were 700 men and women employed. Thereafter the casting industry was depressed but the Second World War brought more work. The firm was taken over in 1946 by the Drayton Group of London. The original foundry site (ST 776482) has been redeveloped for housing although the firm still survives in the town.

Taunton's founders and engineers included C. Allen & Son of the Tone Foundry & Engineering Works in Bridge Street. In 1887 they were advertised as 'ironfounders and steam boiler makers', supplying portable, vertical and horizontal steam engines, water-wheels, pumps, turbines, mill gearing, sawbenches, iron hurdles and fencing. They also made 'The Somerset' improved portable steam engine, suitable on estates for threshing machines, corn grinding mills, chaff cutters and sawbenches. In the same town, Easton & Waldegrave of the Whitehall Iron Works were manufacturers of horizontal, portable and vertical

86

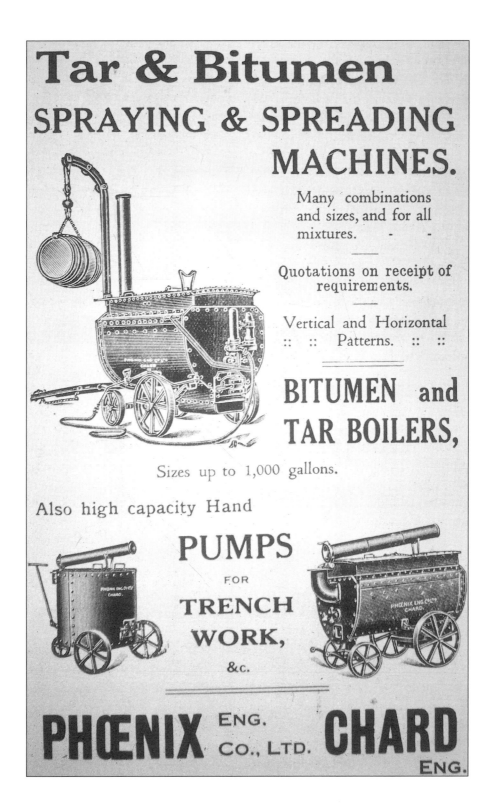

engines, as well as boilers, sawbenches, water-wheels pumps, cranes turbines and hydraulic rams.

At Wellington a foundry was established in about 1835 by William Willmitt, passing to his nephew James Ford when he died in 1866. Ford Brothers & Co.'s Reliance Foundry in Gas Street continued until about 1927. Water-wheels were made at Wellington, such as that for Chipley Saw Mills by Willmitt in about 1859, and for Gerbestone Manor by Ford Brothers in 1898. Other products of Ford Bros included agricultural implements, kitchen ranges, threshing machines, horse gears and water-wheels. They were millwrights, as were Bishop Brothers of the Wellington Foundry in North Street, who made steam engines, boilers, water-wheels (as at Bishops Lydeard Mill) and 'highly approved' kitchen ranges.

Bridgwater had ironfounders of some note. George Hennet built the Bridgwater Iron Works (ST 307363) and a sawmill and timber yard in the 1840s. He was associated with the Stephensons and Brunel and supplied ironwork for Resolven Bridge on the Vale of Neath Railway (1849), Landore Viaduct on the South Wales Railway (1850), wrought-iron caisson lock gates for the Cumberland Basin at Bristol Docks (1846) and pipes for Brunel's South Devon Atmospheric Railway (1847). The firm continued as Hennet, Spink & Else after Hennet's death in 1857. Richard Else had worked with Brunel, and parts for the Royal Albert Bridge at Saltash were supplied from Bridgwater. Hennet, Spink & Else built iron bridges in the 1860s at Hampton Court, Walton-on-Thames and Weybridge, generally condemned as 'ugly'. In Somerset, their ironwork was used in the since-altered Marsh Bridge across the Barle near Dulverton (SS 907290). They made cask-cleaning machines and prizewinning agricultural machinery, while the iron lighthouse on the west pier at Watchet is also their work. The foundry was for sale in 1870 and closed eight years later.

Edward Murch was another Bridgwater ironfounder, who has left his name cast with the date 1848 on Hurstbow Bridge at Martock and the Tone Bridge at Creech St Michael. Surviving products of James Culverwell & Co. of Eastover, Bridgwater, include a horizontal steam engine now preserved by the Westonzoyland Trust and two water-wheels, for the Holford tannery (ST 151405) and Stogursey Manor Mill (ST 204426). Mileposts, apple mills and field rollers were also made. W. & F. Wills Ltd, who moved to the Perseverance Works, Bridgwater, in the 1890s manufactured steam engines including a fine little horizontal engine still running under steam in the care of

The cast-iron Hurstbow road bridge at Martock was made in 1848 by Edward Murch of Bridgwater. July 1995.

the Westonzoyland Engine Trust. This is believed to have worked at a local brickyard. They also made pumps and fitted out the eroder boats which used hoses to keep the River Parrett channel clear of mud.

Petter is one of the great names in the world of engine manufacturing. James Bazeley Petter acquired an ironmongery business in Yeovil in 1865 and soon set up a foundry with a partner to manufacture agricultural implements and machinery at Hendford. Petter invented the 'Nautilus' iron fire grate which was marketed across the country; even Queen Victoria had them installed at Osborne House and Balmoral Castle. Ernest and Percy Petter joined their father and in 1892 produced a self-propelled oil engine. Benjamin Jacobs, who joined the firm from the Parrett Works, designed a single-acting high-speed steam engine, the 'Yeovil Engine', and with the Petter brothers designed a simple oil engine which proved to be immensely successful. In 1895 they made a 1hp engine for a 'horseless carriage', an early motor car that was made by Messrs Hill & Boll at their carriage works in Park Road. This was not really a success, but in 1902 a 30hp agricultural tractor was exported to European countries including Russia.

James B. Petter & Co. Ltd was formed in 1902 and became Petters Ltd in 1908. The new large Nautilus Works was opened at Reckleford (ST 559162), with a drawing office, pattern, casting, machine, erecting and paint shops, the whole powered by two 100hp gas engines and generators which supplied electric lighting to the works and part of the town. Agricultural and marine engines were manufactured here after the Great War. The Seaton-Petter car was made briefly in 1926–27, with hopes of colonial markets, but the main business was

Cast-iron signposts destined for Norfolk were among the many products of W. & F. Wills of Bridgwater, early-twentieth century. Note also the telegraph pole in the background.   I. & M. MILES COLLECTION

This horizontal steam engine provided power in W. & F. Wills Ltd's Perseverance Works at Bridgwater from 1896.

I. & M. MILES COLLECTION

Three-cylinder Petter diesel engine and electric generating set in the Norton quarry power house, Ham Hill, July 1992. Many such power units by Petters and other makers still exist, although abandoned, throughout Somerset.

with their heavy oil industrial and marine engines of all sizes from 1½ to 400hp. Engines were supplied for agricultural use, sawing timber, pumping, generating electricity, and the marine engines for fishing boats, river tugs and barges all over the world. The Nautilus Works closed in 1939 when the Brush Group purchased Petters Ltd and manufacturing was moved to Loughborough. Parts of the Reckleford works have become a bus depot or have been put to industrial uses.

Meanwhile, Petters formed an aircraft division in 1915 at the Westland Works, West Hendford (ST 542154), to build Short Brothers' seaplanes for the Admiralty. Other wartime aircraft included Sopwith fighters and de Haviland and Vickers bombers. An airfield was established in 1917 and Westlands designed their own aircraft, including small civilian aircraft such as the Westland Limousine and the three-engined Westland Wessex. The Westland Wapiti of 1927 was a successful military plane, and the Westland Lysander proved most reliable for special duties in the Second World War. Other aircraft were made under contract and the Westland Dragonfly helicopter of 1948 was an improvement on an American Sikorsky design. From the 1950s onwards Westlands grew to become Britain's leading helicopter manufacturer. The expanded works contains some original buildings.

Paper was made around the Mendips and at other sites, where plentiful water was an important part of the process. Large quantities of linen rags, old hemp rope, sacking or sailcloth were taken to the paper mill where they were first sorted according to quality by women and children. This raw material was then washed and ground in a mill or beating engine to a pulp which was put into a vat or tub. Into this the paper maker placed a mould (a square wooden frame covered with a fine wire cloth), and lifted it out so the pulp drained to form a sheet on the wire mesh. The moulded sheets were laid on a cloth and pressed before being dried in lofts at the top of the paper mill. The sheets had to be sized, pressed in reams and packed for sale. The making of paper by hand was labour-intensive and a long process from start to finish. Machines were invented in the 1800s to make paper in a continuous stream from pulp to drying, polishing and cutting. Such machines could also make sheets of much larger dimensions than possible by hand. There was an expansion in larger paper mills after the duty on paper was repealed in 1861.

Paper mills required to be sited on supplies of fast-flowing clear water, such as could be found springing from the foot of the Mendip Hills. Much water was used in making the pulp but a good stream also provided power. There were eight paper makers recorded in 1830, five at Wookey, Bleadney and Cheddar on the edge of Mendip, two others at Watchet and one at Bishop's Hull. Only four remained in the first half of the twentieth century. The three most important sites were the Hodgkinsons' mill at Wookey Hole, the Wansbrough Mill at Watchet and Somerville's mill at Creech St Michael.

Many visitors to Somerset will have toured the famous caves at Wookey Hole and the attractions of the old paper mill (ST 532478). This is a classic site for a paper mill, close to a reliable spring of clean water at the source of the River Axe. It is also an early site, with paper making first recorded in 1610. Joseph Coles was a paper maker here in 1788 (James Coles was at Lower Wookey or Henley Mill), but in 1830 Wookey Hole was worked by John and James Snelgrove. The buildings seen today date

in part from the 1840s, with a front block of 1899. The mill was rebuilt after a fire in 1855.

William Sampson Hodgkinson, a London wholesale stationer, came here in 1856 with a partner, William Burnside, but the mill was really developed with his son. A description of 1858 gives a good idea of the layout when the Wookey Hole Mill had 'approved modern machinery, capable of producing two tons of hand-made paper weekly'. A turbine waterwheel by Donkin & Co. drove a 'considerable portion' of the mill. There was also a 12-inch horizontal steam engine. The main three-storey building had rag and drying lofts at the top, rag sorting and cutting rooms in the middle and presses and glazing machines on the ground floor. Behind, a two-storey mill had five iron 'engines', two stone chests, four circular stuff chests with agitators and gearing, four knotters and vats and a press, and a second drying room. In addition there was a size boiling house, warehouse, third drying room, rag boiling house, bleaching house, boiler house with two Cornish boilers and a 'lofty' brick chimney. There were also six workers' cottages and stabling in front of the mill.

A celebrated court case took place in 1860 when the paper mill successfully sued the St Cuthbert's Lead Works at Priddy for polluting the water. A trace dye proved that contaminated waste water was emerging at the spring source of the Axe. Production increased in the 1860s, with ten vats producing high-quality vellum, drawing paper, bank and indenture papers. In 1863 banknote paper was supplied for the Confederate bank in Richmond, Virginia. Later in the century a new boiler was installed, a tall chimney built and the present front of the mill added. Hand-made paper continued alongside machine-made paper. The Hodgkinsons sold the mill in 1951 to the Inveresk Paper Co. who worked the St Cuthbert's Mill downstream. They kept Wookey Hole Mill for dry-pressing paper before the site was sold in 1973 to Madame Tussaud's. A beater room, vat house and drying loft were brought back into use and hand-made paper is now demonstrated to visitors.

There were other paper mills along the edge of the Mendip Hills. There were three at Cheddar, the last being owned by the Wansbrough Paper Co. until closure in 1900. The Upper Paper Mill closed in about 1860 and became a shirt factory. Pirie, Wyatt & Co. Ltd had the St Cuthbert's Paper Mill at Wookey station in 1902. St Cuthbert's Paper Works Ltd was here by 1927 and the mill was later acquired by the Inveresk Paper Co. Today, Inveresk plc work the St Cuthbert's Mill (ST 531466), producing high quality mould-made artists' papers and pre-impregnated furniture papers. There was another mill further down the Axe at Bleadney from at least 1784 until 1850.

West Somerset has a working paper mill at Watchet (ST 065429). In the eighteenth century farmers worked part-time paper mills in the area at Egrove Mill (Williton) and Snailholt (Watchet). In 1750 William Wood was a cider and paper maker employing seven workers at Snailholt, and his grandson Isaac was here in the 1820s when the paper mill was transferred a little downstream. This proved a successful location, for the stream was suitable and the harbour was used to import rags which were first cleansed by boiling in lime from the local kilns. Gypsum quarried from the cliffs was used as a 'loading' in the paper from the 1880s to 1914. The year after a big

fire in 1845, John Wansbrough came here from Cheddar and introduced machinery such as Roberts' continuous web machine followed later by Fourdrinier machines. Rags, sacking and hemp rope waste were all used as raw materials. The factory produced brown wrapping papers for shops and coloured blue for sugar-wrap paper. Steam drying was used. A tall chimney was built up the hill near St Decuman's church to improve the draught and was in use until 1962 when gas was introduced. The Wansbrough Paper Co. Ltd went public in 1896 but there was a large fire two years later and the firm soon went into receivership.

William Reed of Silverton Paper Mill in Devon took over in 1903 and the Wansbrough name was retained. At this time, the foreman Pearse bought up machines and started the Exmoor Paper & Bag Co. in the former Stoates' flour mill (ST 069432). This closed in the mid-1970s and has been put to other uses, but a 45hp Gilkes turbine of 1927 survives. In both world wars the Wansbrough Mill used straw as a substitute for wood pulp, imports of which did not resume until 1946. In 1950 five machines were making up to 300 tons of paper every week from waste paper and wood pulp imported through the harbour.

A disastrous fire at the Wansbrough Paper Mill in 1898. Such hazards were commonplace in many industrial processes. The iron church on the left was brought here from the abandoned mining village of Brendon Hill.

The Wansbrough Paper Mill at Watchet is still active after a long history. The old mill chimney rivals the tower of St Decuman's church on the hill above.

Production increased and St Regis International acquired the mill in 1976, with a later management buy-out creating the St Regis Paper Co. Ltd.

R. Somerville & Co. Ltd opened another large paper mill in 1875 at Creech St Michael (ST 269254), taking advantage of a good water supply and proximity to the Great Western Railway. It was equipped with a 100in (2.54m) wide machine for making engine-sized writings and fine printings. In 1907 its products included writing, drawing, printing, envelope, tobacco, art, chrome and enamelled papers. The mill had an exceptionally tall chimney, now demolished, but the architectural detail of some of the buildings is of note. Since closure in 1982 the site has been turned over to other industrial uses.

Paper was made at Dulcote from 1752 until about 1898 when the Dulcote Leather Board Co. began making a thick fibre board used by the shoe industry. The mill burnt down in September 1904 and a century later its ruins and a chimney survive next to the mill house (ST

565448). A similar leatherboard used for shoe stiffeners and insoles was made at Bowlingreen Mill (ST 489372) on the edge of Street for over one hundred years. This had been the Clarks' leather works since the 1830s, with a tannery added in 1853, but it became a leatherboard mill in 1877. A steam engine was bought in 1878 and there were many additions and expansions over the years down

Brick gables at the Creech St Michael Paper Mill, opened in 1875 by R. Somerville & Co. Ltd. It closed in 1982.

to the 1960s. The Avalon Leatherboard Co. eventually closed in the 1980s and the site has been redeveloped. An attractive stone block facing the street dates from 1891 and 1906 and has been converted to housing.

Printing works have a close connection with the paper industry and it is worth noting the Selwood Printing Works at Frome (ST 773482). This is the impressive building of Messrs Butler & Tanner, now converted to flats. In 1855 Butler started the *Somerset & Wilts Journal*, which merged with the *Somerset Standard* in 1925. Date-stones of 1866 and 1876 indicate how the works expanded. Some 500 people were employed in 1890. Steam powered the presses but the works converted to electricity in the early 1900s.

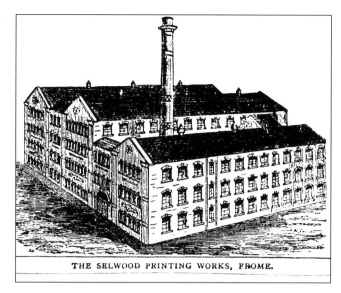

THE SELWOOD PRINTING WORKS, FROME.

This datestone inscribed 'SPW 1866' indicates the quality of the architecture of the Selwood Printing Works which has now been converted to flats.

15

ROADS

Somerset can perhaps claim the first 'roads' in the prehistoric timber trackways discovered during peat cutting on the moors near Meare. The Sweet Track, a purposely constructed timber causeway dated to 3806BC, was followed in later centuries by trackways of hurdles or brushwood. However, the Romans brought the first properly engineered roads and their Fosse Way is still in use today. Another road crossed it north of Shepton Mallet and ran along the Mendip ridge ostensibly to serve the lead mines, but lesser roads have been ploughed out. Then the condition of roads deteriorated for centuries, while they were maintained to varying degrees by local parishes. The only lasting works of the medieval period are stone-arched river bridges.

Established post routes between London and Exeter passed through Somerset by the eighteenth century when efforts were at last made at real improvements by the creation of turnpike trusts. These were initiated by landowners, merchants and others who wished to improve their roads to increase trade and therefore benefit their town or district. Acts of Parliament gave authority to improve existing routes, build new ones and to maintain them. The trusts were empowered to raise tolls to make a return on money invested and to pay for the works and maintenance. Each trust was renewed periodically and their renewal Acts often indicate the dates of changes and new routes. John Billingsley was delighted with the trusts in 1798, writing:

Nothing so much contributes to the improvement of a county as good roads; before the establishment of turnpikes, many parts of this county were scarcely accessible.

The first trusts in historic Somerset were at Bath (1707) and Bristol (1727), the latter becoming the largest in England. The Bridgwater Trust followed in 1730, but the busy 1750s saw the creation of 11 trusts with another four in the 1760s. The Taunton Trust began the episode in 1752, followed in the next year by the Chard, Ilchester, Langport, Somerton & Castle Cary, Shepton Mallet, Wells and Yeovil trusts. In all, 20 new trusts were created in Somerset between 1752 and 1841, the last being the

Wells, Highbridge & Cheddar Trust. The main routes were established by the start of the nineteenth century, after which most of the work involved making branches, realignments and completing links. Lengths of other trusts entered from neighbouring counties, such as Wiltshire's Black Dog Trust in the northeast, or Dorset's Sherborne and Vale of Blackmoor Trusts in the south. Few were ever a financial success, particularly once competition came from the railways. The main-line railways finished off the mail-coach routes and the branch lines did the rest of the work, reducing road transport to local carriers. For example, the Chard Trust's income fell from £1800 in 1837 to £700 in 1866 for this reason. The trusts were gradually extinguished so that road maintenance passed to district authorities and then the county council in 1889. However, one lasting effect of the trusts was to fix the modern road system on the map of Somerset.

One of the trusts established in 1753 was at Chard, a prosperous town at the meeting of routes from London to Exeter and from Taunton to the south coast. The Exeter route began at Haselbury Bridge near Crewkerne in 1753, crossed the hill at Windwhistle and descended to Chard where it turned south through Tytherleigh to Weycroft just outside Axminster. In 1777 a direct route to Honiton was turnpiked via Snowdon Hill, Wambrook, Longbridge and Stockland (then in Dorset) to Cheeseway Ash near Honiton. This could not compete against a new direct road created in 1807 by the Honiton & Ilminster Trust (the modern A303) so it was disturnpiked and alternative routes were built, finally in 1829 with the better-graded line now followed by the A30 to meet the A303 at Devonshire Inn. In 1838 the line up Snowdon Hill was graded with a causeway and cutting.

Important routes from Bristol, Bath, Frome and Shepton Mallet converged on Wells, where a trust was established in 1753. The first two were turnpiked from Rush Hill (A39) and White Post near Radstock (B3139) and the route carried on through Glastonbury to Walton and Pipers Inn where it met the roads of the Bridgwater and Taunton Trusts. The Frome and Shepton roads were turnpiked ten years later. There were adjustments in the

1820s when the ascents from Wells were eased and the route over Wearyall Hill at Glastonbury was avoided. The winding route through the Croscombe valley to Shepton Mallet (A371) was not turnpiked until 1857, replacing the old route along the hill to the south. The railway from Highbridge to Glastonbury (1854) and Wells (1862) took away much traffic and the Bath to Evercreech Junction line of 1874 threatened the turnpike's important brewery traffic. Despite this, the Wells Trust was not wound up until 1883, the last in Somerset.

The Shepton Mallet Trust was also established in 1753 with a main route (now the A37) from a meeting with the Bath and Wells Trusts at Rush Hill, through Shepton Mallet and via the Fosse Way to Red Post at Lydford Park, and others to Pilton and Glastonbury (B3136 and A361). The two north–south routes through Shepton Mallet, via the High Street and Kilver Street (now A37), were considered to be on the main highway from Bristol to the south coast ports of Dorset. The Frome road was turnpiked in 1765 as far as Leighton. It passed just south of Doulting and the present road (A361) through the village was not built until 1871.

The main route of the Langport, Somerton & Castle Cary Trust (1753–1879) ran west to east from Fivehead to Langport (A378) and thence through Somerton to Ansford at Castle Cary (B3153). The last additions in 1824 included a route from Langport towards Bridgwater via Westonzoyland and Chedzoy (A372) and a line south through Muchelney and Kingsbury Episcopi to South Petherton. There was a confusion of roads around Castle Cary where the trust met with the Sherborne, Bruton and Shepton Mallet trusts.

Henry Fownes Luttrell of Dunster was much involved in the creation of the Minehead United Turnpike Trust (1765–1877). Minehead had declined in prosperity by the mid-eighteenth century, due partly to 'deep, heavy and dirty' roads impassable to carriages in winter. Turnpikes from Bridgwater, Taunton and Tiverton approached this remoter area from the margins. The original Minehead Turnpike route to Bampton climbed up to 1345 feet (410 m) at Quarme Hill. This was avoided in 1824 by the opening of an impressive 14-mile road between Timberscombe and Exebridge, now the A396. William McAdam (son of J.L. McAdam) of the Exeter Trust surveyed the route and probably also supervised its construction. To avoid losing height unnecessarily, the road wound up from Timberscombe to the summit at Wheddon Cross before descending the narrow Quarme

and Exe valleys to Exebridge where it met the Tiverton Trust. The inscriptions 'WP 1823' and 'LAWRENCE 1824' carved in the face of a roadside cliff at Bridgetown must relate to this ambitious scheme.

The surface condition of turnpike roads was variable but generally good. In 1798 Billingsley wrote that 'few counties can boast better turnpike roads' than parts of Somerset. For example, between Wells and Bridgwater the road was 'as smooth as a gravel-walk' which was considered to be due to the careful breaking of stones to the size of pigeons' eggs. Whereas seven or eight horses once drew a 2-ton wagon 20 miles a day, the same horses could now draw 5 tons up to 40 miles. Coal was carried in $2\frac{1}{2}$cwt (127kg) loads by packhorses for 15 to 20 miles from the collieries, but after the turnpikes one horse and cart could carry four times as much.

The famous road engineer John Loudon McAdam and his sons were involved in a number of Somerset's turnpike trusts from 1816, although not always harmoniously. McAdam's type of road was relatively cheap but also efficient. The stone was broken to a small size (to go in the mouth!) and laid to a depth of 10in (254mm) and the passage of traffic compacted it without the need for rolling. It also drained well. The quality of road material depended on what was to hand but limestone was particularly favoured. Small gravel pits alongside roads are evidence of early road making.

The archaeology of turnpike routes includes engineering works involving cuttings, embankments and bridges, although many have been subsequently altered or widened so they are passed today with hardly a glance. An abandoned turnpike section (ST 6224601) north of Shepton Mallet was excavated in 1997. The cambered carriageway was 40ft (12m) wide between shallow ditches and constructed with stones of the size recommended by McAdam, although larger stones on one side suggested it was not a true McAdam road. The sandstone road materials were from a local source, including stones apparently picked from the fields. The road had a very short life, having been built in 1821 and disturnpiked in 1842 when the present road (A37) was opened along a kinder gradient to the east. The Wells Trust has two good examples of abandoned routes due to realignments. A half-mile section on the Bath road at West Horrington was abandoned when a new road was constructed in 1821. The Bristol road (now A37), a long and steady climb of about 1 in 20 out of Wells to Pen Hill, was constructed in 1824 to replace a much steeper 1 in 7 route just to the west, which remains as a bridleway.

Bridges are an important part of the archaeology of roads and include packhorse bridges, fine medieval stone arches and iron spans of the nineteenth century. County bridges were administered by justices at the quarter sessions while others were built by the turnpike trusts. Many bridges have been strengthened to take heavier traffic in recent years, although alterations have been sympathetic wherever possible.

Stone bridges across the fast-flowing River Barle on Exmoor demonstrate a variety of types, from the ancient clapper bridge at Tarr Steps (SS 868321) to the five-arched Landacre Bridge (SS 816361) of 1610 or the six-arched Withypool Bridge (SS 845354) of 1866. A splendid stone bridge of the early-nineteenth century crosses the Parrett at Burrowbridge (ST 357304). Its gentle arch of blue lias limestone has granite voussoirs and parapet, with two circular openings in the spandrels designed to relieve floodwater. A granite plaque set in the south parapet explains that John Stone of Yarcombe was the builder in 1826.

Bridgwater's Town Bridge was once the lowest crossing point of the River Parrett. A medieval bridge was replaced in 1797 by a single iron arch with five ribs cast at Coalbrookdale in Shropshire, just eighteen years after the building of the famous Iron Bridge. It lasted until 1883 when the present Town Bridge was erected as a wrought-iron span of 75ft (23m) with seven latticed ribs.

Bridgwater has other associations with iron bridges of the industrial period. These include Hurstbow Bridge (ST 458189) at Martock where the Martock & South Petherton Trust shared half the cost of widening the existing county bridge over Hinton Meads Brook in 1848. This resulted in a pleasing bridge with Ham stone abutments and eight cast-iron ribs supporting the roadway. The inner ribs were replaced in 1975 by a reinforced concrete deck but the outer ribs remain with 'MURCH 1848' cast in the centre. Edward Murch was a Bridgwater ironfounder and his name and the same date

The bridge over the River Parrett at Burrowbridge, c.1900. The riverbank wall is now obscured by mud. Note also the chimney of the Allermoor pumping station in the background.   I. & M. MILES COLLECTION

Bridgwater's Town Bridge of 1883 replaced an iron bridge made almost a century earlier by the Coalbrookdale Co. Looking downstream, with West Quay on the left.

appear on the iron Tone Bridge at Creech St Michael, widened in 1848 (ST 274253). Marsh Bridge (SS 907290) on the Barle near Dulverton had four stone arches before the middle two were replaced in 1866 by cast-iron lattice girders made by Hennet, Spink & Else of Bridgwater. These were replaced in steel in the early-twentieth century but the earlier cast-iron pilasters and parapets remain.

Twenty-four early reinforced concrete bridges were built in historic Somerset in 1909–14, perhaps more than for any other county. Although their inscriptions credit Herbert Chapman, the County Surveyor, they were designed by his assistant Edward Stead. Twenty bridges survive in the modern Somerset, none of them large. Examples include a three-arched bridge at Hartlake (1910, ST5133412) and single arches at Hornshay (1912, ST 142224) and Marston Magna (1914, ST 591224). Stead returned after the war as County Surveyor when 40 more reinforced concrete bridges were built in the 1920s and '30s to relieve unemployment.

Toll-houses are the most obvious legacy of turnpike days. Typically, a toll-house had one or two storeys with a bay

protruding onto the roadside, opposite which stood the gate where the toll was paid to the keeper. A small side gate allowed pedestrians to pass through free. Other toll-houses were adapted from existing cottages. An unassuming house at Chilly Bridge on the Minehead Trust's route down the Exe valley has a side window for watching out for traffic. While the roadside position was ideal for collecting tolls at the gate, modern traffic conditions have made such locations undesirable as dwellings; many have been abandoned and demolished, while others have been lost to road improvements.

Toll-houses and gates were rebuilt or new ones erected on more convenient sites for the collection of tolls. The trusts auctioned tolls annually, the highest bidder to collect an agreed sum. Some were clearly very profitable, such as the Shepton Mallet Trust's 'Downside Gate with the Side Gate and Weighbridge, and Mendip-Road Gate' on the road to Bristol and Bath, worth £802 in 1819. In contrast, the Pilton and Charlton Gates on roads to the west and east of the town were worth a mere £71 and £91.5s each. Such figures, published annually by the trusts, give an indication of traffic volumes on different routes.

Toll-houses

Clockwise from top left:

Kilmersdon toll-house, January 2001.

Toll-house at Burrowfield, Bruton, June 1992.

The toll-house in the High Street at Wincanton, altered but still recognisable. August 2001.

The attractive Snowdon Hill toll-house is on the A30 just west of Chard.

Shawford Lodge toll-house on the A36 near Woolverton.

Ansford toll-house near Castle Cary.

Muchelney toll-house is an almost perfect match with another at Kingsbury Episcopi.

The houses were required to display a prominent toll board, but the only one left in position is at South Cheriton (ST 692248). This Horsington Gate toll board of the Vale of Blackmoor Trust (Dorset) gives a good impression of the charges for use of its roads. Dated 1824, the board declares a toll of 4½d

> *For every Horse or other Beast drawing any Coach, Stage Coach, Berlin, Landau, Landaulet, Barouch, Chariot, Chaise, Chaise Marine, Calash, Curricle, Phaeton, Sociable, Gig, Chair, Car, Caravan, Van, Hearse or Litter, or other such like Carriage.*

Indeed, a detailed challenge to confound anyone attempting to evade the toll! Cheaper tolls were charged for commercial or farm vehicles, with a discount for wider and less-destructive wheels, while droves of cattle were charged 10d per score and sheep and lambs 5d per score. Asses were a penny each.

Very few houses are of the same design, although those at Kingsbury Episcopi (ST 435213) and Muchelney (ST 429251) of the Langport, Somerton & Castle Cary Trust are a matching pair. The attractive toll-house at Snowdon Hill (ST 312088) outside Chard has an overhanging thatched roof supported by pillars. It was built in 1838 by the Chard Trust to serve two gates at the junction of the old and new routes. A similar toll-house, with a slate roof, stood at Tytherleigh (in Devon!) until the 1950s. Galhampton's toll-house (ST 637303) was also strategically placed to control a meeting of roads to Castle Cary and Bruton (now the B3152 and A359). The Langport, Somerton & Castle Cary Trust may have built it in the mid-nineteenth century to replace two other gates at Shepherds Cross and Hadspen. At Wells, the Stoberry toll-house (ST 551465) of 1754 has been altered since the end of the turnpike. It was here in 1773–802 that the Wells Trust had its only weighing machine which could weigh 'Nine Tunns'. Also in Wells, the Keward toll-house (ST 542449) replaced an earlier one in 1842 but it lost its bow front on the orders of the Highway Board in 1883.

Some toll-houses were built outside Somerset where their trusts' routes strayed into neighbouring counties. Two examples are an octagonal toll-house of the Minehead Trust at Exebridge in Devon (SS 933243), and a handsome toll-house of the Yeovil Trust on the A30, literally a stone's throw inside Dorset (ST 574160). The toll-houses and gates were sold off when the trusts were abandoned, although one was maintained in use at the vital crossing at Burrowbridge until 1944. Toll-gates have

South Cheriton toll-house has its toll board fixed in place.

A toll-gate of the Wells Trust is preserved at the end of Brutasche Terrace in Street. A toll-house stands nearby in Glaston Road.

rarely survived, but the Street Gate of the Wells Trust is preserved at the end of Brutasche Terrace (ST 485371).

The turnpikes were obliged to erect milestones or mileposts along their routes. Milestones of different shapes were carved with Roman or arabic numerals giving

Milestones and Mileposts

Milestone at Bayford, near Wincanton. August 2001.

Milestone at Roborough Gate, Brendon Hills.

Milestone at Nunney Catch. August 2001.

Milepost on the Bath road at Frome (Black Dog Trust).

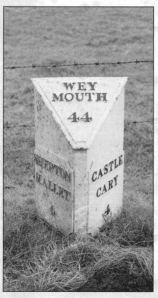

Milepost at Galhampton (A359), cast by John Wightman of Chard. January 1992.

Milepost at Pecking Mill (A371). January 1992.

Milepost at North Down, Blackdown Hills, giving the distance to Taunton to the nearest eighth of a mile.

Milepost west of Kilmersdon. January 2001.

Somerset finger post at Wheddon Cross with 'SCC' finial and direction boards cast with older-style lettering.

Above left: *Cast-iron plate displaying road distances in the Market Place at Shepton Mallet.* Above right: *Signs of the past: AA box and Somerset County Council finger post on the A39 near Holford, both now gone. May 1976.*

the distance to the nearest named towns. A variation was to attach a cast-iron plate with details in raised or incised letters. The plate might be square, but a rounded top was a variation used in the case of the Minehead Trust. In 1786 the Wells Trust demanded that all milestones 'be forthwith repaired and faced with iron plates upon the Plan of the First Mile Stone leading from Wells towards Shepton Mallet,' a stone that survives today without its plate (ST 561453). Other milestones were reused in this way and there is an example at Hadspen House near Castle Cary (ST 658309). Not all milestones were well maintained, for William Marshall observed in September 1794 that those between Somerton and Shepton Mallet were 'shamefully defaced; but how easy to remedy the defect, with paint.'

Cast-iron mileposts in a variety of forms were a handsome alternative in the nineteenth century and often replaced older stones. Mileposts with a triangular shape

but hollow at the back were cast by Wightman of Chard for the Langport, Somerton & Castle Cary Trust and can be seen on the A359 at Galhampton, for example (ST 632294). The two angled faces present the information to the approaching traveller. These triangular types were also used by the Wells Trust, which in 1847 ordered John Kelway to supply 14 iron mileposts at 30 shillings (£1.50) each between White Post on the Bath Road and Glastonbury. Triangular mileposts on the B3170 south of Taunton give precise distances with eighths of a mile. Rectangular cast-iron mileposts with pediments stand at the approaches to Frome and Wells.

Most direction or finger posts in Somerset date from the twentieth century, and early examples with older-style lettering are becoming rarer. Occasionally a finger post is cast with the maker's name. Some warning signs were placed by the Somerset Automobile Club and similar organisations in the early-twentieth century.

Other examples of miscellaneous 'street furniture' include drain covers, manhole covers, lamp standards (gas or electric lighting) and horse troughs. Pillar and wall letter boxes date from the mid-nineteenth century onwards and telephone kiosks became familiar street items in the twentieth century. Since the 1980s many of these have been replaced by modern designs.

Coaching inns are part of the archaeology of roads, particularly of the turnpike days, and there are good examples in most towns. Although now closed, the Red Lion in Somerton's Market Place would seem wholly appropriate, being where the trustees of the turnpike met.

Welcome to Watchet, May 1976.

16

CANALS AND RIVER NAVIGATIONS

Water transport handled much greater loads than the roads and big names in the world of canal engineering were involved in Somerset. The historic county had three river navigations and seven canals, most of which were surprisingly late and did not last long in the face of competition from the railways. The 1830s and '40s were therefore not good times to be building a successful canal.

Some rivers were navigable in historic times, such as the Parrett, Tone, Brue and Axe. The Romans had a wharf at Ilchester on the River Yeo, a tributary of the Parrett. The Brue and the Axe were navigable to Glastonbury and beyond in the medieval period, thanks to artificial cuts, and many rhynes across the moors took agricultural traffic.

Acts of 1699 and 1707 provided for 'making and keeping the River Tone navigable from Bridgwater to Taunton.' The Tone Navigation was administered by Conservators who collected tolls on tonnages carried, for the water-way's maintenance and the benefit of the poor of Taunton. In 1724 Daniel Defoe described the Tone as a

very fine new channel, cut at the expence of the people of Taunton, and which, by the navigation of it, is infinitely advantagious to that town, and well worth their expence, first by bringing up coals, which are brought from Swanzy in Wales by sea to Bridgewater, and thence by barges up this river to Taunton; also for bringing all heavy goods and merchandizes from Bristol, such as iron, lead, oyl, wine, hemp, flax, pitch, tar, grocery and dye stuffs, and the like.

Barges first followed the Parrett from Bridgwater to Burrowbridge, then turned west into the Tone. By the late-eighteenth century 14,000 tons of traffic were carried, mostly coal which was then distributed from Taunton by road into south Somerset and east Devon. In 1823 the Navigation carried 28,500 tons of coal to Taunton with a further 7385 tons to Ham Mills, which was a distribution point for road traffic to Ilminster. The Tone Navigation was bought in 1832 by the Bridgwater & Taunton Canal Co. (with whom relationships had never been smooth), who maintained it until the 1870s, with traffic coming up to Ham until 1929. Ham (ST 289253) was the site of the first lock of the main navigation

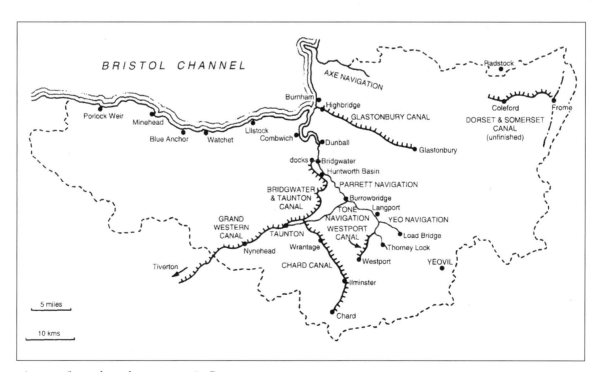

A map of canals and waterways in Somerset.

onwards to Taunton. There were three other locks at Obridge, Bathpool and Creech St Michael, as well as four half locks. In Taunton itself the North Town wharf, or Dellers Wharf, retains just a feel of its former use (ST 227249).

Being tidal far inland, the Parrett was always a commercial waterway and the 'bore' was made use of by boats travelling upstream. As well as navigating the Tone, barges on the Parrett could work their way southwards to Langport where warehouses were built on quays above and below Great Bow Bridge (ST 416266). Rev. Francis Kilvert noted in his diary on 19 July 1870 sailing boats on the Parrett:

> *Sometimes these white sails may be seen gliding along above the flat green meadows and, the river being invisible, they look as if the boats were sailing on land.*

The Parrett Navigation Act was passed in 1836 to improve the waterway. Langport's medieval Great Bow Bridge, with nine small arches, was a major obstacle to traffic coming up from Bridgwater and cargoes had to be manhandled across to smaller boats waiting on the other side. A new three-arched bridge designed by Brunel's assistant William Gravatt was built in 1840–41 to allow barges to pass upstream to Thorney, where there was a half-lock (ST 429226). The Navigation also had four full locks, at Stanmoor (above Burrowbridge), Oath, Langport (just below the bridge) and Muchelney. The principal barge carriers Stuckey & Bagehot took 27,605 tons to Langport in 1843, but much of the river traffic was lost after the railway branch from Durston to Yeovil was opened ten years later through Langport and Thorney. Decline and lack of maintenance caused flooding and the Navigation was closed in 1878 by the Somersetshire Drainage Commissioners. Locks were subsequently removed as part of the drainage management schemes, although the Thorney half-lock survives.

The tributary River Yeo was also navigable above Langport. An Act was passed in 1795 for an Ivelchester & Langport Canal, 'for improving and supporting the Navigation of the River Ivel, otherwise Yeo, from the town of Ivelchester to Bicknell Bridge,' with a navigable cut to the Parrett below Great Bow Bridge. The main traffic was to be coal upstream and agricultural produce downstream. Little work was done but the river was navigable in the nineteenth century for 5-ton barges to a wharf at Load Bridge (ST 467238). A large amount of

Warehouse and Great Bow Bridge at Langport, once a thriving place of trade on the River Parrett Navigation.

Load Bridge, with its enlarged arch to allow the passage of boats further up the River Yeo. Larger trading boats stopped at a quay here. March 1994.

Welsh culm destined for the limekilns to the north was no doubt included in the 9302 tons of goods landed here in 1843. Load Bridge has been much altered and its higher central arch allowed occasional smaller barges to pass through and go higher upstream to Pill Bridge.

The first canals were built to open up wider markets for the Somerset coalfield. The Somerset Coal Canal of 1805 was the only success, with branches from Radstock and Paulton connecting with the Kennet & Avon Canal. However, this interesting canal now lies outside modern Somerset. The Dorset & Somerset Canal was intended to be a link between Bristol and the English Channel, and an Act was passed in 1796. Robert Whitworth, consulting engineer to the Thames & Severn Canal, surveyed the route which was to leave the Kennet & Avon Canal (then under construction) near Bradford on Avon, pass through Frome and Wincanton and into Dorset where there were two alternative routes to Poole or Wareham. Coal was envisaged as the main traffic and for this an 11-mile branch from Frome to Nettlebridge in the coalfield proved to be all that was built before the money ran out in 1803. And no wonder; there were costly aqueducts at Coleford and Murtry, a tunnel at Coleford and a flight of revolutionary locks at Barrow Hill.

Only sections were finished, so the branch was not continuous even to Frome and was barely used. Yet much of interest survives, starting from the basin at Edford (ST 669488) where the canal is crossed by a packhorse bridge carrying a track descending from the collieries. At Coleford, a 'noble and stupendous' aqueduct crosses a side valley (ST 685488) and one would be forgiven for mistaking this tall structure for a railway viaduct. The towpath and a clear section of the canal contours around the hillside to the east of Coleford and the line can be

The tall arches of the Coleford aqueduct on the Dorset & Somerset Canal. January 1992.

detected again near Vobster Cross (ST 710494). At Barrow Hill, James Fussell of Mells tried out his patent balance lock or boat lift in 1800 and 1802. Its twin chambers contained two counterbalanced caissons that lifted and lowered two 10-ton boats 20ft (6.1m) successfully. The lock site and four unfinished lock pits descend the side of the hill (ST 750501). The three-arched Murtry Aqueduct (ST 762498) of 1798 crosses the Mells River, and the dry bed of the canal can be traced alongside the river. The canal never quite reached Frome and the last significant feature is a high retaining wall at Whatcombe, locally called the 'Roman Wall' (ST 771493).

The Dorset & Somerset Canal was not the only proposal to join the north and south coasts. At the same time the Grand Western Canal was planned to link the Bristol Channel, via Taunton, with the Exe estuary. Yet another north–south route was the English & Bristol Channels Ship Canal scheme of 1825, which sought to avoid the hazards of rounding Land's End. It was to have run for 44 miles from Stolford on the Bristol Channel coast north of Combwich, past Bridgwater to a summit near Chard and thence down the Axe valley to the English Channel at Seaton. The canal was planned to take 200-ton ships, and there were to be 58 locks with water supplied from four reservoirs.

The Bridgwater & Taunton Canal was the most conventional of the Somerset canals. The scheme began with an ambitious Bristol & Taunton Canal in 1811 but the designer James Hillinsworth shortened the route to the Bridgwater–Taunton section only, for which an Act was passed in 1824. When it opened in 1827 the Bridgwater & Taunton Canal started from a lock and basin at Huntworth on the River Parrett a mile upstream from Bridgwater. The meandering route included four locks before ending at Firepool in Taunton. A lock connected the canal with the Tone Navigation but there were continuous squabbles between the two rivals until 1832 when the canal company bought out the Tone Conservators. They were, however, required to maintain a navigation on the Tone. The canal came too late to be a lasting success. It was extended from Huntworth to the new floating dock at Bridgwater in 1841, just one year before the Bristol & Exeter Railway was opened through to Taunton. Inevitably, the railway bought out the canal in 1867 and it was closed to commercial traffic in 1907.

Having lain derelict for so many years, the canal was fully restored in 1994 and there is much of interest for the industrial archaeologist. The canal leaves the floating dock at Newtown Lock and curves around the back of

The Dorset & Somerset Canal's Murtry aqueduct crosses the Mells River. January 2002.

The 1841 extension of the Bridgwater & Taunton Canal passes through this stone-walled cutting under West Street at Bridgwater.

The Crossways swing bridge at Huntworth, Bridgwater & Taunton Canal.

Bridgwater through a stone-walled cutting and a tunnel beneath West Street. The original Huntworth Basin has gone, but the nearby Crossways swing bridge (ST 309353) has replaced one that retained its original mechanism. Twelve of these swing bridges were fixed when the derelict canal became a defensive line in the Second World War. More permanent brick-arched bridges cross the canal and towpath at many places. There are four locks in a 2-mile length at North Newton between Standards Lock and Higher Maunsel Lock. The paddle mechanisms are unusual, each having a round iron counterweight on a

Lower Maunsel lock and bridge, Bridgwater & Taunton Canal.

Paddle posts at Lower Maunsel lock.

The Firepool lock joins the Bridgwater & Taunton Canal with the River Tone at Taunton.

A beam engine at the Charlton pumping station supplied water to the Bridgwater & Taunton Canal. The long disused building was under conversion in 2003.

chain. There is still a lock-keeper's cottage at Lower Maunsel Lock (ST 308298). At Firepool in Taunton, the lock joining the canal with the Tone (ST 231253) has double bottom gates to prevent water loss from the canal when the river is lower during drought. A coal wharf and limekilns were built here at the time of the opening of the Chard Canal in 1842.

Water was also supplied to the upper pond by the Charlton pumping station (ST 287261) where a James Watt beam engine of 1826 pumped water from the Tone. New boilers were put in by the Great Western Railway in the 1870s and in 1900 two compound steam engines and Tangye centrifugal pumps were installed, working until the 1920s. The beam engine was scrapped in 1942. The GWR used part of the pumping station to supply water to the pick-up troughs situated between the railway tracks nearby. The pumping station stood dilapidated for many years and, although it has lost its tall brick chimney, this landmark beside the canal was converted to accommodation in 2003.

James Brindley had surveyed a route between the Bristol and English Channels in the 1760s, but it was not until 1796 that an Act was passed for making a canal from the River Tone at Taunton to Topsham on the Exe. James Rennie was appointed engineer in 1810 and a first 11-mile section of canal without locks was opened between Tiverton and Holcombe Rogus in 1814. Hopes of reaching the Exe were abandoned but plans for the missing 13 miles down the Tone valley to Taunton were revived after the Bridgwater & Taunton Canal was opened in 1827. James Green, a former assistant to Rennie, was employed as engineer and he designed a narrow tub-boat canal with seven balance lifts and an inclined plane to overcome the 262ft (80m) difference in level and poor water supply of this difficult section. The canal joined with the Bridgwater & Taunton Canal at Taunton and there was a new 'Parliamentary Cut' to the River Tone at French Weir, so tub-boats could work all the way through from Bridgwater to Tiverton. The canal was built in 1831–38 but its livelihood was threatened almost immediately by the opening of the Bristol & Exeter Railway to Exeter in 1844, made worse by a branch to Tiverton four years later. The railway bought the canal in 1865 and closed the Somerset section in 1867. The Devon length carried stone traffic to Tiverton until the 1920s and has been restored by the county council since 1971.

Much of the canal's course can be explored and a few places are still in water. The Higher Wellisford incline

(ST 102216) carried the tub-boats on wheeled cradles but problems with the water-wheel here led to its replacement by a 12hp steam engine. The semi-detached cottages for the keeper and assistant are now a single house near the course of the 440ft (134m) long incline. James Green's seven lifts (Taunton, Norton, Allerford, Trefusis, Nynehead, Winsbeer and Greenham) were a means of changing between levels rapidly, while saving over 90 per cent of the water compared with locks, although in practice they proved troublesome to work. These balance lifts had two caissons connected by chains over large iron wheels. Tub-boats were floated into the caissons at the top and bottom levels and the extra weight of the top caisson (when water was added) was enough to make it descend whilst raising the other. Greenham had the highest lift of 42ft (12.8m), but the site is now buried (ST 078198).

Excavations by the Grand Western Canal Trust have taken place to conserve the substantial arched masonry chamber of the Nynehead Lift (ST 144218). The change of level here was a mere 24ft (7.3m) but the structure is impressive. A short length of re-watered canal leads away

A re-watered section of the Grand Western Canal and Wharf Cottage at Nynehead.

The Grand Western Canal's aqueduct over the old drive to Nynehead Court.

James Green's tub-boat lift at Nynehead on the Grand Western Canal has been recently excavated.

Grand Western Canal aqueduct over the River Tone near Nynehead. An iron trough is set within the low stone arch.

The Chard Canal aqueduct over the River Tone at Creech St Michael, once handsome but now much deteriorated.

Chard Canal aqueduct abutment at Wrantage. August 1991.

The north portal of Crimson Hill Tunnel, Chard Canal. August 1991.

to the site of Nynehead Wharf and the wharf cottage. The Nynehead site also has an aqueduct over the former drive to Nynehead Court. It is built of sandstone ashlar, presumably to enhance the private drive, and carries a cast-iron trough for the canal. Not far away, an aqueduct across the River Tone has a second cast-iron trough enclosed by low stone arches (ST 147224). A road bridge over the canal course at Trefusis Farm (ST 166232) has cast-iron ribs and is now the sole survivor of this type

since the Silk Mills Bridge near Bishop's Hull was demolished during road improvements in 1977.

If Somerset's canals were late, then the Chard Canal was the last and doomed from the day it opened in 1842 in the year the Bristol & Exeter Railway came to Taunton. Its fate was sealed when a branch line opened to Chard in 1866, and it was bought and closed by the railway company within two years. This short-lived canal was designed for tub-boats by James Green, who was appointed engineer in 1831. For its 13½ miles the Chard Canal was an interesting one, with a major aqueduct, four inclined planes, three tunnels, a large reservoir and just one lock. There was a stop-lock where the canal left the Bridgwater & Taunton Canal at Creech St Michael, soon crossing the Tone by a fine three-arched aqueduct of brick and lias stone (ST271253). The aqueduct has lost its parapet but the canal course crosses the fields on an impressive embankment pierced with flood arches. At Wrantage (ST 308225) can be seen the stone abutment of a demolished aqueduct over the A378, with the embanked canal course on either side. To the south is the north portal of the 1800ft (549 m) Crimson Hill Tunnel (ST 312221), through which the tub-boats were hauled using brackets in the roof.

A stone bridge over the Westport Canal. Note the space for the towpath on the right. March 1994.

A warehouse at the canal terminus in Westport.

The other tunnels were at Lillesdon near Wrantage and Herne Hill, Ilminster. Three inclines had wheeled caissons into which the tub-boats were floated, at Thornfalcon (ST 285242), near the tunnel at Wrantage (ST 310222), and at Ilminster (ST 357141). The fourth incline, which descended south at Chard Common (ST 337098), used wheeled cradles to carry the tub-boats and was worked by a water turbine fed from the Chard Canal Reservoir (ST 337103), which in turn was fed by a 2-mile leat from the River Isle. The canal ended at a basin in Chard (ST 329092), where a yard and canalside warehouses were enclosed by a wall. All were demolished in 1999 and redeveloped.

Two canals of the Somerset Levels were distinct from river navigations. The Glastonbury Canal was opened in 1833 from a sea lock at Highbridge Wharf to Glastonbury after advice from John Rennie. It was large enough to take Severn trows carrying coal and other goods, but it was never a great success and physical difficulties were encountered where it crossed the peat moors and there were conflicts with the need to control

flooding in the area. The Bristol & Exeter Railway bought the canal in 1848 and sold it to the Somerset Central Railway who used it for carrying construction material for their line alongside. The canal was closed in 1854 when the railway opened, although a short length at Highbridge continued in use until 1936. There are the remains of a lock chamber at Highbridge (ST 318472) and traces of another at Shapwick Heath (ST 412418). The stone abutments are all that remain of an aqueduct over the South Drain at Ashcott (ST 451396).

The 2-mile Westport Canal took traffic deep inland when it was opened in 1840 from the River Isle, a tributary of the Parrett. It was controlled by a half-lock at Middlemoor Bridge (ST 405224) and there was another lock where the Isle and Parrett met (ST 416234). Large warehouses were built at the terminus basin (ST 384198) and the canal carried 10,402 tons in 1843. However, the canal had to close in 1878 along with the Parrett Navigation. The Westport Canal, Parrett Navigation and Chard Canal were all in direct competition for traffic from the Ilminster area.

17

RAILWAYS AND TRAMWAYS

Steam lives on in Somerset in the form of the preserved West Somerset Railway, which is the longest such line in England, while there is also activity on the East Somerset Railway. The story of steam locomotion in historic Somerset goes back to 1826–27 when an experimental locomotive was designed and built by William Ashman of Clandown to run on the Somerset Coal Canal's tramway between Radstock and Midford, but it seems to have been too heavy for the rails. Mineral and industrial lines are discussed below. The early developments of Somerset's public railways witnessed rivalries between broad and narrow gauges but, once resolved in favour of the latter, the network settled down until it was decimated by the closures of the 1960s. The remaining routes, interestingly, include the first to be built.

Somerset's main railway network began with Brunel's drive to the west. Work on the broad gauge Bristol & Exeter Railway was soon under way following the opening of the Great Western Railway from Paddington to Bristol. The railway was inaugurated by an Act in 1836 and opened to Bridgwater in June 1841, in a momentous year for the port town which also saw the opening of a new floating dock. The B&ER reached Taunton a year later. The new line stopped at a temporary station at Beambridge to the west of Wellington while the Whiteball Tunnel was being driven into Devon. The railway was fully opened to Exeter on 1 May 1844. Its effect on the Grand Western Canal was inevitable and dramatic. The major engineering feats were the tunnel and earthworks in the hillier country to the west of Taunton, while most of the route crossed the Levels apart from a cutting at Puriton. The B&ER was closely associated with Bridgwater, where it established a coach and wagon works. An exisiting tramway to a quay on the Parrett was acquired in 1863 and a bridge over the river took it into the newly acquired docks in 1871.

Although smoother and faster running was obtained by the broad gauge (7ft $0\frac{1}{4}$ in) there was competition from railways using the narrow gauge (4ft $8\frac{1}{2}$ in), which is now called standard gauge. The B&ER submitted to laying a third rail to take mixed gauge trains, but this compromise was never convenient and lines were gradually changed to

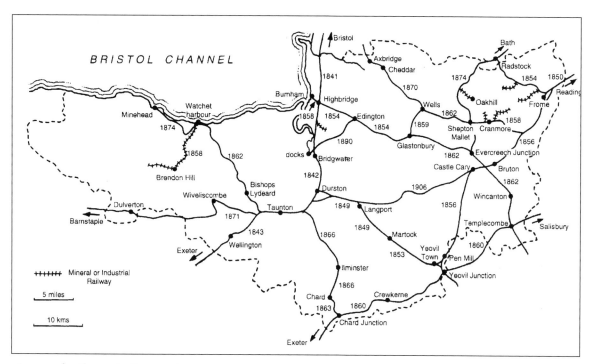

A map of railways in Somerset.

N. GRIFFITHS

standard gauge. The Great Western Railway leased the B&ER in 1876 and what remained of the broad gauge system was converted over a weekend in an impressive feat of planning in 1892.

The first of the B&ER's broad gauge branches was completed from a junction at Durston to Langport and Martock in 1849 but it was not until 1853 that it was opened to Hendford, Yeovil. Railways in Yeovil became complicated, with physical connections made from the Town Station (1861) to stations on other lines at Pen Mill (1856) and Yeovil Junction (1860). The Yeovil branch ran as a mixed gauge until 1879. It was closed to passengers in 1964, although part is incorporated in the GWR's Reading to Taunton main-line route via Castle Cary. Yeovil's Town Station closed in 1966.

A second broad gauge branch left the B&ER at Norton Fitzwarren. The West Somerset Railway, authorised in 1857, was opened in 1862 to Williton and Watchet, where there was a turntable and engine shed until the line was extended to Minehead in 1874. Conversion to standard gauge came in 1882. There was increasing holiday traffic to Minehead in the twentieth century, but the line was closed in 1971. However, the WSR was reopened in 1979

and continues to operate steam trains on this attractive route. The Chard branch from Taunton via Ilminster was opened in 1866 and finished off the young canal. The gauge was not converted until 1891. It was linked at Chard to a branch from the south but the line closed in 1962.

Taunton was already at the hub of five railway routes when a sixth was added in 1871. This was the 43-mile Devon & Somerset Railway from Norton Fitzwarren to Barnstaple. Authorised by an Act of 1864, the first section was not opened to Wiveliscombe until 1871 and it was another two years before it reached Barnstaple along a difficult route involving tunnels and viaducts. This late broad gauge railway (converted to standard gauge in 1881) filled in a route through a sparsely populated area with limited local traffic, but the 1930s did see through-expresses to Ilfracombe for the holiday trade. The D&SR was absorbed into the GWR in 1901. It closed in 1966.

Another early GWR-sponsored broad gauge line entered Somerset and, like the B&ER, this line remains open today. The Wiltshire, Somerset & Weymouth Railway was opened to Frome from Trowbridge and Westbury in 1850. It reached Castle Cary and Pen Mill at Yeovil in

A broad gauge locomotive of the Bristol & Exeter Railway at Williton station in the early days of the West Somerset Railway.

1856, so within three years Yeovil had acquired two stations bringing broad gauge lines from two different directions. From Pen Mill the line continued into Dorset, opening through to Dorchester and Weymouth in 1857. The coal-mining town of Radstock received its first railway branch from Frome in 1854. A second branch, the East Somerset Railway, was opened from Witham to Shepton Mallet in 1858 and reached Wells in 1862. The WSWR was converted to standard gauge in 1874 and the line was doubled a few years later. Although closed to passengers, the Radstock branch continued to carry coal from the remaining Writhlington colliery until 1973. The track is still in place. The first part of the Shepton branch from Witham is now a branch to Merehead roadstone quarry, while a preserved length beyond is operated by the steam East Somerset Railway.

While the GWR came to dominate the routes through Somerset, the rival narrow (standard) gauge London & South Western Railway from Waterloo to Exeter entered the county in 1860 as the Salisbury & Yeovil Railway. It opened through Templecombe and Milborne Port to Yeovil Junction and then climbed to Crewkerne before descending the Axe valley into Devon. Opened as a single track, the LSWR was doubled within ten years. There was an important junction with the Somerset & Dorset Railway at Templecombe and branches linked Yeovil Junction with Yeovil Town and Pen Mill stations. In 1863 a branch (promoted by the Chard Canal Co.) was made from Chard Road Station (Chard Junction from 1872) to Chard Town Station, from which a tramway continued to the canal basin. Chard Joint Station was opened when the broad gauge arrived from Taunton three years later. The GWR ran the whole route from 1917 and closed the Town Station. The second station, renamed Chard Central in 1949, closed in 1962 but the attractive brick and Ham stone building survives (ST 329092). The section of the branch from Chard Junction remained for freight traffic until 1966.

The Somerset & Dorset Joint Railway endeared itself to railway enthusiasts and the public alike. The Somerset Central Railway between Highbridge Wharf and Glastonbury was promoted by Glastonbury businessmen, including James Clark, and was opened as a broad gauge line in 1854 along the Glastonbury Canal's course. The B&ER worked the line, although the SCR kept the harbour. The railway was extended to Burnham in 1858 to develop a cross-channel service to Wales. There was a branch to Wells in 1859 and the line was extended to Bruton in 1862 where plans to join the WSWR were

never fulfilled despite construction of the earthworks. This was mixed gauge until 1870. Meanwhile, the Dorset Central Railway had been developed northwards from the LSWR at Wimborne and the two companies amalgamated as the Somerset & Dorset Joint Railway in 1862. A physical connection was made at Cole near Bruton, but the full course south of Templecombe was not completed until 1863, thus creating a coast to coast route from Burnham to Poole. After financial difficulties, the 26-mile link between Bath and Evercreech Junction was opened in 1874 through Radstock and Shepton Mallet and this dramatic route over the Mendips had steep gradients to the Maesbury Summit, seven viaducts and five tunnels. Through-trains now ran from Manchester to Poole and Bournemouth, of which the 'Pines Express' was the best known on this nostalgic route. High winds on the Mendips were said to delay train times dramatically! The S&DJR closed in 1966, steam-worked to the very end.

When the B&ER opened the Cheddar Valley & Yatton Railway into Wells in 1870 it gave the town a third station. It was broad gauge until 1875 and carried dairy produce and strawberries as well as passengers from Wells, Cheddar and Axbridge. It closed in 1964.

Somerset's last major railway construction was the GWR's 15½-mile link from Castle Cary to Langport to complete the direct Reading to Taunton route. It was built in 1903–06 and involved deep cuttings and embankments, a tunnel and three viaducts. At both ends it incorporated parts of the old WSWR route and the Yeovil branch. The junction of the latter with the old B&ER was altered at Cogload in 1932 when a lattice steel flyover was built to carry the down Bristol line over the Castle Cary lines. At the same time the route was quadrupled to Norton Fitzwarren and Taunton station was rebuilt.

Railway works made a tremendous impact on the landscape and even after closure there are positive traces along many routes. Whether still running or abandoned, the archaeology of railways includes engineering works such as cuttings, embankments, bridges, tunnels and stations. A typical rural railway station had a platform with a building incorporating a booking hall and waiting rooms, a stationmaster's house, signal box and water tower. Any second platform had lesser accommodation and was approached by a footbridge. A yard with sidings might have a goods shed and cattle pens and perhaps even an engine shed and turntable.

Frome station still retains its timber all-over cover or train shed from the days of Brunel.

The level crossing gates at Blue Anchor are worked from inside the 1904 signal box. West Somerset Railway.

Firepool pumping station, beside the canal at Taunton. Water was supplied to the railway on the embankment behind during the days of steam. The faded writing on the iron tank reads: 'BRITISH RAILWAYS TAUNTON FREIGHT CONCENTRATION DEPOT'.

On the main B&ER line, Bridgwater station (ST 308370) dates from Brunel's time, and some early buildings survive at the larger and much-altered Taunton station (ST 227253). Brunel designed the up and down stations on the same side at the latter, causing considerable delays as traffic increased until a single station was built in 1868. There are large goods yards and depots here and the nearby Firepool pumping station (ST 232255) supplied water to the railway. The tall brick house was built upon a pair of stone limekilns beside the canal's coal wharf and a large iron roof tank was added in 1877. The original pumps and engine were replaced in 1889 by steam-powered Pearn three-throw pumps which worked until the 1960s.

Frome station (ST 785476) retains its original 1850 covered roof with timber trusses and wrought-iron ties designed by Brunel's architect J.R. Hannaford. This train shed is a rare survivor of a common feature of broad gauge days. Down the same WSWR line, are neat station buildings in stone at Castle Cary (ST 635335) and Pen Mill (ST 570163). Hardly altered stations (in use!) on the West Somerset Railway include Bishops Lydeard (ST 165290), Williton (ST 085416), Watchet (ST 071432), Washford (ST 044412) and Minehead (SS 975463). Blue Anchor (SS 995447) has a 1904 signal box and original GWR level crossing gates. The much smaller East Somerset Railway has its headquarters at Cranmore station (ST 667429).

Crewkerne station (ST 433085) is a good example of several station buildings designed by Sir William Tite along the LSWR line. Templecombe station (ST 711227), which was closed between 1966 and 1983, has a stylish art deco signal box of 1938, now in part a ticket office.

Sites on the S&DJR include the station and stationmaster's house at Maesbury summit (ST 603472), West

Yeovil's Pen Mill station was opened in 1856 on the Wiltshire, Somerset & Weymouth Railway and has an unusual island platform.

A steam train from Minehead arrives at Bishops Lydeard station on the preserved West Somerset Railway. The original station building of 1862 is on the left and the near platform was added in 1906.

The tall building of Crewkerne station (1859) is typical of others designed by Sir William Tite for the London & South Western Railway. August 2002.

The art deco signal box of 1938 at Templecombe station.

Pennard station and goods shed (ST 567396), Ashcott station (ST 449397) and a crossing keeper's cottage (ST 472392). Cossington station (ST 358408) is the only survivor on the Edington to Bridgwater branch (1890–1952). There are also surviving buildings at Evercreech Junction station (ST 639365), where the Highbridge and Bath lines met. Stations or goods sheds of the Cheddar Valley line remain at Axbridge (ST 433546), Cheddar (ST 454532) and Wells (ST 543456), while tucked away at Dulverton, the former Carnarvon Arms Hotel had incorporated the station and engine shed (SS 927256) once at the terminus of the Exe Valley Railway (1885–1963).

Railway construction included countless bridges. Viaducts are the most spectacular legacy, such as the S&DJR's curving Charlton Viaduct (ST 628436) with 27 arches at Shepton Mallet. It was built of stone in 1874 and brickwork shows where it was later widened, a feature seen on a second viaduct (ST 622443). A third viaduct to the south at Prestleigh has been demolished. A grassy embankment approaches the Chard Railway's disused viaduct across the Tone at Creech St Michael (ST 269253), and both run close to the Chard Canal's aqueduct and embankment. Somerset's last viaducts, of dark engineering brick, were on the GWR's Castle Cary to Langport link of 1906. The Somerton viaduct (ST 492292) and a much longer one at Langport were opened at the same time as a 105ft (32m) iron girder span (ST 415273) over the Parrett, where the foundations are 50ft (15m) deep.

The Somerset & Dorset Joint Railway's Charlton Viaduct at Shepton Mallet has 27 arches in a long curve. It was opened for a single track in 1874 and was widened later.

The Great Western Railway's iron bridge over the River Parrett at Langport. A long brick viaduct nearby is also part of this 1906 route.

The B&ER's Somerset Bridge (ST 311357) over the River Parrett to the south of Bridgwater is of historical engineering interest. Although replaced by a girder bridge in 1904, it contains the abutments of Brunel's original low-arched bridge which caused him great problems when the foundations shifted and it had to be replaced by a timber bridge. A most unusual bridge across the Parrett at Bridgwater is the Black Bridge (ST 300374), built in 1871 by the B&ER to carry a branch into the docks. The central part was telescopic so shipping could pass to East and West Quays. It was built by Warburton Bros of Bristol with ironwork from Lloyds Foster & Co. of Wednesbury. An opening of 78ft (23.8m) was achieved by rolling back the eastern span, using a small steam engine. The bridge last opened in 1953 and now serves as a footbridge.

The B&ER's Whiteball Tunnel (ST 095182) is 1092yd (998m) long and brick lined. Fourteen shafts were sunk along its course during construction by over 1000 navvies in 1842–44. The GWR's Castle Cary to Langport link entailed deep cuttings and a tunnel almost as long at Somerton (ST 470274). The D&SR had two tunnels, at Venn Cross (ST 046246) and Bathealton (ST 064250).

Mineral and industrial railways are of special interest throughout Somerset. The West Somerset Mineral Railway was promoted by the Brendon Hills Iron Ore Co. for transporting ore down to Watchet for shipping to South Wales for smelting. An Act of 1856 authorised a standard gauge line to run from the port via Roadwater to the summit of Brendon Hill and then serving mines to the west. The crowning achievement was the 1100yd (1106m) Comberow incline, taking a double track 803

feet (245m) up onto Brendon Hill in 1858 although it was not fully ready until 1861. The line was extended westwards to Gupworthy by 1864 and a siding ran into iron mines at Raleigh's Cross, Carnarvon Pit, Burrow Farm and Langham Hill. A circuitous and steeply graded 8-mile extension to the Eisen Hill mines was planned in 1864 but never realised. Steam locomotives worked the sections above and below the incline. Some passenger traffic was also carried but after the mines closed in 1883 the railway struggled on until 1898. There was a brief reprieve in 1907–10 when the Somerset Mineral Syndicate reopened some mines and ran a 2ft (610mm) gauge tramway 2 miles from Colton Pit to the head of the incline. The section between Watchet and Washford was last used in 1911–12 to demonstrate an automatic train control system. The railway remained independent and was never joined to the West Somerset Railway.

Although overgrown, the earthwork of the 1 in 4 Comberow incline (ST 029352 to ST 023344) is the outstanding legacy of the railway. The winding house, built into the embankment at the summit but subsequently altered, has massive bolts protruding from the floor where two 18ft (5.5m) diameter winding drums were held. These were intended to be self-acting but were helped by a small stationary steam engine. Brendon Hill station (ST 022344) later became a house. Good sections of the railway course, sometimes with earthworks, run west along the hilltop to the site of Gupworthy Pit and the terminus at Goosemoor, where the station building survives (SS 962356). Down at Watchet, the station and goods shed have been converted to flats and garages (ST 070434).

The Black Bridge of 1871 carried a railway into Bridgwater docks and was telescopic to allow navigation in the river. It is now a fixed footbridge but the rollers can be seen beneath on the east side.

The incline winding house at the top of Brendon Hill. Many years after abandonment, it was converted to other uses and the walls were rebuilt with iron-framed windows. The trees on the embankment have since grown up. May 1976.

The great Comberow incline of the West Somerset Mineral Railway, c.1890. This well-known view never fails to impress.   C. TILLEY COLLECTION

The course of the West Somerset Mineral Railway on Brendon Hill near Burrow Farm.

Inside the Comberow incline winding house. Large bolts in the floor held the winding drums and the arched tunnel behind carried a cable to the top of the incline.

The upper section of the West Somerset Mineral Railway was worked by this robust steam locomotive supplied in 1856 by Nielson & Co. of Glasgow. M. J. MESSENGER COLLECTION

Up on Exmoor, Frederic Knight planned a railway from Simonsbath to descend by two inclines to Porlock Weir to serve the iron mines and open up this part of the moor. Although the rails were never put down, the course was prepared and much of the 9-mile route can be traced, for example near Larkbarrow Corner (SS 820416).

Tramways and sidings from the main railways served limestone quarries in the eastern Mendips, and Merehead and Whatley Quarries rely on the railways today. For example, quarries at Vallis Vale were served from the late-nineteenth century by tramways which took the stone to Hapsford for crushing and screening before being transhipped to the main railway. Bridge abutments can be seen where the old quarry tramways crossed the Egford Brook and Mells River (ST 755491). The course of the old standard gauge mineral railway branch to Whatley Quarry, replaced by a new diversion in 1974, winds through the valley here.

By the 1880s the Mendip Granite & Asphalt Co. Ltd had built a stone works and exchange sidings near Cranmore station on the East Somerset Railway. A 2ft gauge tramway ran up to quarries at Waterlip and Moons Hill and in the early-twentieth century it was continued as a steam railway eastwards to Downhead Quarry. The section between Cranmore and the limestone quarry at Waterlip Quarry (ST 661444) later became a standard gauge siding from the main railway.

There were smaller quarry tramways just to the west at Doulting. From the late 1880s Trask & Co. had a horse-tramway from the Chelynch quarries to their stone works (ST 653425) which had a siding from the East Somerset Railway. Until about 1900 stone from their Bramble Ditch Quarry was carried to the works by a second horse-tramway, crossing the main railway by a bridge.

The course of the old tramway linking Vobster Colliery and Vobster Breach Colliery is just visible as a low bank crossing this field. January 2001.

Industrial tramway sidings at the Eclipse Peat Co.'s headquarters near Meare. This lightweight track was ideal for traversing soft ground and a network ran out into the peatlands. October 1965. M.J. MESSENGER

On the Somerset coalfield, the Westbury Iron Co. built the Newbury Railway by 1863 as a branch from the broad gauge Frome–Radstock line to their Newbury Colliery. Much of it followed the course of the abandoned Dorset & Somerset Canal. A narrow gauge tramway linking Vobster Breach and Vobster Collieries (its course survives) was planned to climb to meet the railway near Vobster Cross, although it is unclear if this last part was ever built. There were sidings from the Newbury Railway to Mells Colliery and Vobster limestone quarry, and a separate line to Bilboa Quarry was added in 1925. After the Newbury pit closed in 1927, the railway was kept open to sidings at Vobster Quarry (ST 705495) until 1966.

The Oakhill Brewery overcame transport problems, uniquely, by operating its own 2ft 6in (760mm) gauge industrial railway in 1904–19. Two steam locomotives (the *Mendip* and *Oakhill*) hauled wagons laden with beer barrels for nearly 3 miles to Binegar station on the Somerset & Dorset Railway. Other industries had extensive private sidings from the main-line system, including the Westland aircraft works (1913–67) at Yeovil, the British Cellophane factory at Bridgwater and the Royal Ordnance Factory at Puriton. There were also sidings into the military stores depot, initially established by the US Army in c.1942, at Norton Fitzwarren and now the Taunton Trading Estate.

Finally, it is said that Taunton had the shortest tramway with the longest name. The Taunton & West Somerset Electric Railways & Tramways Co. Ltd, later the Taunton Electric Traction Co. Ltd, ran a 3ft 6in (1067mm) gauge tramway from a depot at East Reach to the railway station, with an extension to Rowbarton, but clearly not the full length intended in 1901. After only twenty years it was closed in 1921.

Taunton's short-lived electric tram system is seen in this postcard view of Fore Street and the Market House, pre-1913.　　　D. WARREN COLLECTION

18

PORTS AND SHIPPING

Somerset's coast is noted for its high tidal range and trade from its small ports was traditionally in and around the Bristol Channel, with Bristol and South Wales, the latter particularly in the coal trade, and as far as Ireland too. Bridgwater had the only true floating dock and was by far the largest port in the Age of Steam. Watchet, a tidal harbour between piers, thrived briefly on iron ore traffic after the 1850s and was a commercial port in the late-twentieth century well after Bridgwater's dock

had closed. There were smaller harbours at Highbridge, Minehead, Porlock Weir and Lilstock, and even places where beach landings could be made.

Somerset's principal port of Bridgwater was some miles inland on the Parrett where it was in a position to receive river-borne cargoes from a wide hinterland. It had been a port since Saxon times, later with quays on both river banks below the Town Bridge. Disadvantages, which

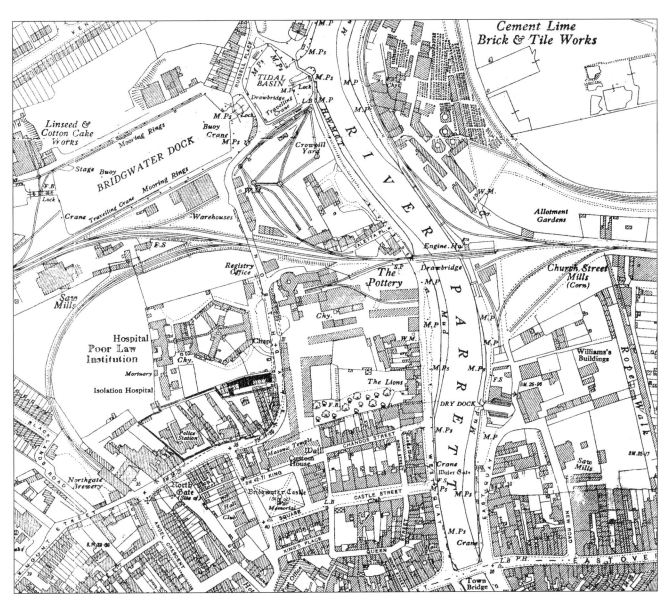

Industries concentrated around Bridgwater Dock and the River Parrett are clearly seen in this portion of the Ordnance Survey 25-inch map of 1929.

ORDNANCE SURVEY: CROWN COPYRIGHT RESERVED

became more apparent as trade increased in the eighteenth and early-nineteenth centuries, included the extremely high tidal range and the 'bore' which Defoe noted

sometimes it comes in with such furious haste, as to come two fathoms deep at a time, and when it does by surprize, it often does great damage to ships, driving them foul of one another, and oftentimes oversetting them.

The winding course of the Parrett from Combwich Reach was difficult to navigate and there were continuous problems with silting so that in the early-nineteenth century larger ships could not reach Bridgwater during neap tides and were offloaded into barges at Combwich (itself once a port in the medieval period). There were then four shipbuilders and trade almost doubled in ten years from 1822, with many townspeople involved in shipowning.

Numerous schemes were put forward for a ship canal from Combwich to a river basin, but none came to fruition. However, in 1837–41 the Bridgwater & Taunton Canal was extended from its original basin at Huntworth to a new floating dock and basin at Crowpill downstream from the town (ST 297375). Thomas Dawe Maddicks was the engineer and the works included a ship lock and smaller barge lock from the Parrett into an outer tidal basin before entering the main basin which measured 600ft (183m) by 200ft (61m). Lock gates maintained the water level as a floating dock. The canal entered the basin at the far end. Clay spoil was either tipped beside the basin, forming a hillock called the Mump, or burnt in kilns to make bricks and tiles. The new dock opened on 25 March 1841 and could take vessels of 600 tons. Steam paddle tugs towed sailing ships up and down the river.

Ingenious methods were employed to deal with silting from the river (so much loved by the Bath brick industry!). Maddicks installed sluicing culverts in the outer tidal basin (perhaps after consulting with Brunel) to keep the river entrance clear, and in 1844 the *Bertha* mud scraper was set to work. Designed by Brunel, a steam engine on the boat pulled it across the dock by chains while a long adjustable scraper blade scoured the dock floor as it went. This curious vessel worked at Bridgwater until 1971. It was subsequently displayed at the Exeter Maritime Museum, but currently resides many miles from home at Lowestoft.

Vessels still used the West and East Quays in the river.

There was a dry dock and a shipbuilding yard at East Quay where F.J. Carver & Sons launched the last sailing ketch in 1907. There were also timber quays belonging to the many brick and tile works along the river, the nearest being Barham Brothers' brickworks opposite the dock entrance. In the river, mud was kept clear from the banks by the *Pioneer* and then the *Eroder*, a 62ft (19m) steel-hulled steam vessel built by W. & F. Wills with movable water jets and a deck gun. It worked from 1910 to 1927 along the river, washing out the entrance to the docks, clearing the berth of the Parrett Bath Brick Co., and was even employed at Highbridge harbour.

The Bristol & Exeter Railway bought the docks in 1866. Over 200,000 tons of goods passed through the port in 1878 but this traffic declined. Coal from South Wales had

Three-masted schooner Anna *at Bridgwater. She loaded a cargo of bricks here just before the Great War but was sunk by a U-boat in 1918. Railway trucks are seen in Sully & Co.'s coal yard and the corner of Ware's warehouse is on the right.*

I. & M. MILES COLLECTION

Sail and steam shipping alongside Ware's warehouse in Bridgwater Dock. From an early postcard.

SOMERSET STUDIES LIBRARY

Above: *Ware's warehouse at Bridgwater Dock in May 1976. This fine building has since been converted to flats.*

Right: *Old hand crane at Bridgwater Docks. Hard-wearing granite coping stones were used around the entrance to the outer basin.*

Below: *Bridgwater's ship lock at the entrance to the tidal River Parrett, disused and well silted in 1986.*

Crane base at the west end of Bridgwater Dock.

been a major import, as at other Somerset ports, but the developing railway network could now bring it easily from Radstock and, after 1886, from Wales via the Severn Tunnel. Coal, timber and fertilisers were imported but the docks continued to decline after the Second World War and were officially closed in 1971. Somerset County Council bought the docks in 1974 and the site has been redeveloped as a marina. Dock features remain, however. The four-storey Ware's Warehouse of 1841 has been converted to flats but retains something of its brick and stone appearance. Other features of interest include the double-leaf bascule bridge between the basins, which replaced an earlier one in 1907, a hand crane, bollards and quayside details such as the sluicing mechanisms around the outer basin. Bowering's animal feed mill, still operating, completes the scene at the upper end of the dock.

Further downstream on the Parrett's east bank, Dunball Wharf (ST 309409) was established in 1844 for importing coal. There was a siding to the B&ER and the lime and cement works. The railway company later took over and extended the wharf. Petroleum was imported in the mid-twentieth century; today, sand is discharged and some commercial traffic comes here too.

Highbridge Wharf (ST 316473) was developed by the Somerset Central Railway which had its terminus here in 1854 and coal and other goods were imported until 1955. The railway was extended in 1858 onto a 900ft (274m) pier at Burnham with the intention of developing passenger traffic with Wales. The railway company formed the Burnham Tidal Harbour & Railway Co. in 1860 and operated a 'fast steamer service', claiming the shortest and cheapest route for goods and passengers between South Wales, the South West and South of England. The S&DJR's brief attempt to run a passenger service from

Poole to Cherbourg in 1865–66 created a rather bizarre direct route between South Wales and France. The Severn Tunnel finished off the Burnham to Wales service. Highbridge Wharf was closed in 1949 and has been redeveloped. Nearby, John Burnett & Co.'s bonded store of 1900 remains of interest (ST 319471). Attempts to build a harbour further along the coast at Brean Down failed and the harbour works were washed away in a storm in 1872.

Watchet harbour (ST 072435) is held to be the place from which Coleridge's Ancient Mariner sailed, for the poet visited here in 1797 when there was just a simple west pier. The Earl of Egremont, as lord of the manor, was involved in works during the early-eighteenth century to repair and improve an old storm-damaged pier. In 1797 William Jessop advised the building of an east breakwater but only a line of piles was constructed. In 1838 the west pier was extended and a new east breakwater was built at last. However, the tidal harbour was in a poor condition and the piers were hardly used. Instead, cargoes were handled by carts brought alongside ships lying aground at low tide.

This was the situation by the 1850s when the Brendon Hills iron mines and the West Somerset Mineral Railway were being developed with plans to ship thousands of tons of ore to South Wales. There were difficult negotiations with Egremont but a Watchet Harbour Act of 1857 set up harbour commissioners with representatives from the mining and railway companies. The harbour had been put in good order by 1862 when 500-ton ships could use it. A wooden extension to the west pier and a new east pier enclosed 10 acres, although the harbour remained tidal. The WSMR ran onto a new jetty built into the harbour from the west pier, where a special hydraulic tipper was installed in 1874. Over 40,000 tons of iron ore were shipped in the 1870s and the ships returned with coal, but then the mines closed in 1883. A great storm in late December 1900 wreaked great damage to the harbour and shipping within it. The Watchet Urban District Council took over and rebuilt the harbour in 1902–04, the west pier in sandstone and concrete. Shiploads of wood pulp were imported for the paper mill, ship-breaking took place at the west pier in 1920–25, and paddle-steamers called until 1929. As well as traffic for the paper mill, Watchet became a thriving port for exports in the 1970s but it later closed to shipping and part was opened as a marina in 2002. The west pier retains its 1862 lighthouse and there is a trace where the iron ore jetty once joined the pier.

A steam crane discharges coal from a sailing trader at Minehead pier, c.1930s. Tourism is competing with the shipping industry for quay space.　　　　D. WARREN COLLECTION

The West Pier at Watchet, with the site of the iron ore shipping wharf in the foreground.

Minehead (SS 972471) was mentioned as a port in the fourteenth century, but its position was moved westwards in 1604–16 when George Luttrell built a stone quay, subsequently extended in 1682. Wool and hides were imported from Ireland and oak bark for tanning and grain were exported. The pier was extended and repaired several times in the early-eighteenth century and coal and culm were imported from South Wales. Other ports had eclipsed Minehead by the 1800s and the harbour, once considered one of the best and safest in the Bristol Channel, fell into decline. There was some shipbuilding, the last in 1881 when the two-masted schooner *Perriton* was launched for the local Ridler ship-owning family. Coal also came down the Bristol Channel from the Forest of Dean and exports included pit props for the mines. Local sailing traders continued to call, apparently right down to the 1950s when coal was brought for the gasworks and unloaded by a steam crane 'of immense antiquity' on the pier. The famous White Funnel paddle-steamers called at Minehead and other Bristol Channel ports, and the company's 690ft (210m) pier stood here from 1901 until 1940.

Porlock Weir (SS 864480) has a small basin served by lock gates, with a small quay and warehouses. It was developed in 1855 by Col G.W. Blathwayt who was anticipating the building of an iron ore railway from Simonsbath. Oak bark and bricks were exported and coal, culm and limestone were imported for the local limekilns. Some shipbuilding took place and there were locally owned vessels of up to 85 tons. The last cargo of coal came in 1948. A pebble ridge protects the dock, much as it must have done for the earlier harbour back in the 1420s. There were also places along the coast where

Solid masonry was used in 1855 for building the lock entrance to the harbour at Porlock Weir.

Navigational Aids

Burnham high lighthouse, with Trinity House accommodation below. This disused light stands inland from the shore and is surrounded by residential houses.

The cast-iron lighthouse on the West Pier at Watchet.

This navigation buoy of 1860 served shipping in the Parrett estuary and has been recently restored. It is displayed upside down at Bridgwater Dock and a similar buoy can be seen at Combwich.

Burnham low lighthouse stands on timber piles. The sea front at Burnham-on-Sea is in the background.

boats could be beached to unload culm and limestone from South Wales for burning, the nearest good example being the limekiln on Bossington Beach. Gypsum from the cliffs was shipped off from Blue Anchor.

A fascinating little harbour at Lilstock (ST 173453) was formed in the 1820s and '30s by Sir John Acland of Fairfield, Stogursey. It had a breakwater parallel to the shore, with gates and sluices for keeping the entrance clear. A stone pier was added to the breakwater in about 1860. Most of the cargoes were coal, culm and limestone for the estate's houses and limekilns and there were storehouses and a limekiln beside the harbour. Paddle-steamers called briefly in the 1860s and '70s. The storm that devastated Watchet in 1900 also destroyed Lilstock. Although now overwhelmed by a pebble bank, there are still traces of the breakwater, sluice gate recesses, a limekiln and stores.

Navigational aids include the Burnham high and low lighthouses to protect shipping from the Gore Sand at the entrance to the Parrett estuary. They were built in 1832 by Trinity House to replace an earlier pair of 1801. The high lighthouse (ST 304505) is now redundant, standing 98ft (30m) tall amid a residential part of Burnham-on-

Lilstock's ruined stone pier is revealed on the shore at low tide.

Sea. In contrast, the timber-built low lighthouse (ST 299504) is on piles on the tidal shore and has been kept as a guiding light. The only other lighthouse in Somerset is on the end of the west pier at Watchet. This simple octagonal tower of cast iron was made in 1862 by Hennet, Spink & Else of Bridgwater. It survived the great storm of 1900 when much of the pier was severely damaged. Originally lit by oil lamp, it was later converted to gas and then electricity.

WATER SUPPLY AND DRAINAGE

The earliest water supplies for villages and towns came from springs and wells, and for some places this continued into the twentieth century. Fountains and pumps were erected and occasionally benefactors set up conduits for the benefit of the townspeople. The last of Ilminster's stone conduits, for example, is 'The Stook' in the Square. The small stone Patwell pump house at Church Bridge, Bruton, is another example. Somerton had a strong spring at Roger's Well (ST 488283) with enough force to supply five spouts, while Stogursey's St Andrew's Well (ST 202427) has two springs, one supplying fresh water said to be softer than the other. Springs at Glastonbury supplied a reservoir holding 31,500 gallons at the top of the High Street from which five conduits served the town. Drinking fountains were installed in the mid-nineteenth century, with a pump house (ST 507396). Some were quite elaborate, such as a water fountain, trough and lamp standard made by the Coalbrookdale Co. to commemorate King Edward VII's coronation, in Broad Street, Somerton (ST 491287).

Doulting, where St Andrew's Well is the source of the River Sheppy, has a humble example of water supply developments by a local benefactor. In around 1850 the lord of the manor, William Mellior Foster Mellior, provided a 6ft (1.83m) diameter overshot water-wheel and pumps to feed a small reservoir in the village. By 1886, supply to the village and two farms was increased by the building of a new pump house downstream containing a 12ft (3.66m) diameter backshot water-wheel and pumps. The pumps were replaced in the 1920s by two twin-piston pumps by Godwin of Quenington, Gloucestershire, and worked until about 1960 when they were replaced by an electric pump. Incredibly, the system still works today and the remains of both water-wheels survive.

Hydraulic rams provided, as they still do in some cases, a constant water supply to farms and villages. The world's oldest manufacturers, Green & Carter, are located at Ashbrittle and they are connected with the Easton family, originally from Bradford-on-Tone in Somerset, who manufactured rams back in 1814. Water could also be obtained for farm use by wind pumps.

Pollution from wells increased as the population and its demands for water rose, but the problem was overcome. For example, sickness was reported in the early 1890s among the population of the hamlet of Holford on the edge of the Quantocks, where water was taken from a well and two streams. The immediate cure was the building of a covered reservoir and piped water supply in 1896. In 1876 an artesian well was sunk to a depth of 258ft (79m) at Bow Street in Langport and a new public pump was installed above it. The town of Chard used springs from about 1570 until 1928. Water was piped to under half the

Somerton's water fountain, trough and lamppost to commemorate Edward VII's coronation in 1902 was cast by the Coalbrookdale Co.

population, but the rest relied on wells until a deep well with electric pumps supplied a reservoir on Snowdon Hill in 1928.

The water supply 'industry' followed the Public Health Act of 1848 which demanded good-quality piped water for the increasing populations in the towns in the wake of cholera and typhoid scares. By the second half of the nineteenth century local authorities were establishing water supply companies. The Shepton Mallet Water Works Co. was established in 1859 and a 'plentiful supply of pure water' from springs on the Mendips to the north of the town was conveyed in cast-iron pipes to a reservoir at Lower Downside. A second source from Beacon Hill began in about 1894. The Highbridge waterworks pumped water from a borehole in 1886–1906. Only its octagonal brick chimney remains (ST 317470).

It became usual to pump water from a good source to a holding covered reservoir or water tower from which it was fed by gravity through pipes to households, and this is particularly well illustrated at Wellington where some remarkable landmarks of the water industry remain. The Wellington Sanitary Authority, later the Urban District Council, built the Westford pumping station (ST 123204) in 1885 to replace 286 wells, many of which contained water of a dubious quality. The first water source was the Rackfield spring, later enlarged by a second spring and well at the pumping station. Two gas engines, with their own producer gas-making plant, were installed to work two sets of three-throw pumps manufactured by Glenfield & Co. of Kilmarnock. Together they could deliver 14,500 gallons per hour. They were not a great success and there were at least two explosions involving one of the engines. Town gas was also used, although when the main was fractured by a traction engine the gas supply was lost and so was Wellington's water. One gas engine was kept for emergencies in 1902 when a steam engine was installed with a Cornish boiler housed in the producer gas room. The final change came in 1935 when

One of the two Ruston diesel engines in the Westford water pumping station near Wellington. WESSEX WATER HISTORICAL ARCHIVE

Westford pumping station was built for Wellington's water supply in 1885. The chimney was added when a steam engine was installed in 1902. Two Ruston diesel engines were installed in 1935 and are still inside the building.

two Ruston diesel engines were installed to work the original Glenfield pump sets. The pumping station was closed in the 1960s but the brick building still stands with its 1902 chimney, and contains the pump sets and Ruston engines inside. The building had been threatened with redevelopment.

From the beginning, water from Westford was pumped to a water tower holding 44,000 gallons at Rockwell Green (ST 126200). The tank of riveted iron plates stands atop a round brick tower and an opening provides access to an iron platform and ladder to the tank. The tank was provided with a water level indicator which was visible from the pumping station. Alongside the tower (which has the profile of a lighthouse) is a taller concrete tower erected in 1935. Meanwhile, another water tank had been built in 1896 at Dark Lane, Wellington. A tank made of three rows of cast-iron panels by Ford Bros & Co. of Wellington stood over a two-storey brick dwelling made for a water company employee. Having been made redundant, most of the tank was removed and the accommodation converted to a house.

Bridgwater received its water from wells and a pumped supply engineered by Richard Lowbridge in the early part of the eighteenth century. The water engineer Thomas Hawksley first planned a scheme to replace this supply in 1866 and Bridgwater Corporation completed the Ashford Water Treatment Works (ST 236385) in 1879. Water from the Currypool Stream was pumped to a reservoir at Wembdon. The pumping engine house contained two James Watt beam engines with two Cornish boilers providing the steam. They reverted to standby when replaced in about 1920 by a horizontal single cylinder oil engine working Hathorn-Davey three-throw pumps.

Building the draw-off tower and pitching the dam for Ashford Reservoir in 1934. WESSEX WATER HISTORICAL ARCHIVE

A contrast in styles at Rockwell Green where the water towers date from 1885 (right) and 1935 (left).

The completed Ashford reservoir, with the pumping station building beyond, 1934. WESSEX WATER HISTORICAL ARCHIVE

Ashford water treatment works and pumping station at the time of completion in 1879. The main building survives today but the chimney has been felled.

In the 1930s plans were drawn up for a reservoir and treatment works at Durleigh in response to British Cellophane's intended new factory in Bridgwater. Ashford Reservoir was built in 1934 and the treatment works enlarged, and the new Durleigh Reservoir and works were commissioned in 1938. Ashford's capacity was increased again when Hawkridge Reservoir was built and opened in 1962.

Until the 1950s Taunton's water supply came from a series of tapped springs in the Blackdown Hills. Three open reservoirs were built to impound the water from the springs, at Blagdon in 1886, Leigh in 1893 and Luxhay in 1905. They are still in use today, feeding Fulwood Water Treatment Works. The almost circular Cheddar Reservoir was an artificial creation of the Bristol Waterworks Co. Completed in 1937 on the Levels between Cheddar and Axbridge, water was pumped to the company's Blagdon Reservoir on the far side of the Mendip Hills. Other reservoirs in Somerset, such as Clatworthy or Sutton Bingham, date from the 1950s onwards.

While one side of the water industry was supplying water, the other was concerned with removing it from the Levels.

The basins of the Parrett, Brue and Axe were, and are, liable to flooding because the waters are held back by a belt of marine clays along the coast. Early attempts to drain parts of the Somerset Levels were made by the abbeys of Athelney, Muchelney, Glastonbury and by Wells Cathedral. Watercourses were straightened, such as the River Brue to the west of Meare. The main period of drainage was from 1770 to 1830 when agricultural improvements created much of the landscape of the Levels seen today. The moors were enclosed and drained by means of straight rhynes (drainage ditches) feeding into major drainage channels that led to a clyce (sluice) at the sea. William Jessop advised on several large schemes at the turn of the century, with his assistant Robert Anstice who later became the first County Surveyor for Somerset. The King's Sedgemoor Drain was cut in 1791–98 from the River Cary at Henley Corner (ST 435327) to a clyce into the Parrett at Dunball (ST 310408), a total length of $12\frac{1}{2}$ miles. Improvements also took place on the Brue (1801–06) and Axe (1803–10). The clyce at Highbridge deteriorated and was rebuilt in 1801 when a new Western Cut and South Drain were made. A new clyce was built at Bleadon, which prevented shipping reaching the old medieval quay at Rackley further up the Axe.

In the Parrett basin the first main scheme was at Northmoor, with rhynes feeding a main drain which ended at a clyce on the Parrett. An Act in 1830 allowed for enclosing and draining lands in Othery, Middlezoy and Westonzoyland. One of the problems of the early schemes was that water could not drain through the clyce when the River Parrett was flowing high, so the answer was to pump the water up to the level of the embanked river. Windmills were not used for pumping, as on the Norfolk Broads, but steam power was used from 1830.

The Westonzoyland pumping station (ST 340328) had the first steam pumping engine on the Levels and by chance the site has been preserved by the Westonzoyland Engine Trust. The engine house, boiler house and attendant's house beside the River Parrett are dominated by a tall and superbly-shaped chimney. In 1830 a 27hp beam engine was installed here to work a scoop wheel to help drain some 1600 acres. This was found to be inadequate and the building was altered in 1861 to take an Easton & Amos Drainage Machine which continued in use until 1951. This has been restored to work by steam today. Dominated by a large flywheel, it is a twin

Top: *The preserved 1861 Easton & Amos pumping engine at Westonzoyland.*

Above: *Maker's name on the Westonzoyland drainage engine.*

Left: *Westonzoyland drainage pumping station with its distinctive chimney in 1986. Note the very small replacement diesel pump house at the end of the rhyne. The River Parrett is behind the main pumping station.*

cylinder vertical steam engine atop a cast-iron well casing. At the bottom, and driven by the engine, is a centrifugal pump designed in 1850 by John George Appold. James Easton, of a Somerset family, had formed a partnership with C.E. Amos in 1836 at Southwark and their firm gained a reputation in supplying water pumping engines worldwide. They were joined by William Anderson in 1864 and the firm moved to Erith, Kent. Their pumping engines were installed all over the Somerset Levels.

Westonzoyland was followed by other schemes and engines, such as at East Saltmoor (ST 353308) where a 6hp Easton & Amos steam engine was installed in 1838, and Southlake (1846). An Act of 1861 established Internal Drainage Boards and three were formed in 1864 at Chedzoy, Currymoor and Stanmoor. William Amos was the surveyor for the first two and all the pumping stations had steam engines by Easton & Amos. As well as the engine with its house and boiler house, each scheme required an attendant's cottage and work on the rhynes and bridges.

The Northmoor Board of 1867 installed the only engine with a name cast on it: 'The Good Hope. 1867'. This was an engine similar to the Westonzoyland and Currymoor ones. The old engine at Southlake pumping station was replaced by a new Easton & Amos one in 1869, the same year that the Allermoor Board was the last to install a steam pump. The pumping station (ST 357306) was built at Burrowbridge, a little distance from Allermoor, and the old Cary river channel was used as the engine rhyne. This 30hp engine was said to lift 60 tons of water a minute against a 6ft head, consuming 3 tons of coal a day. It should be noted that such engines were never capable of draining the Levels completely but were only used during the few weeks of the year when flood levels had lessened.

The individual drainage boards were independent and had little control over the main drainage channels. The Somerset Drainage Act of 1877 gave the Somersetshire Drainage Commissioners an overall view of matters on the Levels. It coincided with the agricultural depression which left less money available, but work was done on the main channels. Highbridge Clyce, which had caused problems in 1869, was rebuilt and a steam grab dredger was used on the main channels in 1882–89. Further work on clearing mud from the channels and rivers was done by eroder boats fitted out with pumps and hoses by W. & F. Wills, engineers of Bridgwater. The steam-powered *Pioneer* and *Eroder* pumped jets of water at the banks to remove excess silting between 1894 and 1927.

Saltmoor pumping station, near Burrowbridge.

The Somerset Rivers Catchment Board built the West Sedgemoor pumping station at Stathe on the Parrett in 1944.

The Somerset Rivers Catchment Board took over drainage management in 1930, and a widening of the King's Sedgemoor Drain was begun in 1939. Large quantities of water (4.5m gallons a day) were required for the new Royal Ordnance Factory at Puriton and the Board constructed Huntspill Cut to provide both flood relief for the River Brue and a reservoir for the factory. The Gold Corner pumping station (ST 367431) had four 240hp Crossley diesel engines powering Sulzer pumps. The King's Sedgemoor Drain also provided a backup supply. The Catchment Board built a new pumping station worked by Ruston diesels at Stathe (ST 376286) where the West Sedgemoor Main Drain meets the Parrett. Diesel engines replaced steam in the 1940s at Chedzoy, East Saltmoor, Northmoor, Southlake and Stanmoor.

The Somerset River Board was formed in 1950, responsibility subsequently going to the Somerset River Authority, Wessex River Authority and now the National Rivers Authority. Westonzoyland stopped in 1951 but the pumping engines at Allermoor and Currymoor continued to be steamed until 1955. The former was made redundant but the latter was replaced by diesel. In addition to the Westonzoyland steam engine, the Allermoor engine survives in its redundant pumping station, and two others have also been brought here. Westonzoyland's tiny diesel pump house could not be in greater contrast to the tall steam pumping station that it replaced. Thanks to the dedication of the Westonzoyland Engine Trust, the public can still experience steam in action at this site.

20

LIGHT, HEAT AND POWER

The first trial use of gas for lighting in Somerset dates from 1816, but it was not until the 1830s that town supply companies became well established, such as the Frome Gas Co. (1831) or the Bridgwater Gas Light Co. (1834). By 1866 there were 16 gas undertakings in Somerset. Coal gas was first supplied for street lighting, and then domestic lights before cooking and heating were added as the gas companies expanded their industry. In 1902 there were gas companies at Axbridge, Bridgwater, Bruton, Burnham, Castle Cary, Chard, Cheddar, Crewkerne, Frome, Glastonbury, Highbridge, Hinton St George, Ilminster, Langport, Martock, Milborne Port, Milverton, Minehead, Shepton Mallet, Somerton, Taunton, Watchet, Wedmore, Wellington, Wells, Wincanton, Wiveliscombe and Yeovil. Each supplied its locality and was completely isolated, but some companies had already integrated when the gas industry was nationalised in 1949. A grid main was laid to supply the outlying towns with gas from the larger works and the small uneconomical ones were closed during the 1950s. The discovery of North Sea natural gas in 1964 resulted in the closure of all traditional gasworks, although the last at Minehead remained until the 1970s.

Bituminous coal was heated to about 800°C in horizontal retorts placed in rows in the retort house, leaving coke. The exhauster drew gas from the retorts to pass it through the condenser for cooling and separating the tar, the scrubber to remove ammonia in water, and the purifiers which used lime or iron oxide. A steam engine drove the exhauster and pump for the scrubber. Later retorts were vertical, which could be used continuously. The purified gas was stored in a gasholder which was sealed with water at the base. Early gasholders were held between columns but spiral guided types were invented in 1890. Gas was supplied to consumers by a network of pipes laid by the company. By-products which could be sold were coke, tar, ammonia and fertilisers.

Taunton was a pioneering centre of gas in Somerset. Here, John Wride had lit his house with gas in 1816 and a Taunton Gas Light Co. was formed to light the town's streets. This failed and a second company was set up in 1821 to make gas from various oils (including whale, seal and linseed) but it was not very successful and in 1833 coal gas was used for lighting the streets and Cox's lace factory. The Taunton Gas Light & Coke Co. Ltd was formed in 1845 and a new works was built in the Tangier district. There were then 208 consumers in addition to the street lights. Lights were open flames but the invention of the gas mantle in the 1890s was a timely development when electricity was becoming a rival. By then paraffin oil lamps were also a viable alternative to gas. Higher mains pressures made gas heating and cooking available in the late-nineteenth century. In the 1930s appliances, including the 'ever popular' gas irons, were made at a works next to the Taunton gasworks site.

Taunton Gasworks, an undated view of part of this large works.   SOMERSET STUDIES LIBRARY

Wedmore's tiny gasworks dates between 1870 and 1947 and the retort house, manager's house and showroom still survive.

The 1930s saw amalgamations and closures. The Taunton & District Gas Co. absorbed gas companies and their works at Milverton, Wiveliscombe, Ilminster and Langport, although gas making continued at these last two until 1954–55. After nationalisation in 1949, Somerset came within the South West Gas Board, with the exception of the small Milborne Port Gas Co. which went to the Southern Gas Board. Gas making ceased at Taunton in 1957.

Despite demolition and redevelopment of what were regarded as ugly and smelly urban sites, physical evidence of the once important gas industry does survive in Somerset, including retort buildings, offices and houses. A good example of a small town gasworks still in a recognisable form, although now a private residence, was built in 1870 two years after the formation of the Wedmore Gas Co. When it became a limited company in 1909 the gasworks consumed 150 tons of coal annually and served 51 consumers and 36 street lights. It was bought by the Weston-super-Mare Gaslight Co. in 1946 and closed in 1947. Although the gasholder has gone, the tiny site contains the retort house with a coal store, gas engine pump house and a decorative chimney. The showroom faces the road, with the manager's house behind (ST 437479).

Somerton gasworks (ST 495288) was established below the town in 1857 and was converted to a milk depot (!) after closure in 1955. The site is now derelict but the gable of the retort house is still recognisable. Cheddar gasworks (ST 458528) was built in 1869 and a small retort house, manager's house, boundary wall and gateposts survive. Ilminster did not have a gasworks until 1880 and the Ilminster Gas Light, Coal & Coke Co.'s red-brick retort house survives as a retail warehouse at Cross to the south of the town centre (ST 360141). The extensive stone buildings of the Frome gasworks (ST 776486), which closed in 1937, remain in good order in the occupancy of CEP Ceilings Ltd. The site at Welshmill Lane is below the railway where there was a siding and coal drop. A director of the Frome Gas Co. was Edward Cockey, whose iron foundry in the town manufactured gasworks equipment and gasholders.

A number of industries and private estates also had their own small gasworks, mainly for lighting. Fox Bros at Wellington had an early gas plant for their Tonedale Mills and the Neath Abbey Ironworks supplied a new gasworks in 1843, nine years after building the town's gasworks. The mill was lit with gas until 1895 when electricity was

Ilminster's brick retort house was built in 1880. The gasworks closed in 1954 and the buildings are now a retail warehouse.

The stone-built retort house and other buildings of the gasworks in Welshmill Lane at Frome have accommodated other industries since closure in 1937.

generated by two Crossley suction gas engines (replaced by diesels in 1930). The mill used ammoniacal liquor from the gasworks, and that in the town, for bleaching textiles. In Chard, gas was first made by Wheatley & Co. to light their lace mill (and to burn off the fluff from net lace) and excess gas was sold in 1833 to private consumers. The Chard Gas & Coke Co. Ltd was formed in 1870. The gasworks closed in 1956, but the manager's house and altered showroom survive.

Clarks of Street and Somerville's paper mill at Creech St Michael also had their own gasworks for lighting. The Somerset & Dorset Railway had two gasworks at Templecombe (1870–1921) and Highbridge station, where oil gas was produced and stored in pressure cylinders for lighting railway carriages. The Oakhill brewery's gasworks was used to light the village streets, while in the same east Mendip area there were gasworks at Downside Abbey and the Lunatic Asylum (Mendip Hospital) near Wells. The St

Audries estate at West Quantoxhead had its own gasworks from the mid-nineteenth century to about 1925. The Gothic-style retort house survives as a listed building (ST 104428). Welsh coal was carted up from a beach landing to the works. Another private gasworks at Hinton St George served Hinton House, the church and village.

Acetylene was another form of gas, used in private houses from the largest mansions to the smallest cottages. Dunster Castle had a plant around the turn of the century and one survives at Morden House, North Curry. This was made by the Acetylene Corporation Ltd who installed over 3000 plants nationwide between 1895 and 1913. They claimed acetylene to be 'the safest, simplest, cleanest, cheapest, also the most reliable and pleasing, and the best for the eyesight and decorations of all the many forms of country house lighting'. North Petherton may have been the only town in the country lit by acetylene. The North Petherton Gas & Carbine Co. was formed in 1906 and it was not until about 1931 that a town gas main was brought from Bridgwater.

Electricity began to rival gas from the late-nineteenth century, first for lighting and then for power and heating. The twentieth century saw great advances in the industry.

In the early years water-wheels, turbines or stationary gas engines drove small generators for local consumption. There were scattered town power stations or 'electricity works' until the 1930s when the Central Electricity National Grid was created to distribute power via pylons and substations more efficiently from larger generators outside the region. The old generating sites often became substations or depots, although Minehead continued to generate until 1952. The contrast could not have been greater when just five years later construction began on the first Magnox nuclear power station at Hinkley Point. It was commissioned in 1965.

Once introduced, electricity soon became indispensable for domestic lighting and heating, street lighting and the power for running most industrial machinery. For consumers, electricity was a safer and more convenient alternative to gas. Distribution by wires and poles brought mains electricity to the remotest farms and hamlets, especially when the industry was nationalised after the Second World War. Until then small generator sets were used in larger houses, some institutions and factories, either driven by water, gas, steam or petrol. Water mills powered small generators for their own consumption or private estates.

Pylons over the Parrett at Hay Moor near Bridgwater: a national grid first came to Somerset in the 1930s and many of the early pylons may be considered to be part of industrial archaeology.

As with gas, Taunton was a pioneering town for electricity. Back in 1879 football matches here and at Wellington had been lit by arc lamps, perhaps the first time anywhere in the country. Henry Massingham introduced the first public electric light supply in the West Country here in 1886. He was a boot and shoe manufacturer but clearly saw the future in this new form of power. His Taunton Electric Lighting Co. obtained a contract with the Corporation to light the streets with arc lamps and there were private customers too. Massingham used an engine supplied by Easton & Waldegrave of the Whitehall Ironworks and Thompson-Houston arc lighting generating sets at his Fore Street 'Electric Lighting Depot'. A larger site was opened at St James Street in 1889 because of increasing demand, but after difficulties the company was bought by Taunton Corporation. This 'Electricity Works' was expanded to include three Bellis & Morcom steam engines driving British Thompson-Houston alternators, and from 1919 steam turbine units were installed. From 1912 electric cookers and water heaters were hired out and Taunton's short-lived tramway was supplied with electric power in from 1901 to 1921. The power station was closed after the Central Electricity Board Grid came to Taunton from Bridgwater, although it saw service again in 1948 because of a lack of generating capacity in the post-war years. The South Western Electricity Board took over at nationalisation.

Taunton was certainly at the forefront of electricity. The Newton Electrical Works at Taunton gained a high reputation in the industry, making fuse and switchgear, motors, generators and other electrical equipment from 1891 until 1934. Francis Murray Newton was an associate of Massingham and brought out his first patent in 1882. His activities were not restricted to Somerset, for in 1892 his lighting system was installed in the new Fordington roller mill at Dorchester, Dorset.

Suction gas engines were used in the power stations at Bridgwater and Minehead. These had vertical cylinders and had a direct drive but could be noisy. They were ideal for smaller stations, such as at Burnham (1914–26) where the two lighthouses were among the customers, or Chard where three engines used wood waste from Salter & Stokes' saw mill at Chard Junction. The Bridgwater & District Electric Supply & Traction Co. Ltd's generating station (1904–35) had two Westinghouse suction gas engines each with 200kV DC generators. Anthracite coal provided the feedstock for the producer gas. By the time of closure there were five of these engines and two diesels. Minehead's generating station (SS 978455) in Marshfield Road, Alcombe, worked from 1916 to 1952. There were four suction gas engines, all from different manufacturers. The Minehead Electricity Supply Co. Ltd had operated at Quay Street since 1902 but noise from the engines had forced them to move to Alcombe. The site is currently vacant.

The Wedmore Electric Light & Power Co. was started in 1908 by William George Burrough, a solicitor. Electricity was enthusiastically received in the town and it was used for lighting as well as for heating, grinding corn, churning butter, kneading bakers' dough and working cider apple mills. Such was the local promoter's enterprise that in comparison the larger town Wells did not get an electricity supply until 1924. Wedmore became a substation in 1928 when it was taken over by the North Somerset Electric Light Co. As well its gasworks, Wedmore's generating station also survives, with the date 1908 and 'ELECTRIC STATION' over the main doorway (ST 435477). Two suction gas engines were here, the larger being reserved for work in the evenings.

Hydro-electric power operated on Exmoor. The Dulverton Electric Light Co. of 1906 was established in an old paper mill with a water-wheel and an oil engine made by W.H. Pool & Sons of Chipstable. It became the West of England Generating Co. in 1926 when a new hydro-electric power station was set up with two Armfield turbines at Brushford (SS 919269). These were replaced by larger Escher Wyss turbines ten years later by the Exe Valley Electricity Co. However, this power station was mothballed in 1938 and closed in the early 1950s. The Porlock Electricity Co. (1909–32) generated electricity at two sites. The corn mill at Hawkcombe (SS 885463) was rebuilt internally where a new overshot wheel drove a generator with belts. The second site at the Wheelhouse (SS 884467) was powered by a 15ft (4.57m) wheel, and both wheels continually operated to charge up batteries. When a gas engine was later installed at Hawkcombe, followed by a diesel set, the Wheelhouse plant was used by Thomas Pearce & Sons' tannery until 1939.

Industrial generators included the Anglo-Bavarian Brewery at Shepton Mallet which had its own plant as early as 1880. In addition to their gas plant, Fox Bros had two Crossley suction gas engines for generating electricity in 1916–30. From 1910 a gas engine generated electricity at their Wiveliscombe mill, for lighting and powering looms. At Yeovil, Petters Ltd's own power station lit the centre of town with electricity.

21

HOUSING AND RECREATION

We have seen where the people worked, but where did they live and what facilities were provided for their welfare in the Age of Steam? This social side of industrial archaeology should not be neglected. There are many instances where industrialists provided housing for their workforce, most frequently in remote areas or whole communities within existing towns.

Textile workers' houses are to be found in Frome. The Trinity area was one of the earliest extensive developments of industrial housing in England, from the late-seventeenth century. Trinity Street (ST 772483) was built in 1718–22 and is just such a place referred to by Defoe when he described the town as

so prodigiously increased within these last twenty or thirty years, that they have built a new church, and so

many new streets of houses, and those houses are so full of inhabitants, that Frome is now reckoned to have more people in it, than the city of Bath.

There are weavers' workshops and dwellings at Sheppards Barton, developed over time by Sheppards, the leading clothiers; some date from 1700, others are 1840. Rich clothiers' houses are to be found in this town and at Shepton Mallet.

Different examples of housing around the county include stone terraces of about 1864 along South Street in Crewkerne, not far from Viney Bridge Mills. Fox Bros of Tonedale Mills, Wellington, built terraces of houses for their workers and the same is true of the Hodgkinsons at Wookey Hole paper mill. In Taunton there is terraced housing for E. & W.C. French's tannery workers at Eastgate Gardens, Tancred Street, while there are

John Boyd, the horsehair manufacturer, lived at Ochiltree House in Upper High Street, Castle Cary.

This terrace at Eastgate Gardens in Taunton was built for E. & W.C. French's tannery workers.

Wilfrid Terrace was built in 1885 for C. & J. Clark's shoe workers in Street. The factory is just visible to the left.

semi-detached houses built by the London & South Western Railway near Templecombe station. An interesting but long since demolished site was 'The Crescent', built in the late-eighteenth century for workers at the Albion or Milton Silk Mill near Evercreech (ST 659377). There were eight cottages of five rooms and an owner's house of 11 rooms, but it is unclear if the latter was at the centre of this unusual block. In 1813 there was accommodation for 150 workers and apprentices. Many child employees were living here, mostly young girls brought from many miles distant.

Street has the finest examples of housing provided by an industrial employer. Much of the town owes its development to C. & J. Clark who built terraced housing for their shoe makers. Most of the employees were outworkers in the 1860s when houses were built in Orchard Road and provided with a 'backshop' for their work above a rear kitchen and accessed by a ladder and trap-door. By the end of the century most workers were employed in the factory itself, but the Clarks continued to provide houses of a high standard, characteristically terraces with gables at intervals. Wilfrid Terrace was built almost opposite the

London & South Western Railway workers' cottages alongside Templecombe station.

High Street factory entrance in 1885, with Cobden Terrace (1889) and Lawson Terrace (1891) in the same street. Not far away are Grange Terrace (1898) and Brutasche Terrace (1902). All have carved names and dates, as do single and semi-detached houses named after trees such as 'The Limes, 1892'.

Coal miners' houses around Coleford and Radstock were of a generally good standard but, in contrast to these and Street's comfortable housing, remote miners' settlements on Exmoor and the Brendon Hills were provided with industrial housing in the true sense. They were short-lived, for the lure of iron minerals was their only reason for existing, and most now lie in ruins. Frederic Knight built cottages for the Dowlais Co.'s miners on Exmoor in the 1850s. Nine miners and their families were living in cottages at Cornham Ford by 1856 and there were other cottages built at Wheal Eliza, the latter now in ruins above the mine (SS 784381). The Plymouth Co. built rows of cottages at Simonsbath, while in some places cowsheds were converted to cottages, but activities did not last long.

On Brendon Hill (ST 024344), however, quite a community was established when the iron mines and mineral railway were developed in the 1850s. By the 1870s there were over 250 people living here in 60 cottages, some of which only had one bedroom. The Brendon Hills Iron Ore Co. leased Sea View House near the top of the railway incline for its mine captains in 1854, but by 1863 they had built four cottages at Raleigh's Cross Mine, six cottages each at Church Cottages and Beulah Cottages, and three in Somerset Terrace at Sminhays. A scheme was started in 1865 to build 30 more but only half were completed. The railway company had also erected ten wooden houses in their goods yard. Seven cottages of Brick Row were built on the site of demolished 'Turf Huts' near the incline.

There were three chapels at Brendon Hill. The Beulah Chapel was built in 1861 by the Bible Christians, the Wesleyans had a chapel above the stables of Sea View House, and the Anglicans erected a corrugated iron church which was also used as a school. There were shops and Brown's Temperance House, with seven 'superior cottages' built nearby. The house later became Davis's Stores. The company village was strongly teetotal and the Brendon Hill & Gupworthy Temperance Society was among the organisations here. In 1865 a miners' reading room and institute was incorporated into the horizontal winding engine house at Raleigh's Cross Mine.

Once the mines closed, the miners moved away and the village and its cottages soon became deserted. By 1890

Above: *Only the foundations remain of the miners' cottages at Wheal Eliza on Exmoor.*

Top right: *Beulah Chapel was built in 1861 for iron miners and their families at Brendon Hill. It was restored in 1910 and remains in use as the Brendon Hill Methodist Church.*

Bottom right: *'Beulah 1861' maintains the memory of a strong Nonconformist name.*

Trinity Street in Frome, with early textile workers' houses and the Holy Trinity church of 1838.

The Boden Institute in Mill Lane at Chard, with the Boden lace factory beyond. Henry and Walter Boden opened their workers' institute in 1892.

only the terraces at Beulah and Sminhays had survived demolition. The 'Iron Church' was dismantled and re-erected at the Wansbrough paper mill down in Watchet. Only Sea View House, the Temperance House (now a farmhouse), Beulah Chapel and a few overgrown foundations remind us of this once thriving place at 1000ft (305m) above sea level. Further west there was a smaller community of about 100 at Gupworthy (SS 967353) where miners and their families lived in terraced cottages of The Square and Pleasant Row. A Bible Christian chapel was converted from two cottages in The Square. The nearest inn was 2 miles away. The mining company owned a few other cottages, including two at Bearland Wood Mine and three at Eisen Hill.

Churches and chapels were built for workers elsewhere. The Lawton family were Wesleyans and provided a chapel at their Stapley Silk Mill (ST 188136). After the mill closed it was used by the Blackdown Hills Mission in 1884–1904. Frome's strong tradition of Nonconformity is illustrated, for example, by the complex of Wesleyan Methodist Chapel (1810), with manse, schoolroom and headmaster's house at Wesley Slope. Rivalling this, Christ Church was built along Christchurch West in 1818 for the 'labouring poor' on Packhorse Field where Radstock colliers' packhorses had grazed, while Trinity Church (1838) blocks off the end of Trinity Street in an impressive manner.

Institutes were provided by industrialists for the general improvement of the working classes. Frome's Literary Institute was built in 1868 as a gift by the clothier John Sinkin. Boden's Institute was built in 1892 by Henry and Walter Boden next to their lace factory in Mill Lane, Chard, to benefit their employees' education. It was later the town's public library before that moved into Holyrood Mill. At Street, William Stephens Clark built Crispin Hall in 1885, a handsome building in the High Street containing a working-mens' club, a hall with a capacity of 1100, a geology museum and a library, with a gymnasium added five years later.

Architecture of the industrial period is an important feature of this final chapter. There are many other buildings or structures worthy of consideration but space permits, literally, the briefest mention of this potentially broad subject. These include schools, hospitals, workhouses, prisons, market halls, inns, cinemas and public parks. Williton, for example, has an outstanding example of a workhouse of 1840 designed by George Gilbert Scott, while Vivary Park at Taunton is an excellent late-Victorian public park, complete with cast-iron gates, bandstand and elaborate fountain. These deserve our attention as much as the mines and mills because they were all monuments erected during Somerset's Age of Steam.

SELECTED FURTHER READING

GENERAL

M. Atkinson, ed., *Exmoor's Industrial Archaeology* (Tiverton, 1997)

R. Atthill, *Old Mendip* (Newton Abbot, 1964, with later editions)

R. Atthill, *Mendip: A New Study* (Newton Abbot, 1976)

C.A. & R.A. Buchanan, *The Batsford Guide to the Industrial Archaeology of Central Southern England* (1980)

D. Defoe, *A Tour Through the Whole Island of Great Britain* (1724–26)

W. Marshall, *The Rural Economy of the West of England* (vol. 2, 1796)

B.J. Murless, 'Whither (or Wither?) Somerset's Industrial Heritage?', in C.J. Webster (ed.), *Somerset Archaeology* (Taunton, 2000), 111–16

W. Page, ed., *Victoria History of Somerset*, vol. 2 (1911), 353–433

H. Riley & R. Wilson-North, *The Field Archaeology of Exmoor* (Swindon, 2001)

D. Warren, ed., *Somerset's Industrial Heritage* (SIAS Survey No.8, 1996)

G. Watkins, *Stationary Steam Engines of Great Britain, Vol. 7* (Ashbourne, 2003)

SIAS Bulletins: Somerset Industrial Archaeological Society, 1975–2003

FARMING IN THE INDUSTRIAL AGE

S. Bartlett, 'Hinton Mill, Mudford', *SIAS Bulletin*, 82 (December 1999), 2–4

J. Billingsley, *A General View of the Agriculture in the County of Somerset* (2nd ed., Bath, 1798)

F. French, 'Athelney and the Withy Industry', *The Somerset Year Book*, 21 (1922), 65–67

B. Hook, A.P. Ward & B.J. Murless, 'Horse gins in Somerset', *SIAS Jnl*, 1 (1975) 31–34

M.H. Jones, 'Simonsbath Sawmill', *SIAS Bulletin*, 77 (April 1988), 2–13

B.J. Murless, 'Gerbeston Manor Mill', *SIAS Bulletin*, 71 (April 1996), 14–17

J. Penoyre, 'Drayton – A Victorian Farmstead', *SIAS Bulletin*, 67 (December 1994), 18–22

D. Rabson, 'The turbine house at Hornshay Farm, Nynehead', *SIAS Bulletin*, 88 (December 2001), 2-9

D. Walker, *Somerset Farming: A Hundred Years of Change* (Tiverton, 2001)

A.P. Ward, 'A Withy Boiler at Burrow Bridge', *SIAS Jnl*, 1 (1975), 12–15

D. Warren, 'Water-power on Farms in West Somerset', *SIAS Jnl*, 1 (1975), 5–11

M. Williams, *The Draining of the Somerset Levels* (Cambridge, 1960)

SOMERSET STONE

Anon, 'Newland Quarry', *SIAS Jnl*, 3 (1981), 38–39

P. Daniel, 'Notes on Site Visit to Snowdon Caves, Chard, *SIAS Bulletin*, 71 (April 1997), 12–14

H. Prudden, *Geology and Landscape of Taunton Deane* (Taunton, 2001)

P. Stanier, *Stone Quarry Landscapes* (Stroud, 2000), 76–82

C. Tilley, 'The West Somerset Slate Industry', *SIAS Bulletin*, 61 (December 1992), 20–24

C. Trask, *Norton-sub-Hamdon: notes on the parish and the manor and on Ham Hill* (Taunton, 1898)

F.S. Wallis, 'Draycott Stone and Marble, Somerset', *Proc. Bristol Nat. Soc.*, 32 (1973), 275–280

D.W. Warren, 'Newland Quarry', *SIAS Jnl*, 2 (1977), 36–39

LIME BURNING

Anon, 'Limekilns at Milverton', *SIAS Jnl*, 1 (1975), 46

Anon, 'Tengore Lane Limekilns', *SIAS Bulletin*, 44, (April 1987), 5–6

M. Anderson, 'Lime Kilns in Stoke Saint Mary', *SIAS Bulletin*, 43 (December 1986), 3–4

P. Daniel, 'Limeburning in Somerset', *SIAS Bulletin*, 45 (September 1987), 10–12

P. Daniel, 'Limekilns at Castle Hill, Wiveliscombe', *SIAS Bulletin*, 49 (December 1988), 10–13

P. Daniel, 'Limeburning and geology in Somerset', *SIAS Bulletin*, 55 (December 1990), 6–14

P. Daniel, 'A Limeburning Miscellany', *SIAS Bulletin*, 69 (August 1995), 2–7

P. Daniel, 'Limeburning at Great Elm, near Frome', *SIAS Bulletin*, 82 (December 1999), 5–11

P. Daniel, 'Limeburning in Priddy', *SIAS Bulletin*, 86 (April 2001), 8–15

P. Daniel & B.J. Murless, 'Limekilns at Warren Bay', *SIAS Bulletin*, 62 (April 1993), 2–8

P. Daniel & B.J. Murless, 'A limekiln complex at Down End, Puriton', *SIAS Bulletin*, 65 (April 1994), 15–22

B. Murless, 'Tengore lane Limekilns', *SIAS Bulletin*, 43 (December 1986), 13–16

E. Taylor, 'Limekilns on Mendip', *BIAS Jnl*, 18 (1986), 10–11

A.P. Ward, 'A Limekiln near Fitzhead', *SIAS Jnl*, 1 (1975), 39–43

MINING FOR METALS

Anon, 'Kennisham Hill Engine House', *SIAS Jnl*, 3 (1981), 40

P. Bell, 'Langham Pit – Ropeway from Kennesome Hill', *SIAS Bulletin*, 55 (December 1990), 17–20

J.W. Gough, *The Mines of Mendip* (Newton Abbot, 2nd ed., 1967)

J. Hamilton & J.F. Lawrence, *Men and Mining on the Quantocks* (Bracknell, 1970)

F. Hawtin, 'Industrial Archaeology at Charterhouse-on-Mendip', *Industrial Archaeology*, 7 (1970), 171–175

M. Jones, 'Excavations at Chargot Wood and Langham Hill', *SIAS Bulletin*, 70 (December 1995), 9–13

C.J. Schmitz, 'An account of Mendip calamine mining in the early 1870s', *PSANS*, 120 (1976), 81–83

W.I. Stanton & A.G. Clarke, 'Cornish Miners at Charterhouse-on-Mendip', *Proc. Univ. Bristol Spelaeol. Soc.*, 17 (1984), 29–54

M. Todd, Charterhouse on Mendip: interim report on excavations in 1994', *PSANS*, 138 (1994), 75–79

COAL MINING

J. Cornwell, *Collieries of Somerset & Bristol* (Ashbourne, 2001)

C.G. Down, & A.J. Warrington, *The History of the Somerset Coalfield* (Newton Abbot, 1971)

S. Gould, *The Somerset Coalfield* (SIAS Survey No.11, 1999)

S. Gould, 'Coke Ovens at Vobster Breach Colliery', *Inds. Arch. Review*, XVII (1994), 79–85

S. Gould & P. Bell, 'Coke Ovens at Vobster Breach Colliery', *SIAS Bulletin*, 69 (August 1995), 20–24

B.J. Murless, 'Vobster Breach Colliery', *SIAS Bulletin*, 55 (December 1990), 15–16

S. Miles, 'Oil at Kilve', *SIAS Bulletin*, 70 (December 1995), 19–23

CLAY INDUSTRIES

R. Coleman-Smith, *Donyatt Pottery 11th century – 1939* (SIAS Survey No.9, 1996)

F. Hawtin & B.J. Murless, 'Bridgwater Glasshouse', *SIAS Jnl*, 3 (1981), 2–5

L. Isaac & I. Parrott, *Brickmaking in Wellington* (Wellington, 3rd ed., 2002)

M. Maxwell, 'Bath bricks', *SIAS Jnl*, 3 (1981), 41

B.J. Murless, 'The Bath brick industry at Bridgwater: a preliminary survey', *SIAS Jnl*, 1 (1975), 18–28

B.J. Murless, 'Taunton Brickyards', *SIAS Jnl*, 3 (1981), 28–35

B.J. Murless, *Somerset Brick & Tile Manufacturers: A Brief History & Gazetteer* (SIAS Survey No.13, 2000)

E. Wide, 'Brick making at Bishop's Hull, 1940–1950', *SIAS Bulletin*, 68 (April 1995), 4–14

CORN MILLING

M. Allen, 'The Spillers of Bridgwater', *SIAS Bulletin*, 73 (December 1996), 17–23

M. Bodman, *Mills around Wiveliscombe: Watermill sites on the upper River Tone and Hillfarrance Brook* (SIAS Survey No.12, 2000)

M. Bodman, 'Mills along the Alham, *SIAS Bulletin*, 86 (April 2001), 16–25

C.A. Buchanan, 'Shapwick Windmill', *SIAS Jnl*, 1 (1975), 16–17

A.J. Coulthard & M. Watts, *Windmills of Somerset and the men who worked them* (1979)

B. Shingler, 'Gants Mill, Bruton', *SIAS Bulletin*, 92 (April 2003), 4–12

D. Warren, *Mills of the Isle and its tributaries* (SIAS Survey No.15, 2001)

M. Watts, 'Windmills of Somerset', *BIAS Jnl*, 6 (1973), 21–31

M. Watts, *Somerset Windmills* (Keynsham, 1975)

M. Watts, 'Documentary evidence of windmills at Walton', *SIAS Jnl*, 2 (1977), 31–32

BREWING AND MALTING

F. Davis, *The Anglo: The History of the Anglo Bavarian Brewery, 1864–1994*, (Shepton Mallet, 1994)

S. Fussell, 'Sidney Fussell & Sons Limited, Cross Keys Brewery, Rode, Somerset', *SIAS Bulletin*, 90 (August 2002), 20-24

F. & P. Hawtin, 'Stogumber Brewery, 1840–1973, *SIAS Jnl*, 2 (1977), 15–19

M. Miles, *Hancock's Brewery Wiveliscombe* (SIAS Survey No.2, 1985)

M. Miles, 'Oakhill Maltings', *SIAS Bulletin*, 44 (April 1987), 13–15

M. Miles, 'Halse Malthouse', *SIAS Bulletin*, 45 (September 1987), 3–9

M. Miles, 'Halse Maltings, Somerset', *Inds. Arch. Review*, XI, No.2 (1989), 136–140

CIDER AND CREAM

A. Heeley & M. Vidal, *Joseph Harding, Cheddar Cheese-Maker* (Glastonbury, 1996)

P. Legg, *Cidermaking in Somerset* (Glastonbury, 1984)

TEXTILES

S. Buchanan, 'The Woollen Industry and its Successors in the Taunton Region', *SIAS Bulletin*, 61 (December 1992), 8–15

J. Coles, 'Ilminster's Shirt and Collar Industry', *SIAS Bulletin*, 92 (April 2003) 22–24

J. Doble, B. Hodgson, G. Lindsay, B. Shingler, L. Snelgrove & P. Stokes, *The Silk Industry in Evercreech* (Evercreech, 2001)

J. Hagen & M.P. Fox, *More Than Two Hundred Years: Wellington and the Foxes* (Wellington, 2000)

L. Hoskins, *A Plain Net Centenary 1895–1995* (Chard, 1995)

K. Rogers, *Wiltshire & Somerset Woollen Mills* (Edington, 1976)

C.G. Taylor, 'William Henderson and the Horsehair Power-loom', *SIAS Bulletin*, 89 (April 2002), 18–27

D. Warren, 'Snowdon Collar Works, Chard', *SIAS Bulletin*, 85 (December 2000), 14–24

M. Williams & S. Ely, *John Boyd's Horsehair Factory (the Ansford Factory), Castle Cary, Somerset: English Heritage Buildings Report* (Swindon, 2001)

LEATHER INDUSTRIES

L.H. Barber, *Clarks of Street, 1825–1950* (Street, 1950)

L. Brooke, *Glove-Making in Yeovil and District* (Yeovil, 1993)

J. Harper, *Sheep, Donkeys and the Pig: 400 Years of Gloving* (Yeovil, 2000)

P. Lawson-Clarke, *The Glovers of Yeovil* (South Petherton, 1996)

P. Lawson-Clarke, 'The Glovers of Yeovil', *SIAS Bulletin*, 82 (December 1999), 13–21

FOUNDERS AND ENGINEERS

Anon, 'Parrett Ironworks', *SIAS Jnl*, 3 (1981), 36–38

M. Bodman, 'William Willmitt, Wellington iron founder', *SIAS Bulletin*, 70 (December 1995), 16–18

K. D'Maurney Gibbons, *A Path to the Door: A Chronicle of Petters' Inventions, Businesses, People, Engines and Aircraft, 1895–1995* (Stroud, 1995)

K. Gifford & R. Gallop, *Fussells Ironworks Mells* (Bristol, 2000)

P. Petter, *The Story of Petters Ltd* (Westbury, 1989)

R. Stiles & J. Cornwell, 'Fussell's ironworks Mells, Somerset', *BIAS Jnl*, 8 (1975), 14–16

D. Warren, 'Chidgley's Foundry, Watchet', *SIAS Jnl*, 3 (1981), 6-9

D. Warren, *A village industry: W.H.Pool and Sons, Engineers, Chipstable* (SIAS Survey No.4, 1988)

D. Warren, *Dening of Chard: Agricultural Engineers 1828–1965* (SIAS Survey No.6, 1989)

D. Warren, 'Joseph Hawker and the development of the crawler tractor', *SIAS Bulletin*, 72 (August 1996), 12-19

D. Warren, 'The Buckland St Mary Rake and Gate Manufactory', *SIAS Bulletin*, 76 (December 1997), 2–9

PAPER MAKING

N. Edwards, 'Paper making at Watchet', *SIAS Bulletin*, 62 (April 1993), 9–12

M. McGarvie, *Bowlingreen Mill: A Centenary History* (Street, 1979)

A.H. Shorter, 'Paper and Board Mills in Somerset', *SDNQ*, XXV, pt CCXLIV (1950), 245–57
D. Tomlin, 'Paper Making in Somerset', *SIAS Bulletin*, 60 (August 1992), 4–9
M. Watts, 'Wookey Hole Paper Mill', *BIAS Jnl*, 7 (1974), 26–7

ROADS

J. Bentley & P. Daniel, 'Investigation of Turnpike Road North of Shepton Mallet', *SIAS Bulletin*, 77 (April 1998), 15-17
J. Bentley & B.J. Murless, *Somerset Roads, Parts 1 & 2* (Taunton, 1985 & 1987)
C.A. Buchanan, 'The Langport, Somerton and Castle Cary Turnpike Trust', *SIAS Jnl*, 2 (1977), 20–23
C.A. Buchanan, 'The Wells Turnpike Trust', *SIAS Jnl*, 3 (1981), 10–16
S. Buchanan, 'The Shepton Mallet Turnpike Trust', *SIAS Bulletin*, 77 (April 1998), 17–21
Chard History Group, *The Roads, Canals and Railways of Chard* (Chard, 2001)
L.A. Clarke, *The Minehead United Turnpike Trust* (SIAS Survey No.16, 2002)
D. Gerhold, 'The Whitmarsh Family, Carriers and Coachmasters of Taunton and Yeovil', *PSANS*, 143 (1999), 117-31
D.J. Greenfield, 'The County Bridge Papers', *SIAS Jnl*, 2 (1977), 27–30
R. de Z. Hall, 'John Loudon McAdam and his descendants in Somerset', *SDNQ*, XXVII, pt CCLXX (1959), 258-61
R.H. Spiro, 'John Loudon McAdam in Somerset and Dorset', *SDNQ*, XXVII, pt CCLXIII (1956), 85–92

CANALS AND RIVER NAVIGATIONS

Anon, 'Grand Western Canal: Notes & News', *SIAS Jnl*, 1 (1975), 43–45
G. Body & R. Gallop, *The Glastonbury Canal* (Bristol, 2001)
G. Body & R. Gallop, *The Parrett Navigation* (Bristol, 2002)
C.A. Buchanan, *The Bridgwater and Taunton Canal* (SIAS Survey No.1, 1984)
K.R. Clew, *The Dorset and Somerset Canal* (Newton Abbot, 1971)
B. George, *James Green: Canal Builder and County Surveyor* (Tiverton, 1997)
A. Graham, 'A survey of the mid-19th-century buildings of the Chard Canal basin and wharves,' *PSANS*, 143 (1999), 141–49
A. Graham, 'The Buildings of the Chard Canal Basin and Wharves, *SIAS Bulletin*, 83 (April 2000), 2–11
D. Greenfield, 'The Tone Aqueduct at Creech St Michael', *SIAS Bulletin*, 90 (August 2002), 2–7
C. Hadfield, *The Canals of South West England* (Newton Abbot, 1967)
H. Harris, *The Grand Western Canal* (Newton Abbot, 1973)
T. Haskell, *By Waterway to Taunton – A History of the Bridgwater and Taunton Canal and the River Tone Navigation* (Tiverton, 1994)
D. Warren, 'Charlton pump house', *SIAS Bulletin* 50 (April 1989), 4–10

RAILWAYS AND TRAMWAYS

C.G. Down & A.J. Warrington, *The Newbury Railway* (1979)
M. Hawkins, *Somerset and Dorset Then and Now* (Wellingborough, 1986)
M.H. Jones, 'The Prehistory of the West Somerset Mineral Railway', *SIAS Jnl*, 2 (1977), 4–14
C.G. Maggs, *Branch Lines of Somerset* (Stroud, 1993)
M. Oakley, *Somerset Railway Stations* (Wimborne, 2002)
R. Sellick, *The West Somerset Mineral Railway and the story of the Brendon Hills Iron Mines* (Newton Abbot, 2nd ed., 1970)

PORTS AND SHIPPING

G. Body & R.Gallop, *Dunball Village, Works & Wharf* (Bristol, 2001)
C. Handley, *Maritime Activities of the Somerset & Dorset Railway* (Bath 2001)
B.J. Murless, *Bridgwater Docks and the River Parrett* (Taunton, 1983)
D. Warren, 'Lilstock Harbour', *SIAS Bulletin*, 52 (December 1989), 1–3

WATER SUPPLY AND DRAINAGE

C. Doble, 'The hydraulic ram and its Somerset connections', *SIAS Bulletin*, 80 (April 1999), 7–11
D. Gledhill, 'The Gas Engines at the Westford Pumping Station', *SIAS Bulletin*, 73 (December 1996), 13–16
E.R. Kelting, 'The Rivers and Sea Walls of Somerset', *PSANS*, 112 (1968), 12–20

I. Miles, *Bogs and inundations* (SIAS Survey No.7, n.d.)

I. Miles, 'Westonzoyland Pumping Station', *SIAS Jnl*, 3 (1981), 26–27

M. Miles, 'Steam Eroding Boats of the Somerset Levels', *SIAS Bulletin*, 61 (December 1992), 4–7

M. Miles, 'Eroding Boats, Part Three', *SIAS Bulletin*, 66 (August 1994), 14–20

B.J. Murless, 'Dark Lane Water Tower, Wellington', *SIAS Bulletin*, 70 (December 1995), 14–15

D. Warren, 'Westford Pumping Station Survey', *SIAS Bulletin*, 47 (April 1988), 11–13

D. Warren, *Rural Water Supply in Somerset* (SIAS Survey No.10, 1998)

D. Warren, 'Doulting Water', *SIAS Bulletin*, 84 (August 2000), 10–19

M. Williams, *The Draining of the Somerset Levels* (Cambridge, 1970)

LIGHT, HEAT AND POWER

D. Gledhill, *Taunton Gas 1816-1949* (SIAS Survey No.5, 1989)

D. Gledhill, 'Gas in Somerset – A Few Notes', *SIAS Bulletin*, 52 (December 1989), 4–8

D. Gledhill, 'Gas engines and water-wheels in Somerset power stations', *SIAS Bulletin*, 70 (December 1995), 2-8

D. Gledhill & P. Daniel, 'Wedmore Gasworks', *SIAS Bulletin*, 66 (August 1994), 2–9

D. Gledhill & P. Lamb, *Electricity in Taunton 1809–1948* (SIAS Survey No.3, 1986)

H. Hudson, 'Wedmore Electric Light and Power Company: A Recollection', *SIAS Bulletin*, 81 (August 1999), 8-17

P. Lamb & E. Lodge, 'Christy Brothers in the South West', *SIAS Bulletin*, 87 (August 2001), 21–25

D.P.J. Stafford, 'The Listed Hole – St Audries Gasworks', *SIAS Bulletin*, 59 (April 1992), 12–14

D. Warren, 'Acetylene Street Lighting in North Petherton', *SIAS Bulletin*, 44 (April 1987), 11–12

HOUSING AND RECREATION

R. Leech, *Early Industrial Housing: The Trinity Area of Frome* (1981)

Several of the books and papers in this short list cover more than one industry, although they are only named once, and most will give further sources of information. Robin Atthill's classic *Old Mendip* is a good case in point. Originally published in 1964 during the formative years of industrial archaeology as a discipline, it contains chapters on many different aspects of industry and transport. Angus and Sandy Buchanan's survey of Southern England's industrial archaeology, now more than twenty years old, includes a significant chapter on Somerset. A more recent gazetteer, edited by Derrick Warren for SIAS, portrays the state of industrial archaeology in Somerset in 1996.

Railways, of course, have been very widely published and there is some material there for the industrial archaeologist. In addition, maps, guidebooks, trade directories (Kelly's, Harrod's, Pigot's, etc) and newspapers all create a useful picture of industrial activity. Periodicals with occasional references to industries include the *Somerset & Dorset Notes & Queries (SDNQ)* and the *Proceedings of the Somerset Archaeological & Natural History Society (PSANS)*. All these and more can be consulted at the Somerset Studies Library in Taunton, or some local libraries.

I have deliberately drawn on the publications of the Somerset Industrial Archaeological Society, all of which are held in the Somerset Studies Library, Taunton. Much work has gone before me and I hope in some way to have brought this together into a readable account. Because of the wealth of published material, primary sources were not consulted for this book. However, the Somerset County Record Office in Taunton contains archives covering a very wide range of industries and a visit is highly recommended. There is also potential research to be found in those industries and topics hardly touched on here.

INDEX

A

acetylene 145
aeroplanes 9, 86, 90
agriculture 7, 8, 11, 15–18
airfields 12
Albion Silk Mill 73, 148
Allen, C. & Co. 13, 83, 84, 86
Allerford 49–51, 53, 110
Allermoor pumping station 97, 141, 142
Anglo-Bavarian Brewery 9, 60, 63, 146
Ansford 68, 77. 78. 96, 99
Aplin & Barrett 10, 68
Appold. J.G. 141
aqueducts 105, 106, 110, 111, 112, 113
Armfield, Joseph 53
Arnold & Hancock Ltd 60, 62, 63
Ashford Water Treatment Works 138, 139
Ash Priors 28
Ashton Windmill 56–58
Avalon Leatherboard Co. 94
Axbridge 8, 36, 117, 121, 139, 143
Axe, River 91, 92, 103, 139

B

bacon factory 68, 73
Bakelite Museum 53
Barham Brothers 43, 44, 46, 128
barite 36
Barle, River 18, 32, 88, 97, 98
Bason Bridge 68
Bath & West Show 12, 84
Bath brick 8, 44, 46, 47
Bath Trust 95
Battscombe Quarry 23, 25
Bearland Wood Mine 32
Bertha mud scraper 11, 128, 151
Billingsley, John 7, 15, 25, 69, 95, 96
Bird, R. & Co. 76
Bishop Bros 13, 88
Bishop's Hull 44, 46, 69, 91, 113
Bishops Lydeard 16, 49, 55
Bishops Lydeard Mill 49, 83, 88
Bishops Lydeard Station 118, 119
Black Bridge 122
Black Dog Trust 95, 101
Blackdown Hills 7, 19, 27, 31, 101
Blackland Iron Mine 33
Blackmoor Lead Works 34, 35
Blathwayt, G.W. 132
Blue Anchor 46, 118, 134
blue lias 8, 20, 22, 24, 27, 28, 30
Board & Co. 30
boat lifts 10, 110
Boden & Co. 73, 74, 150, 151
Bossington Beach limekiln 29, 30, 132
Bowlingreen Mill 80, 93, 94
Boyd, John 77, 78, 147
Brean Down 12, 130
Brendon Hills 8, 11, 12, 24, 28, 30–32, 101, 122, 130, 149
Brendon Hills Iron Ore Co. 31, 32, 122
breweries 59–66
brickyards 8, 14, 43–48
bridges 9, 10, 84, 88, 95, 96, 97, 98, 108, 113, 117, 121, 122, 140

Bridgwater 5, 7, 8, 9, 10, 11, 12, 13, 43-47, 55, 66, 88, 89, 97, 98, 106, 107, 115, 118, 122, 127, 128, 130, 133, 138, 139, 143, 145, 146
Bridgwater & Taunton Canal 5, 11, 13, 30, 103, 106–110, 113, 128
Bridgwater Dock 11, 55, 106, 127-130, 133
Bridgwater Gas Light Co. 143
Bridgwater Iron Works 88
Bridgwater Steam Flour Mills 9, 55
Bridgwater Town Bridge 10, 97, 98, 127
Bridgwater Trust 95
Bristol & Exeter Railway 11, 13, 30, 46, 70, 106, 110, 113, 114–118, 122, 128, 130
Bristol Channel 110, 127, 132
Bristol Trust 95
Bristol Waterworks Co. 139
British Cellophane Ltd 12, 126, 139
Broomfield Consols Copper & Silver-Lead Mining Co. 36
Brown & May 23
Brown family 72
Browne, John & Co. 44, 46, 47
Brue, River 79, 103, 139, 142
Brushford 146
brush making 9, 14, 78
Brunel, I.K. 11, 88, 115, 118, 122, 128
Bruton 49, 52, 69, 73, 96, 99, 100, 117, 135, 143
Bryscombe Quarry 19
Buckingham Mine 8, 36
Buckland Dinham 39, 40
Buckland St Mary Rake & Gate Manufactory 84
Burcott Mill 49, 53
Burnham 7, 11, 44, 61, 66, 117, 130, 133, 134, 143, 146
Burrowbridge 97, 100, 103, 141
Burrow Farm Mine 31, 32, 122, 124
Butler & Tanner 94
butter 9, 15, 67, 68

C

calamine 8, 35
Callow Hill Quarry, 23, 25
canals 10, 11, 37, 103–114
Cannington 36
canvas 9, 68, 74, 76
Carnarvon Pit 31, 122
Castle Cary 9, 22 68, 69, 73, 77, 78, 86, 95, 96, 100, 102, 116, 122, 117, 118, 143, 147
Castle Hill limekilns 27
cement making 8, 30, 41, 47, 84, 130
Chaffcombe 67, 68
Chaingate Mill 54
Chandos Glass Cone 47
chapels 12, 149–151
Chard 7, 9, 12, 14, 19, 40, 53, 67, 68, 69, 72, 73, 74, 78, 83, 85–87, 95, 100, 106, 110, 113, 114, 116, 135, 136, 143, 144, 146, 150, 151
Chard Canal 10, 110, 112, 113, 114, 116, 120
Chard Junction 68, 117, 146
Chard Station 117
Chard Trust 95, 100
Chargot Wood 32
Charlton Adam 25, 28
Charlton Brewery 60, 64
Charlton Mackrell 22

Charlton pumping station 13, 109, 110
Charlton Viaduct 121
Charterhouse 8, 33, 34, 35
Cheddar 9, 23–25, 34, 55, 67, 91, 117, 121
Cheddar reservoir 11, 139
Cheddar Valley & Yatton Railway 117, 121
cheese making 9, 15, 67
chert 19
Chelynch quarries 21, 22 124
Chewton Lead Works 35
Chewton Mendip 34
Chidgey, John 9, 16, 84
Chilton Street Mill 55
Chilton Tile Factory 46
Chilton Trinity 44, 46
cider 9, 15, 62, 67, 92, 146
Clapton Mill 49, 51, 54
Clark, C.& J. 9, 79, 80, 81.144, 148, 149
Clark, Son & Morland 79, 80
clay industries 8, 43-48
coal mines 7, 8, 12, 37-41
Coates & Co. 78
Cockey, Edward 9, 12, 83, 86, 144
Cogload junction 117
coke ovens 39
Coker Works 74
Coldharbour Mill 70, 76
Coleford 8, 37, 38, 105, 149
collar making 9, 78, 86
Colley Lane Patent Tile & Pottery Works 44
Colthurst, Symons & Co. Ltd 44, 46
Colton Pits 31, 122
Comberow Incline 122–124
Combe St Nicholas 53
Combe Sydenham 49, 53
Combwich 36, 41, 44, 106, 128, 133
Coombs, C. 53
copper mines 7, 8, 32, 33, 36
Cornham Ford 31, 33, 149
corn mills 7, 8, 9, 14, 15, 17, 49–58, 146
Court Mill 53
Cow & Gate 68
cranes 20–23, 83, 86, 129–131
Cranmore Station 24, 118, 124
creameries 8, 67, 68
Creech St Michael 9, 12, 88, 91, 93, 98, 104, 112, 113, 121, 144
Crewkerne 7, 9, 12, 14, 44, 46, 49, 60, 61, 69, 74, 77, 78, 95, 118, 120, 143, 147
Crewkerne United Brewery 60
Crimson Hill Tunnel 113
Croscombe 54, 94
Cross Keys Brewery 65, 66
Culverwell, J. & Co. 66, 80, 88
Currymoor pumping station 141, 142
Cutsey Farm 17

D

dairies 8, 15, 67, 68
Darshill 70, 73
Dawe, J. 76
Day, A. & H. 84
Day, F. 78
Defoe, Daniel 7, 9, 10, 11, 67, 69, 80, 103, 128, 147
Dening & Co. 85, 86

Devon & Somerset Railway 9, 22, 28, 116
diesel engines 18, 54, 67, 70, 90, 136–138, 142
Dodington 8, 36
Donne, T.S. & Sons 77, 78
Donyatt potteries 8, 48
Dorset & Somerset Canal 7, 37, 39, 105, 106, 126
Dorset Central Railway 117
Doulting 7, 8, 21, 22, 96, 124, 135
Dowlais Iron Works 33, 149
Dowlish Ford Mills 75, 76, 80
Down End Cement Works 30
Downhead Quarry 24, 124
Downside Abbey 144
drainage 104, 139–142
Draycott marble 19
Drayton Farm 17
Dulcote Leather Board Co. 93
Dulverton 9, 16, 33, 72, 84, 88, 121
Dulverton Electric Light Co. 146
Dunball 8, 12, 30, 44
Dunball Wharf 130
Dunster 22, 48, 69, 72, 84, 96, 145
Dunster Mill 49, 53
Dunwear works 44

E
East Harptree Lead Works 34, 35, 36
East Quantoxhead 30
East Saltmoor pumping station 141, 142
East Somerset Railway 11, 21, 24, 115, 117, 118, 124
Easton & Amos 14, 140, 141
Easton & Waldegrave 13, 86, 146
Ebbw Vale Co. 8, 31
Eclipse Peat Co. 41, 42, 125
Edford 39, 105
edge tools 9, 83, 84
Eisen Hill iron mines 32, 122, 151
electricity 12, 16, 18, 40, 67, 68, 70, 74, 84, 90, 94, 134, 143, 144–146
Elworthy Bros & Co. Ltd 72
engineers 8, 9, 13, 15, 51, 66, 83–90
England, Herbert 55
English & Bristol Channels Ship Canal 106
Ennor, Nicholas 35
eroder boats 88, 128, 141
Evercreech 9, 68, 73, 148
Evercreech Junction 11, 44, 46, 68, 96, 117, 121
Exe Valley Electricity Co. 146
Exford 28
Exford Iron Co. 33
Exmoor 6, 8, 9, 15, 16, 22, 24, 28, 29, 30, 31, 32, 33, 46, 61, 63, 72, 92, 96, 124, 146, 149
Exmoor Mines Research Group 6

F
farming 7, 8, 15–18
Firepool limekilns 30
Firepool lock 106, 109, 110
Firepool pumping station 118
flax 9, 17, 73, 74–76, 77, 78, 84, 85, 103
Ford Bros 16, 88, 138
Fosse Way 10, 37, 68, 95, 96
foundries 9, 83-90
Fox Bros 9, 69, 70–71, 144, 146, 147
French, E. & W.C. Ltd 14, 79, 147, 148
Frome 7, 9, 12, 13, 14, 23, 27, 37, 58, 60, 68-70, 83, 86, 94, 96, 101, 102, 105, 106, 116, 117, 124, 147, 150, 151

Frome Gas Co. 143, 144
Frome station 118
Frome Trust 95
fulling mills 7, 69, 70, 72
Fulwood Water Treatment Works 139
Fussells Iron Works 9, 83, 84
Fussell, James 83, 84, 106
Fussell, Sydney & Sons Ltd 66

G
Galhampton 86, 100, 101, 102
Gane, A. & Sons 22
Gants Mill 52, 53, 54, 69, 73
gas engines 44, 70, 76, 85, 88, 136, 144, 145, 146
gasworks 10, 12, 86, 132, 143–145
generators 145–146
Gerbeston Manor 16, 88
Gifford, Fox & Co. 14, 73, 74
Gilkes, Gilbert 17, 23, 53
Glastonbury 9, 44, 46, 54, 66, 79, 80, 82, 85, 96, 102, 103, 114, 117, 135, 139, 143,
Glastonbury Brick, Tile & Pipe Co. 46
Glastonbury Canal 114, 116
Glenthorne limekiln 27, 30
gloves 7, 9, 10, 80, 82
Gold Corner pumping station 142
Govier, W. 84
Grand Western Canal 10, 106, 110, 111, 113, 115
Grand Western Canal Trust 6, 110
Great Bow Bridge 104
Great Western Railway 22, 93, 110, 115, 117, 121
Green, James 110, 113
greensand 19
Gupworthy 16, 31, 32, 84, 122, 151
gypsum 8, 30, 92, 134

H
Halse malthouse 59
Hambridge Brewery 64, 65
Hambridge Mill 51
Ham Hill & Doulting Stone Co. 21
Ham Hill quarries 7, 8, 19–21, 28
Ham Mills 54, 103
Hancock, W. & Sons Ltd 62
handle houses 70
Hard Stone Firms Ltd 22
Hart, Arthur & Son Ltd 76
Hawker, Joseph 86
Hayward, Richard & Co. Ltd 76
Heasley Mill 72
helicopters 90
hemp 9, 74–76, 103
Hennet, George 82, 88
Hennet, Spink & Else 88, 98, 134
Highbridge 44, 47, 48, 58, 68, 96, 103, 114, 127, 128, 139, 141, 143, 144
Highbridge Waterworks 136
Highbridge Wharf 114, 117, 128, 130
Higher Flax Mills 78
Hinkley Point 12, 145
Hinton Farm Mill 16
Hinton St George 144
Hockey, John 86
Hoddinott, James 13, 73
Hodgkinson, W.S. 91, 147
Holcombe 60
Holford 80, 88, 102, 135
Holt Bros Ltd 66
Holyrood Lace Mill 73, 74, 86, 151
Home Farm 17

Honiton & Ilminster Trust 95
Horlicks 68
horse gin 15, 34, 38
horsehair 7, 9, 69, 73, 77, 78, 147
Hortbridge Mill 78
horticulture 8, 18, 41
houses 12, 22, 40, 64, 68, 134, 147–151
Huish Colliery 12, 41
Huish Episcopi 18, 56
Huntspill 47
Huntspill Cut 142
Huntworth Basin 106, 108, 128
Hurstbow Bridge 88, 97
hydraulic rams 17, 88, 135
hydro-electric power 146

I
Ilchester Trust 95
Ilminster 9, 48, 68, 74, 75, 78, 80, 84, 86, 103, 114, 116, 135
Ilminster gasworks 144
inclined planes 10, 110, 113, 114, 122–124
inns 95, 102, 151
institutes 12, 149, 151
Inveresk Paper Co. 91, 92
Ireland 46, 55, 132
iron foundries 9, 12, 33, 83–90, 144, 146
iron mines 8, 12, 31–33, 122, 124, 130, 149
Isle, River 14, 72, 114
Ivelchester & Langport Canal 104

J
Jessop, William 130, 139
John Boyd Textiles Ltd 77, 78, 147

K
Keinton Mandeville 8, 22, 68
kelp 18
Kelway, James & William 8, 18
Kemp, T. & Sons 73
Kennisham Hill Mine 31, 32
kerb stones 22
Kilmersdon 37, 99, 101
Kilve 8, 18, 30, 40, 41
Kingsbury Episcopi 96, 99, 100
King's Sedgemoor Drain 139, 142
Knight, Frederic 32, 33, 124, 149

L
lace mills 9, 14, 73, 74, 86, 144
Landacre Bridge 97
Langham Hill Mine 31, 122
Langport 8, 18, 22, 66, 83, 104, 117, 121, 135
Langport, Somerton & Castle Cary Trust 95, 100, 102
lead mining 7, 8, 30, 33, 34, 36, 95
lead smelting 8, 33, 34, 35, 135
leatherboard 93, 94
leather industries 9, 10, 79–82, 93
lighthouses 7, 11, 88, 130, 133, 134
Lilstock 30, 134
limekilns 7, 8, 25–30, 105, 110,, 118, 132, 134
limestone 8, 19–22, 25–30, 96, 97, 124, 126, 132, 134
Limington Brewery 66
Load Bridge 28, 104, 105
locks 7, 52, 103, 104, 106, 108, 109, 110, 113, 128, 132
locomotives 35, 13, 115, 116, 119, 123, 126
London & South Western Railway 117, 118, 120, 148

Long Sutton 27, 28, 51, 53
Luxborough 30
Lynch malthouse 59

M
Mackintosh Colliery 38, 39
Maiden Beech Brick, Pipe, Tile & Pottery Co. Ltd 46
Major, H.J. & Co. Ltd 44
malthouses 9, 59–61, 62
Mark 84
Marley, J.B. & Son 46
Marston Magna 67, 98
Marston Magna creamery 67, 68
Marston marble 19
Martock 9, 51, 68, 69, 74, 82, 88, 116, 142
Martock & South Petherton Trust 97
Maesbury 117, 118
Massingham, H. 146
McAdam, J.L. 5, 96
McAdam, W. 96
Meare 10, 41, 94, 125, 139
Mells 9, 38, 83, 84, 106
Mells Colliery 39, 126
Mendip Granite & Asphalt Co. Ltd 24, 124
Mendip Hills 5, 7, 8, 9, 11, 23, 24, 27, 31, 33–36, 56, 91, 95, 117, 124, 136, 139
Mendip Hills Mining Co. 34
Mendip Hospital 144
Merehead Quarry 23, 117, 124
Merriott, 74
Milborne Port 9, 12, 79, 82, 117, 143, 144
Milborne Wick 16
mileposts 10, 86, 101, 102
milestones 10, 84, 86, 88, 100–102
military works 12, 90, 108, 126
millwrights 9, 51, 53, 84, 85, 88
Milton Silk Mill 11, 73, 148
Milverton 28, 142, 144
Minehead 6, 7, 11, 12, 18, 31, 44, 46, 72, 96, 116, 118, 119, 127, 131, 132, 143, 145, 146
Minehead Turnpike 96, 100, 102
mineral railways 11, 30, 31, 32, 33, 37, 84, 122–126, 130, 148
mines 7, 8, 31–41, 94, 122, 124, 130
model farms 15, 17
Montacute 20
Moons Hill Quarry 24, 124
Moorewood Colliery 40
Moss, William 46
Muchelney 96, 99, 100, 104, 139
Murch, Edward 80, 97, 142
museums 8, 14, 33, 37, 43, 44, 53, 58, 67, 70, 73, 80, 84, 85, 86, 128, 142, 151

N
navigational aids 133, 134
Nestle & Anglo Swiss Condensed Milk Co. 68
Nethercott, E. 84
Nether Stowey 80
Nettlebridge 8, 37, 39, 105
Newbury Colliery 38, 39, 126
Newbury Railway 39, 126
Newland Quarry 28
New Rock Colliery 40
Newton Electrical Works 12, 146
Newton, F.M. 146
Nimmer Mills 9, 72, 78
North Curry 18, 54, 145
Northmoor pumping station 141, 142
North Petherton 144, 145

Norton Fitzwarren 60, 62, 67, 116, 117, 126
Norton stone works 20, 21, 90
Norton sub Hamdon 19
Nunney Catch 101
Nurcott 30
nurseries 8, 18
Nynehead 15, 17, 110, 111, 113

O
Oakhampton Quarry 22, 23
Oakhill Brewery 9, 11, 60, 64, 126, 144
Oakhill Maltings 9, 60
ochre 8, 36
oil engines 83, 84, 85, 88, 146
oil shale 8, 40, 41
Orchard Mill 53
Othery Steam Mill 54
Oxley's Colliery 39, 40

P
paddle-steamers 11, 130, 132, 134
paper mills 9, 35, 55, 91–94, 130, 144, 147, 149
Parrett Bath Brick Co. 46, 128
Parrett Navigation 28, 104, 114
Parrett, River 7, 8, 10, 36, 43, 44, 46, 52, 88, 97, 103, 104, 106, 114, 115, 121, 122, 127, 128, 130, 134, 139, 140, 142
Parrett Works 9, 13, 17, 74–76, 84, 85, 88
Parsons, George 9, 13, 17, 74–76, 84, 85
Paulton Engine Colliery 12, 37
Pearce, Thomas & Sons 80, 146
Pearsall, James 14, 73
peat 8, 41, 42, 95, 115, 125
Pecking Mill 101
Pen Mill 53, 79, 116, 117
Pen Mill Station 116, 117–119
Percival, Thomas 73
Perry Street 74
Petters Ltd 9, 10, 67, 83, 85, 88, 90, 146
Phoenix Engineering Co. 86, 87
Picked Stones Mine 33
Piles Mill 50, 51, 53
pillboxes 12
Pitcote Colliery 39
Plymouth Iron Co. 33
Polden Hills 30, 55, 57, 58
Pool, W.H. & Sons 84, 146
Porlock 7, 9, 11, 16, 59, 80, 146
Porlock Weir 11, 33, 46, 124, 127, 132
ports 127–134
pottery 8, 44, 47, 48, 55
power stations 12, 145, 146
Priddy 8, 27, 34, 35, 91
Prideaux, C. & G. Ltd 68
printing works 68, 94
Pritchard, William 22
Prowse's Mill 13, 14, 72
Pudleigh Mill 72
pumping stations 11, 12, 13, 18, 96, 109, 110, 118 136–142
Puriton 12, 115, 126, 142
Pylle 30

Q
Quantock Hills 8, 15, 19, 22, 24, 36, 40, 80, 135
quarries 7, 8, 14, 19–24, 25, 26, 28, 30, 36, 90, 116, 124, 126

R
radio stations 12

Radstock 8, 12, 37, 41, 95, 105, 111, 117, 130, 149, 151
railways 8, 10, 11, 12, 15, 37, 46, 53, 60, 67, 68, 95, 96, 103 115–126
Raleigh's Cross Mine 31, 122, 149
Rennie, James 114
reservoirs 34, 70, 106, 113, 114, 135, 136, 138, 139, 142
retorts 8, 40, 41, 143, 144
river navigations 5, 10, 103–105
roads 10, 95–102
roadstone 23, 24, 117
Roadwater 84, 122
Rockwell Green 11, 138
Rode 61, 65, 66
roller mills 8, 49, 53–55
Roman Lode 31
Romans 7, 8, 10, 19, 25, 31, 33, 34, 37, 95, 103
rope-walks 10, 75, 76, 78
Rowlands Mill 53
Royal Bath & West Agricultural Society 15
Royal Ordnance factory 12, 126, 142
rug making 9, 79, 80, 82
Ruston & Hornsby 54, 136–138, 142

S
sailcloth 9, 14, 74, 78, 85, 91, 174
St Audries 17, 144, 145
St Cuthbert's Lead Works 35
St Cuthbert's paper mill 91, 92
St Ivel 9, 68
St Regis Paper Co. Ltd 93
salt 12
Saltmoor pumping station 141
sandstone 19
sawmills 17, 18
Sealy, John & Co. 44
Selwood Printing Works 94
Shapwick 55, 58, 114
sheepskins 80
Sheppy, R.J. & Son 67
Shepton Mallet 7, 9, 22, 24,13, 60, 63, 64, 67, 69, 70, 72,73, 74, 94, 95, 96,102, 117, 121, 143, 146, 147
Shepton Mallet Trust 95, 96, 98
Shepton Mallet Water Works Co. 136
Sherborne Trust 95
Shipham 8, 35
shirt making 9, 69, 78, 92
shoes 80, 81, 83
Showering Bros 9, 64, 67
Sibley, W. 13, 51, 76, 85
signposts 89, 102
silk mills 9, 12, 14, 72, 73, 148, 150
silver 34
Simonsbath 18, 32, 33
Singer, J.W. 9, 86
slate 8, 22, 23
Smeaton, J. 30
Smith, G.H. 74, 76
Snowdon Collar Works 78, 86
Snowdon Hill 19, 95, 99, 100, 136
Somerset & Dorset Joint Railway 11, 30, 46,68, 117, 118, 121, 126, 130, 144
Somerset Brick & Tile Museum 43, 44
Somerset Bridge 122
Somerset Central Railway 117
Somerset Coal Canal 37, 105, 115
Somerset County Museum 14, 33, 73
Somerset, Dorset & Devon Dairy Co. Ltd, 68

Somerset Industrial Archaeology Society 4, 6, 14, 84
Somerset Levels 8, 11, 12, 18, 139-142
Somerset Lime & Cement Works 30
Somerset Mineral Syndicate 32, 122
Somerset River Board 142
Somerset Rivers Catchment Board 142
Somerset Rural Life Museum 67, 84
Somerset Trading Co. 46, 47
Somerset Wheel & Waggon Co. 51, 85
Somersetshire Drainage Commissioners 141
Somerton 22, 54, 84, 102, 122, 135, 144
Somerton radio station 12
Somerton viaduct 121
Somerville, R. & Co. Ltd 93, 144
South Cheriton 100
South Drain 139
South Petherton 27, 96
Southcombe Brothers 82
Southlake pumping station 141, 142
South Western Electricity Board 146
South West Gas Board 144
Sparkford Vale Co-operative Dairy Society Ltd 68
Sparrow, W. 51, 68, 85
Spiller & Co. 9, 55
Stapley Silk Mill 151
Starkey, Knight & Ford Ltd 66
Stathe 142
stations 117-121
steam engines 9, 12–14, 17, 11, 23, 24, 31, 32, 35, 36, 37, 39, 44, 46, 54, 55, 58, 66, 69, 70, 72, 73, 74, 76, 78, 79, 84, 85, 86–89, 91, 93, 110, 122, 136, 138, 140–142, 146
steam ploughing 15
Stembridge Windmill 56
Stoate, W. 54, 55
Stogumber Brewery 61, 64–66
Stogursey 41
Stone Allerton windmill 58
Stoke St Gregory 18
Stoke Sub Hamdon 19, 82
Stratton Common 39
Street 9, 12, 22, 76, 80, 81, 93, 100, 144, 148, 149, 151
street furniture 102
Stringfellow, J. 9, 78, 86
Sweethayes Court 15
Sweet Track 95
swing bridges 108

T
Tail Mill 14, 74
tanneries 9, 79, 80, 82, 146, 147
Tarr Steps 97
Taunton 7, 9, 11, 12, 13, 24, 30, 33, 43, 44, 46, 53, 54, 60–63, 69, 72, 73, 78, 79, 82, 84, 86, 95, 96, 106, 113, 116, 117, 118, 126, 103, 110, 115, 139, 144, 146–148, 151
Taunton Electric Lighting Co. 146
Taunton gasworks 143, 144
Taunton Station 117
Taunton trams 126, 146
Taunton Town Mills 53, 54
Taunton Trust 95
telescopic bridge 122
Templecombe Station 117, 118, 120, 144, 148
Tengore Lane limekilns 27

textiles 7, 9, 13, 69-78
Theak, F. Ltd 78
Thomas, William & Co. 46
Thompson & Le Gros 73
Thorney 68
Thorney Mill 52, 53
Thurlbear Wood limekilns 26
tiles 8, 44–46, 48
Tiverton 96, 110
toll-gates 100
toll-houses 98-100
Tonedale Mills 9, 13, 70-72, 144
Tone Navigation 7, 103, 104
Tone, River 14, 54, 98, 110–113
Tout Quarry 25, 28
Tracebridge Quarry 23
traction engines 15, 22, 33
tractors 15
trams 126, 146
tramways 21–23, 24, 26, 32, 33, 35, 36, 37, 38, 40, 42, 115, 117,122, 124–126, 146
Trask & Co. 20, 21, 124
Treborough Quarry 22, 23, 30
Treffry & Co. 34
Trull 15
tunnels 113–115, 122
turbines 17, 18, 23, 52-54, 74, 146
turnpike trusts 10, 37, 95–102
twine 74–76

U
Ubley Rakes 34
Unigate 9, 68

V
Vale of Blackmoor Trust 95, 100
Vale of Taunton Deane 19
Vallis Vale 14, 23, 24, 27, 124
Van Heusen, J.M. 78
Velvet Bottom 34, 35
viaducts 121
Viney Bridge Mills 76, 77, 147
Vobster Breach Colliery 39, 125, 126
Vobster Colliery 39, 125, 126
Vobster Quarry 24, 126

W
Wadeford Woollen Mill 72
Wainwright, John & Co. 24
Wallbridge Mill 70
Walton windmill 57, 58
Wansbrough Paper Mill 9, 92, 93, 151
Ward, J.S. 73
warehouses 114, 126
Washford 30, 54, 118, 122, 128–130
Watchet 8, 9, 11, 18, 25, 54, 55, 84, 91–93, 116, 118, 122, 130, 132-134
Watchet Town Mills 55
Watchfield windmill 58
water drainage 139–142
water mills 7–9, 49-55, 84
water supply 11, 135–139
water towers 138
water-wheels 13–17, 23, 33, 37, 38, 39, 49–55, 68, 69, 73, 74, 78, 80, 84, 86, 88, 110, 135, 145, 146
webbing 76–78
Wedmore 12, 143, 146

Wedmore Electric Light & Power Co. 146
Wedmore Gas Co. 143
Wellington 8, 11–13, 44, 46, 67, 69–72, 86, 88, 136–8, 143, 144, 146, 147
Wells 9, 100, 117, 121
Wells, Highbridge & Cheddar Trust 95
Wells Trust 95-97, 100, 102
West Buckland 16
West Coker 76
West Lambrook 74, 84
West Quantoxhead 17, 145
West Sedgemoor Main Drain 142
West Somerset Railway 11, 115, 116, 118, 119
West Somerset Mineral Railway 11, 31, 84, 122–124, 130
West Surrey Central Dairy Co. Ltd 68
Westbury Iron Co. 38, 40
Western Counties Creameries Ltd 68
Western Cut 139
Westford pumping station 136–138
Westford Mills 72
Westland aircraft works 9, 90, 126
West of England Collar Manufacturing Co. 78
West of England Engineering Co. 74, 85
Westonzoyland Engine Trust 6, 13, 14, 66, 88, 89, 140, 142
Westonzoyland pumping station 140–142
Westport Canal 113, 114
Whatley Quarry 23, 124
Wheal Eliza 33, 149
Wheatley & Co. 73, 144
Wheddon Cross 96, 102
Whiteball Tunnel 115, 122
Wightman, J. 85, 86, 101, 102
Williton 16, 49, 53, 116, 118, 151
Williton transmitter 12
Wills, W. & F. 13, 44, 45, 88, 89
Wiltshire, Somerset & Weymouth Railway 116–119
Wiltshire United Dairies 68
Wincanton 68, 99, 101
Wincanton Transport 9, 68
wind engines 17
windmills 7, 9, 55–58, 140
Windsor Hill 24
Witcombe Brothers 66
withy industry 18
Withypool Bridge 97
Wiveliscombe 28, 59, 62, 63, 146
Wivelscombe Slate Quarry Co. 23
Wookey Hole Paper Mill 9, 35, 91, 147
woollen mills 9, 13, 69–72
Woolverton 99
workhouses 151
Wrantage 112, 114
Writhlington 37, 117

Y
Yeo, River 17, 104, 105
Yeovil 9, 10, 15, 44, 53, 68, 79, 80, 82–85, 88, 90, 104, 116, 117, 119, 126, 143, 146
Yeovil Trust 95, 100
Yeovilton 12

Z
zinc mines 8, 35